W9-CLS-254

225.91 May   222186
Meyer.
The early Christians.

The Lorette Wilmot Library
Nazareth College of Rochester

GOOD NEWS STUDIES

Consulting Editor: Robert J. Karris, O.F.M.

Other Titles in Preparation

The Early Christians

*Their World Mission
and
Self-Discovery*

by

Ben F. Meyer

DISCARDED

LORETTE WILMOT LIBRARY
NAZARETH COLLEGE

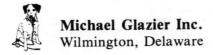

Michael Glazier Inc.
Wilmington, Delaware

About the Author

Ben F. Meyer was born in Chicago and educated in California and Europe (France, Italy, Germany). He is the author, among other works, of *The Aims of Jesus* and editor of vol. II (The Greco-Roman world) in the *Jewish and Christian Self Definition* series. He does hermeneutics and the history of religions at McMaster University in Canada. He is currently at work on the temple theme in Judaism and Christianity.

DISCARDED

First published in 1986 by Michael Glazier, Inc., 1935 West Fourth Street, Wilmington, Delaware 19805.

© 1986 by Michael Glazier. All rights reserved.

Library of Congress Catalog Card Number 85-45550
International Standard Book Number:
  Good News Studies: 0-89453-290-1
  Early Christians: 0-89453-542-0
Typography by Richard Reinsmith.

Printed in the United Sates of America

222186

Contents

To three friends for all seasons

John C. Robertson, Jr.
E. P. Sanders
Gérard Valleé

REFERENCES ABBREVIATED IN THE NOTES

Bauer-Arndt-Gingrich: Bauer, Walter. *A Greek-English Lexicon of the New Testament and Other Early Christian Literature.* Translated and adapted by William F. Arndt and F. Wilbur Gingrich. Chicago: University of Chicago Press, 1957.

Billerbeck: Strack, Hermann L., and Paul Billerbeck. *Kommentar zum Neuen Testament aus Talmud und Midrasch.* 6 vols. Munich: Beck, 1922-61.

Blass-Debrunner-Funk: Blass, F. and A. Debrunner. *A Greek Grammar of the New Testament and Other Early Christian Literature.* Translated and revised by Robert W. Funk. Chicago: University of Chicago Press, 1962.

ET: English translation

EVV: English versions of the Bible

NEB: New English Bible

NAB: New American Bible

PG: Migne, Jacques Paul. *Patrologiae cursus completus. Series graeca.* Paris: Gouthner, 1928-36.

RSV: Revised Standard Version

TDNT: *Theological Dictionary of the New Testament.* Edited by Gerhard Kittel and Gerhard Friedrich. 9 volumes. Translated by Geoffrey W. Bromiley. Grand Rapids: Eerdmans, 1964-74.

TDOT: *Theological Dictionary of the Old Testament.* Edited by G. J. Botterweck and Helmer Ringgren. Translated by David E. Green. Grand Rapids: Eerdmans, 1974 - .

PREFACE

This study derives from participation in a program of research: "Judaism and Christianity in the Greco-Roman Era: the Process of Achieving Normative Self-Definition." Sponsored by the Social Sciences and Humanities Research Council of Canada at McMaster University, Hamilton, Ontario, the research program (1976-81) was dedicated to discovering how and why, by the mid-third century of the common era, Judaism and Christianity alike had achieved a socially effective self-definition: comprehensive, flexible, normative, open to adjustment but firm enough to allow each to discern and reject self-negating revisions. By reference to this large project the present study is very limited. I nevertheless hope that it has been of some service to participants in the research project and that it will be of interest to others, for whom the issue of Christian identity and self-definition is of more than historical interest.

My purpose has been to take the central event in the life of primitive Christianity—the launching of the mission to the gentiles—as a paradigm of changing Christian self-definition and as the force that brought Christian identity into the light of thematic consciousness (see, for example, Gal 2:15f.; 6:15). This has entailed reconstructing the history of the launching of the mission. But the questions to which this reconstruction responds are limited and so, accordingly, is the reconstruction itself. These questions are two: what was there in the earliest Christian self-definition that made a mission to the gentiles first possible and then actual? And what impact did the mission, in turn, have on the self-consciousness of early Christianity?

My answer to the first question belongs to the history of early Christian eschatology. It centers on the distinctive way in which the Greek-speaking Jewish Christians called *hellē-nistai* in Acts appropriated the kergyma of Jesus' resurrection. As to the second question, it was the world mission that brought early Christianity to the full thematic consciousness of not only already belonging in "this age" to "the age to come," but of being called on to become, laboriously, what it already was: a new mankind.

This raises the question: what did the transition from Jewish sect to world-missionary movement mean with regard to Christianity's continuity and discontinuity with its own past selfhood? Gregory Dix took this to be the "main issue" underlying historical debate on early Christianity from Ferdinand Christian Baur to his own time. Was the historic Catholic Church "identical" with the primitive Apostolic community? Though I do not propose a direct answer to this (i.e., Dix's) loaded theological question, I do propose a way of grasping and refining the issue, an effort to prepare the way, at least remotely, for a direct and properly theological answer. The "refinement" bears on how to deal in adequate and responsible fashion with the issues of syncretism and orthodoxy in earliest Christianity.

I hope it is clear that the specific difference of the present study is its reconsideration of the early Christian mission in terms of the historical diversities and developments of early Christian self-definition. This is equally the key to how it differs from a straightforward reconstruction of the mission and to why it exhibits a distinctive set of emphases. The accent on self-definition explains, for example, why we pause to specify in some detail how a historical retrieval of the kerygma differs from the existentialist retrieval put forward by kerygma theology; how a two-line formula (Rom 3:25f.) opens up the new world of thought behind the

Greek-speaking Jewish-Christian sponsorship of a mission to the eastern Mediterranean; how Paul's consciousness of his world-wide mission and Pauline soteriology in its whole sweep illuminate each other; and, finally, how the legacy of Paul's missionary theology was appropriated by his closest followers.

The real thrust of the inquiry, then, is toward an insight into the native character of earliest Christianity. The investigation envisaged here is akin to the archaeologist's vertical trench: the striations brought to light allow one to trace (within the limits of the single but central issue of the world mission) what earliest Christianity owed respectively to the historical Jesus and to the disciples' Easter experience of the risen Christ; to Cephas and the twelve; to the Christian *hellēnistai* of Jerusalem and Antioch; to Paul, and to his most eloquent successors.

Biblical texts are cited in my own translations, which have been especially guided by the *Revised Standard Version* (London: Nelson, 1952) in consultation with *The New English Bible* (Oxford and Cambridge University Presses, 1961) and *The New American Bible* (New York: Kenedy, 1970). In citing the gospels I have taken Mark as a base; for example, "Mark 2:21f.; parr. Matt 9:16f.; Luke 5:36f.; Thomas 47b" means that the citations of Matthew, Luke and (non-canonical) Thomas are parallels (at least in a wide sense to the Markan text. At several points in the pages to follow I have tried to provide full biblical references with a view to serving students and scholars — without, I hope, irritating the general reader.

Chapters One and Two appeared in an earlier form under the title "Early Christian Self-Definition" (Colloquy 37; ed. I. Lawrence, Berkeley: Center for Hermeneutical Studies, 1980). Their revised form is printed here with permission. The appendix on "The Pre-Pauline Formula in Rom 3:25-26a" is a summary of an article of the same title which appeared in *New Testament Studies* 29 (1983): 198-208.

I am grateful for a leave fellowship grant from the Canada Council some years ago (1976-77), for it allowed me to complete *The Aims of Jesus* (London: SCM, 1979), to begin the research in "self-definition" that has culminated in the present work, and to carry out an independent study of early Christian faith-formulas. I wish to thank the librarians of Mills Memorial Library at McMaster University and those of the city and university libraries of Neuchâtel for their efficient and amiable service. Finally, I am much indebted to Phyllis DeRosa Koetting for typing and retyping the manuscript.

Burlington, Ontario
August, 1984

I

The Problem

The following pages deal with a pivotal moment in the history of early Christianity — the launching of the world mission. This was a bold and fateful act; bold in the sovereign proclamation that "there is no longer 'Jew' and 'Greek'" (Gal 3:28; cf. Rom 10:12; 1 Cor 12:13; Eph 2:13-16), fateful in that this abruptly declared abolition of old identities ultimately meant an end to toleration within Israel of the offending —the traitorous— sect. The world mission was therefore much more than an act of expansion. It set the stage for what would in effect be the migration of Christianity from one world to another. It thus not only entailed an effort to bring the gospel into the Greek field of vision, but also generated a change in Christianity itself from its first self-understanding as the vanguard of Israel to its second self-understanding as humanity reborn of the last Adam — a new mankind.

It is at least conceivable that this new development might have been effected without benefit of a world mission, for the theme of "a new mankind" had always been implicit in the theme of eschatological Israel. But in fact the development of an explicit self-understanding as "a new mankind" took place as an aspect of the epoch-making passage of a Jewish sect into the world of the gentiles.

Our task is, first of all, to locate the causes and effects of the world mission in the self-definition of early Christianity. By "causes" I mean those aspects of early Christian self-definition that gave plausibility, purpose, and motive to the notion of a mission to the gentiles and that positively impelled Christians to undertake it in the way they did. By "effects" I mean the changes wrought in Christian self-definition by their inaugurating the mission and adjusting to meet its problems and, above all, by their reflection on the eschatological scenario which took new shape in order to accommodate the transforming impact of the mission on the church that launched it.

Second, our task is to address the central problem that arises from the mission, namely, what did the transition from Jewish sect to world-missionary movement mean with regard to Christianity's continuity and discontinuity with its own past selfhood? This, in a word, is the issue of "identity"; it is a matter of how to interpret fundamental change.

Ever since Ferdinand Christian Baur (d.1860) the interpretation of change has been the most central, divisive, and refractory issue in New Testament studies. Though we have now had one hundred and fifty years of historically informed and consciously critical opinion on change in early Christianity — Baur's conflict of Petrine and Pauline currents, Harnack's hellenization of the gospel, the history-of-religions school and its view of early Christianity as an evolving syncretism, Walter Bauer's positing of heresy before orthodoxy in several Mediterranean centers[1] — all the solutions hitherto proposed have either been discarded or remain under debate. Contemporary opinion on change in early Christianity is a log-jam of incompatible interpretations.

Underlying the welter of disagreements, however, the concrete, controlling issue has always been that of Christianity's historic identity and the more general issue of identity as such, how it is established and maintained and how it

---

[1]On Baur and Harnack, see below, 107f.; on Bauer 107f., and 193f.

is lost. Thus, the separation of Christianity from Judaism is, at root, a matter of the emergence of a new identity; and the question of gentile Christianity's continuity with its origins in the Easter community of Jerusalem comes down to whether Christianity ever had a single ecclesial identity and, if so, whether it was maintained throughout the drama of early Christian development. Gregory Dix observed thirty years ago that "the main issue" in all the phases of the past century of debate about early Christian change has been one and the same: "the 'identity' of the historic Catholic Church with the primitive Apostolic community."[2]

Dix himself dealt with the issue trenchantly if briefly (he did not live to bring his manuscript to its intended completion) in his work *Jew and Greek*. In addressing the same issue today a new and inviting opportunity is presented, it seems to me, by the conspicuous progress made in recent decades in fashioning the tools of intentionality analysis. This analysis, both in the mode of "generalized empirical method" (Bernard Lonergan)[3] and in that of "interpretative" social theory (Alfred Schutz in the wake of Max Weber)[4] — partly paralleling Husserlian phenomenology (Lonergan) and partly registering its direct influence (Schutz) — presents itself as a particularly promising approach to the data on early Christian change. For these are, above all, data of meaning, just the kind of data that intentionality analysis, by contrast with the analytic schemes of behaviorists, functionalists, and voluntarists,

[2]Gregory Dix, *Jew and Greek* (Westminster: Dacre, 1953) 2.

[3]See B. J. F. Lonergan, *Insight* (New York: Longman, 1957) 72, 243 on how the term "generalized empirical method" is related to and distinguished from empirical method in the natural sciences. Also: "The Subject," in *A Second Collection* (New York: Herder & Herder, 1974) 69-86; "The Ongoing Genesis of Methods," *Studies in Religion/Sciences Religieuses* 6 (1976-77): 341-55.

[4]Alfred Schutz, *The Phenomenology of the Social World* (Evanston: Northwestern University Press, 1967). George Walsh, the editor and co-translator of this work, offers an introductory account of the distinctively "interpretative" character of Weber's theory and of Schutz's effort

has been devised to take account of.

The common pitfall is reductionism, among whose guises is, ironically, a devotion to "meaning." For many of the devotees of linguistic meaning — hermeneutists, language analysts, structuralists — have in fact contributed to a new nominalism, one that reduces realities to words and words to "language" (as "world," "game," or "code"). In current New Testament studies it reduces the gospel to its formulas and the formulas to the ensemble of their backgrounds, sources and parallels. From this it follows that early Christianity, for all its own testimony to the contrary, was never "one" but always "many." Moreover, the nominalism at home in this inference is readily combined with a positivist conception of individuality according to which the individual is constituted as such by being cut off from everything else, like a stone. But this, as Collingwood argued, characterizes the world of nature, not the world of meaning or mind, "where individuality consists not of separateness from environment but of the power to absorb environment into itself."[5] On nominalist and positivist premises the Christianity of the world mission could be nothing but a syncretism. When such premises, however, are weighed and found wanting, the effort to relate to one another the self-understanding of the Christians of antiquity (especially their conviction of Christian unity and continuity and root-

---

to add to and revise it. I do not intend to cite Weber or Schutz extensively. I have nevertheless been dependent on both: on Weber, for his reservoir of categories (e.g., for the traits of "communal" versus "associative" relationships, and for the concept of adaptation as not only lining up means to ends but as expressing commitment to values; thus, Christian development in all its phases — including the thrust toward orthodoxy, already evident in the latter first century and case-hardened by the time of Irenaeus — was much less *zweckrational* than *wertrational*); on Schutz, for the *Phenomenology* with its refinement of Weber's categories, and for the experiments in epistemology in vol. II of his *Collected Papers*, The Hague: Nijhoff, 1964.

[5] R. G. Collingwood, *The Idea of History* (Oxford: Oxford University Press, 1946) 162.

age in a common origin) and the analyses of modern scholars (especially their discrimination among the distinct fields of vision characterizing diverse Christian groups) will inevitably take a different direction.

But we postpone until later the question of "identity" and how it is generated, maintained, and lost. For the present we shall merely indicate that there is an ulterior issue — the issue at the root of most if not all of the conflicting interpretations of change in early Christianity offered over the past century and a half — which we must address even if we can only prepare the way for a full and direct answer.

Meanwhile, there are concrete historical problems bearing on the world mission. How is it that, alone of the parties, movements, and sects of first-century Judaism, Christianity discovered within itself the impetus to found gentile religious communities and to include them under the name "the Israel of God". (Gal 6:16)?[6] How can we explain the dynamics of the decision in favor of this impetus? Surely, those who made the decision were aware that it would only sharpen the threat to their own continuing existence within a Judaism to which the Christian cause was increasingly alien. How can we account for the origins of the conception of Christ not only as the fulfillment of the promises to Israel but as the first-born of many brothers (Rom 8:29; cf. Col 1:18; Rev 1:5; Heb 2:10-18), the first man of a new mankind (1 Cor 15:45-49)?

These questions bear on meaning and on that intimate and crucial sphere of meaning which we shall presently describe and name "self-definition." Their density derives from a presupposition to the effect that the main trajectory of early Christian history was self-orienting, that early Christian history was radically determined by dynamics internal to the Christian movement. This is not to deny the impact on the Christian movement either of events that

---

[6]This way of construing Gal 6:16, which corresponds to the view of the majority of scholars, has been recently vindicated again by E. P. Sanders, *Paul, the Law, and the Jewish People* (Philadelphia: Fortress, 1983) 173f.

changed the world in which Christians lived or of non-Christian attitudes and policies toward Christians. It is rather to affirm that the Christian movement from the start had its own built-in set of orientations, its own "deep structure." This is why, though unpredictable in advance, Christian responses to other groups and to great events regularly appear in retrospect to have been "typical," intensely and radically characteristic of the movement, an expression of its idiosyncrasy and spirit. Christianity was never more *itself* than in the launching of the world mission. And here appears a paradox that must at least be acknowledged, if not resolved: on the one hand, the radical commitments determining Christianity's "deep structure" derived from Jesus and the Easter kerygma; on the other, neither Jesus nor the Easter kerygma envisaged the world mission. Is it, then, nonsensical to say that Christianity was never more itself than in the launching of the world mission?

In order to resolve this paradox, we must ask some more general questions. Out of what kind of self-definition did the world mission spring? Where did that self-definition itself come from? What impact on early Christian self-definition did the mission have? What kind of identity, if any, did early Christianity maintain despite (or, possibly, thanks to) its various self-definitions, pre-world-missionary and world-missionary?

By embarking on a world mission the early Christians first of all dramatically revealed a self-definition unique in Judaism. Second, they set in motion the most densely charged event of late antiquity, one sowing the seeds of a radically new order of things: the Christian civilization of Europe and Byzantium, the mother of Western civilization today. Third, they changed themselves. The world mission effected changes of vantage point and horizon, a changed consciousness and changed ambitions. If the earliest Jerusalem community had looked on itself in awe as messianic Israel, the world mission produced a nascent communion of Jew and Greek, the beginnings of a fellowship to be fully realized in history. This, in fact, was soon made to define history's content and goal: the coming to be of "one new man" (Eph 2:15) and his coming to maturity as "perfect man" (Eph 4:13). Christ had broken down the wall of division between Jew and Greek and "made the two of us one" (Eph 2:14). Moreover, he was himself the head, the vital source, of the new man, in whose maturing "Christ [would] come to full stature" (Eph 4:13). Christianity, in short, had become the vanguard of a new humanity.

Obviously, it would be a mistake to suppose that the central concern of early Christianity was to establish its own self-definition. Its central concern was to testify that Jesus of Nazareth had been raised from the dead. From this the proclamation to Israel concluded that he had been enthroned as Messiah and the proclamation to the gentiles that he had been made "Lord (*kyrios*) of all" (Rom 10:12; Acts 10:36; cf. 1 Cor 8:6), of Jew and Greek (Rom 10:12; Acts 20:21; cf. 11:20), the living and the dead (Rom 14:7-9; 2 Cor 5:15), the human and the spirit world (Phil 2:10f.). The central concern of the mission was to proclaim an event, to interpret its sense, to win its acknowledgement, and in so doing to bring to full circle the drama that had opened with creation and rebellion (Gen 1-3), division and alienation (Gen 4-11), the election of Israel and the promise that in it lay God's blessing for the nations (Gen 12). The mission announced that the blessing was now. It consisted in the reign (1 Cor 15:24f.) of the risen Lord (e.g., Rom 1:4; 14:9; cf. 2 Cor 5:15) and it signified a new and final creation of mankind (Gal 6:15; 2 Cor 5:17).

"Identity" and "self-definition" were subjective correlatives to earliest Christianity's celebration of the risen Christ. Eventually we shall specify "identity" as a principle of unity and "self-definition" as a principle of diversity. Let it suffice for the present to say that both the proclamation and the correlative selfhood of the proclaimers were unique and reflected a phenomenon unique in the history of religions: *eschatological reversal realized in historical time.*

There is no real analogy, East or West, to the salient traits of the Christian proclamation of fulfillment, namely, reversal, anticipation, and convergence. Reversal refers to the stunning turnabout by which a slave's death was followed by en-

thronement as Son of God. "Anticipation" refers to the advance
arrival of the end of history, which now entered history to
shape it from within, resurrection taking place in time and
the risen one offering historical mankind the life of the age
to come (1 Cor 15:45). "Convergence" refers to the focusing
of fulfillment on a single figure — a gathering up of the hope
motifs from the covenants, sagas, prophecies, and psalms of
Israel and the poetry, philosophy, and mystery cults of
Greece, to affirm that all human aspiration had come to
flower in him.

The Christian proclamation, then, invited Jew and Greek
alike to step into a spacious circle of fulfillment. At its center
was the risen Christ and the Spirit he received and poured
out (Acts 2:33) to vitalize the new race gathered around him
(1 Cor 15:45). It was resurrection that grounded the con-
verging on him of fulfillment and of hope, and resurrection
that not only grounded but constituted both the reversal
epitomized in "Christ died and lived again" (Rom 14:9; cf. 1
Thess 4:14) and the anticipation epitomized in Christ, the
"first-fruits" of resurrection (1 Cor 15:20, 23) and "first-
born" of many brothers (Rom 8:29; cf. Col 1:18; Rev 1:5;
Heb 2:10-18).

The resurrection was accordingly determinative of the
identity and hence of all the various self-definitions of his
followers. As paradigm of their destiny, it shaped the baptismal pattern of *reversal* (the "putting on" of his death in
the hope of sharing his risen life, Rom 6:3-6; Gal 3:27) that
stamped all Christian existence (Rom 7:4-6; 8:13; 13:14;2
Cor 4:11; Phil 3:10). It gave substance to the eucharistic
pattern of *anticipation* by which "our bread of tomorrow"
(Matt 6:11; par. Luke 11:3; cf. Matt 8:11; par. Luke 13:29)
sustained life, already, today.[7] And it accounted for the
christocentrism of *convergent fulfillment*: "Whatever promises God has made, their Yes is in him" (2 Cor 1:20). Hence,

---

[7]That we should understand the first of the two "we-petitions" of the
Our Father to refer to our "bread of tomorrow" is commended by two
disparate but convergent data: (a) the form closest to the puzzling adjec-
tive *epiousios* is the feminine participle of *epeimi* in the fixed phrase *tē*

change and development in the way men of faith appropriated the resurrection and the role of the risen Christ directed change and development in the self-defining of Christians. Many factors entered into the expansion and differentiation of Christian horizons in the first years of the Christian movement. But, as Paul and Paulinism in particular show, they did so by indirection. New concerns contoured Christian self-definition by being filtered through christological reflection, so maintaining the classic pattern: first Christ, then those who belong to him (1 Cor 15:23).

All this, no doubt, states the matter too succinctly, for it passes over the tensions and quandaries, the hesitations and illusions, the trial runs and errors that also belonged to the drama of developing Christianity. But before dealing with detail we should recall that what emerged was a social phenomenon extraordinary not only for the perspectives it proclaimed but for the assurance with which its spokesmen

---

epiousę hēmera/ nykti, "on the following day / night" (cf. Acts 7:26; 16:11; 20:15; 21:18; 23:11); cf. *tetartaios* formed from *hē tetartē hēmera.* (b) St. Jerome reports that in the gospel of the Nazoreans (a targum-like retroversion of Matthew into Aramaic) he found at this point in the Our Father the word *mahar* (presumably in the form *limhar*). He rightly translated: *panem nostrum crastinum, id est futurum,* "our bread of tomorrow, i.e., our future (bread)."

Epiousios so understood may still refer either to (a) the day just begun or about to begin, or to (b) the "tomorrow" of eschatological consummation (which is how Jerome apparently understood it). That the second of these possibilities was the original sense is commended by three data: first, the antithesis "today"/"tomorrow" (itself paralleled by the antithesis of divine and human forgiveness in the next line); second, the eschatological character of the whole prayer; third, the predominant early Christian interpretation of "bread" as transcending (without necessarily excluding) ordinary bread.

The only real objection to this interpretation is that it seems unusual, isolated, in the language of Jesus. Actually, it has a solid context of parallels. Jesus conceived his table fellowship whether with sinners (see B. F. Meyer, *The Aims of Jesus* [London: SCM, 1979] 166 or with his disciples (see Meyer, *Aims,* 218) precisely as a present anticipation of the eschatological banquet.

proclaimed them and showed themselves ready to attest the truth of their proclamation by dying for it.

Thus far we have used the word "self-definition" in a general sense, a sense adequate to a general introduction. It is time now, however, to convert it into a precise technical term.

II

On Self-Definition

From the Fact of Change to the Consciousness of Change

The first generation of Christians lived through changes in Christianity that for depth and rapidity were unmatched in subsequent Christian history. Yet they emerged from them in the assurance of their own profound rootedness in Christ and the first Apostolic community. How did they so successfully manage to assimilate this experience of change?

Without pausing to refine the question and with no intention of proposing a full answer, we might simply offer an observation of fundamental relevance to it. The first Christians assimilated great changes in perspective and role and purpose by filtering them through christological reflection. Making Christ the touchstone, they fastened on a way of at once riding and reining in the dynamics of development.

But they did not *acknowledge* development. They overlooked it. They suppressed its novelty, intent on ways of relocating the creative aspects of their own historic experience, safely and objectively, in God's eschatological saving act. Like the ancient world generally, early Christianity lacked the resources that would have allowed it to affirm its own enduring identity while frankly acknowledging the novelty and unpredictability of its discoveries and adjustments.

The modern world, by contrast, has cheerfully accepted the reality of development and the category "development" with all its implications. This has opened a chasm between the consciousness of antiquity and that of modern and especially contemporary man. For the present inquiry this chasm poses a methodological quandary. How are we to deal with the combination of insights and oversights typical of early Christianity's historic self-appropriation? Should we be content to search out the forms and modes of self-definition just as they come to conscious expression in ancient Christian writing? Or should we understand the process of self-definition which actually took place to be irreducible to how things were conceived by the early Christians themselves?

Neither alternative will do just as it stands, but some version of both is indispensable. The first alternative will not do, for we are concerned with what happened, with history — and the first alternative falls short of history. It does not aspire to go beyond exegesis, which, be it ever so "historical-critical," does not reconstruct the past but merely secures data for such reconstruction by elucidating intended meanings. These "intended meanings" of the ancients obviously did not focus on history in the modern sense. So, even if they were one hundred percent valid and our grasp of them one hundred percent accurate, they would not put us in possession of history in the sense in which we are concerned with it.

The second alternative — to reconstruct for oneself an approximation of "what happened" — is ambivalent by reason of the opening it offers to reductionists, who, usually bent on saving early Christianity from itself, would systematically transpose all early Christian efforts at self-definition into supposedly better categories. Not all transpositions are reductionist. But those run the risk of reductionism that try to get away from what the movement meant to those who participated in it. Historical reconstruction, however, need not be done in the reductionist manner. An alternative procedure would be to respect the integrity of early Christian perspectives while setting them in the context of a larger analytic scheme. Our present purpose is to sketch just such a larger scheme; and our point of departure is the rise of the historical consciousness at the dawn of the modern era.

The core of an historical consciousness is the recognition that man makes himself to be what he is, and that this self-making is a process whereby, acknowledged or not, all his acts of meaning enter into the forging of his selfhood. This transforming insight has been invoked from Vico to the present day by the most diverse, even antagonistic, movements of the Western world, some celebrating man's total autonomy and especially his emancipation from metaphysics and religion, others, more recently, celebrating Christian man's coming of age as "son" (Gal 4:5) and heir of the world (cf. Rom 4:13). Despite their conflicting interpretations of autonomy, these views represent a radical agreement: by his own acts of meaning man defines and redefines himself, defines and re-defines his world.

In its full sweep and scope, then, self-definition is at the very heart of the process affirmed by the historical consciousness, the process by which man is actively engaged in the shaping of himself and his world. All agents by all their actions, however directed and intended, shape and define themselves in several ways: action tends toward habit and so disposes the agent to a given line of development; moreover, action, once objectified and interpreted by interaction with others[1], is retracted or modified or affirmed and so enters the arena where, positively or negatively, selfhood is engaged and affected. Regardless of its object, action shapes its subject. Human acts, in short, are subject-orienting as well as object-oriented.

---

[1] See the retrieval of George Herbert Mead's analysis of the social origin of meaning in Gibson Winter, *Elements for a Social Ethic. The Role of Social Science in Public Policy* (New York: Macmillan, 1966) 17-29, 88-99.

Self-Definition:
A Structured Process Having Three Moments

If this duality holds for all human acts, special status must be reserved for those acts that are deliberately and directly focused on self-shaping. And just as all deciding necessarily entails some prior act of understanding, so the deciding directly focused on self-shaping necessarily entails some prior act of self-understanding: some question about the self (such as what am I? or what ought I to be? or what do I really want to be?) and some answer to that question. Conscious self-shaping cannot stand alone; some self-understanding is the condition of its possibility.

Moreover, just as conscious self-shaping entails a prior act of self-understanding, so self-understanding entails a prior reservoir of resources: the sum and limit of what one knows and cares about. As sum, it is one's total field of vision; as limit, it is the horizon bounding that field of vision.

Now, as one moves one's horizons change, and this means a change in the aggregate of resources available for self-understanding. Under a variety of influences there may well emerge, in consequence, a new self-understanding and so the goal of shaping a new self. This suggests a preliminary conclusion. What makes the world of self-definition go round? Diverse or changing horizons.

From this sequence of inferences self-definition comes into focus as a structured process having three moments. Let us now consider them analytically and in their proper order: first, "horizons," then "self-understanding," and finally "self-shaping."

"Horizon," literally, is the limit of one's field of vision; metaphorically, it is the limit of one's knowing and caring. This limit implies a subjective pole (namely, the subject projecting the formality under which he knows or cares) and an objective pole (the whole of what falls under the projected formality). The subjective pole of the thief's horizon is the thief with his techniques and ambitions of larceny; the objective pole, commodities as appropriable by theft.

Horizon bounds a field of vision, a world. The world of the earliest Christians was all that fell under the formalities they projected. But what lay beyond one's horizon yesterday falls within it today. Thanks to the modern world's acknowledgment of progress and development, growth and decline, historians today try to trace changes in the field of vision from generation to generation and from culture to culture. So we may expect that the whole world of meaning in which early Christianity lived will have been notably modified between A.D. 30 and A.D. 60 and from the communities of the Levant to those of Egypt, Asia Minor, Greece, and Rome.

Second, self-understanding is man's response to the Delphic oracle's "Know thyself." This precept sets a delicate, difficult, and never-ending task, one not to be accomplished in isolation from others. Selfhood comes to light in differentiation and relations, primitively in the differentiation of one's body as part of oneself and distinct from one's surroundings, more dramatically in the discovery of "thou" and "I" and "we" in a context of communication. How I understand myself hinges in no small part on how I am treated by my world, and my understanding of it is in no small part a projection of what I have learned in interpersonal experience.

"Know thyself" commands the realization of reflex intentionality, the effort to convert wonder about oneself into understanding of oneself; to disengage this understanding from the fleeting moment of its realization and fix it in a concept of what one is; and finally to pass judgment on the adequacy of understanding and concept. If, moreover, the Delphic precept comes to fulfillment in an understanding not only of what one in fact is, but also of what one might be and of what in one's inmost heart one longs to be, there comes to light the compelling phenomenon of one's summoning self — a self strangely, disconcertingly more *me* than my already given, long since familiar self — yet, not me, not yet me, not yet wholly real.

Thus, one finds oneself driven to the third and peak moment in self-definition. This is, first of all, the self-orienting dimension of all human acts. But, second, it is the direct, thematic, deliberate drive to a renewal of selfhood. This "renewal" turns on the recognition that one is not yet in fact what one most truly is. It is epitomized in the Pindaric motif "Become what thou art."

The spontaneous move of attending to and seeking to understand oneself tends to conjure up a summoning self with which to confront one's merely given self. At this existential level there is played out a drama of identity with its own sequence of misunderstandings, peripateias, recognitions. The heart of the matter is the gap between the merely given and the really real. The given self is confronted by the summoning self; and in so far as effective decision closes the gap between them, the summoning self comes painfully and precariously to realization. The self as given yields to the self as pattern, project, vocation. A moment ago we said that one's summoning self is "not yet wholly real." But to the extent that one is actually succeeding in becoming what he is, his projected, summoning self is more real than his given self. It is not only a fuller and freer self, it is precisely the self that is coming to be, whereas the merely given self is in process of eclipse.

To project one's horizon and so to discover one's world, to puzzle out and conceptualize oneself, to weigh and pronounce on the adequacy of this effort, to seek to bring oneself deliberately to realization — what in human terms is achieved by this whole process? In general, it effects one's entry into the world of human meaning as a participant in its construction, maintenance, and modification. This is the properly human world. Its hallmark is language. And just as language is not sound alone but sound and meaning, so meaning enters constitutively into the fabric of this world.

Refinements and Objections

By thus schematizing self-definition as process, we have drawn on intentionality analysis to provide ourselves with a model that should prove useful in the effort to understand how one social group in antiquity realized its own identity, entered more than one world of human meaning, and in the process modified itself as well as those worlds. This model is not a law to which data must be made to conform. It is an instrumental construct conceived as potentially relevant to data. Its point is, first of all, to focus attention on potentially fruitful data. It presupposes a question (how did the earliest Christians make themselves be what they were?) and mediates between the question and the data. But we cannot know in advance how useful the model will be in generating an understanding of any particular cluster of data. Hence, we are satisfied to be in possession of a useful tool, and we shall be neither surprised nor disappointed if its usefulness proves to be limited.

The model has been designed to avoid the Scylla of reductionism and the Charybdis of anachronism. Or, to put the matter positively, it has been designed, on the one hand, to do full justice to the two elements of self-definition that were fully conscious in primitive Christianity: self-understanding (themes such as "the sanctuary of God" and "the body of Christ") and thematic self-shaping (the substantial body of parenesis on the shaping of Christian identity to accord with its summoning self: "Pattern yourselves no longer on this age but be transformed by the newness of your spirit," Rom 12:2). On the other hand, the model is designed to take full account of the *three missing factors* in the primitive Christian consciousness. The early Christians lacked the interpretative resources that would have allowed them, first, to conceive of their own collective identity as perduring and flowering through a sequence of new developments; second, to acknowledge the fact of a changing self-understanding and of the crucial role played therein by changing horizons; third, to recognize that Christian self-shaping was not only a matter of conscious and deliberate effort but was the subject-orienting correlative of every Christian theme, every affirmation of tradition and every new departure, every success and every failure. In short, the early Christians, blind to development, overlooked its typical patterns.

We accordingly resist the limitation of "self-definition" to crisis situations, which demand that social groups engage in line-drawing to determine what is right and what wrong, who is in and who out. Crisis situations regularly punctuated the history of early Christianity from its origins to the age of Tertullian and beyond, and line-drawing was a regularly recurrent Christian enterprise belonging to the process of self-definition. But to limit "self-definition" to the response to crisis situations would tend to make the resolution of the single crisis appear to be more arbitrary or unpredictable than it was and the whole series of such resolutions more random, eclectic, discontinuous than it was. To make "self-definition" include horizons, self-understanding, and self-shaping not only in crises but in the relatively stable situations that preceded and followed them is to focus on the long-term and underlying forces that are indispensable to the understanding of historically unique transitions.

There is no doubt that the proposal to deal with collective, intersubjective self-definition hinges on our usually more determinate and satisfactory grasp of self-definition at the level of the individual subject. The primary analogue in intentionality analysis is this subject. But the individual human subject, naturally social and relatively unintelligible apart from society, relates to the group as a particularly privileged analogue. He is not only a constituent element, a member of the group, flourishing through this membership. He is also its paradigm, for as individual person he already has the interiority and dynamism and unity that the group, as interpersonal collectivity, seeks to arrive at. Hence the commonplace image of society as a "body."

The group is more than an aggregate of individuals or factions. It is a strange but compelling phenomenon that groups — national communities, professional and business associations, clubs and clans and political parties — have personalities that resist easy reversal. And if Niebuhr's phrase "moral man, immoral society" signals the element of diversity in the analogy of the individual and the group, such phrases as "the mind of the church" signal the element of comparability in the same analogy. The use of both sorts of phrases attests a common approval of both ideas, for similarity and diversity between the individual and the group are both real. Finally, that the description of group subjectivity on the analogy of individual subjectivity is both natural and inevitable is shown by the way in which even those who find fault with it (when considering it as a theoretical question) spontaneously adopt it when discussing the activities of any human group. They have no choice. It is obvious that no other idiom is adequate.

Clarification by Contrast

The model we are proposing is in any case loose rather than tight, wide rather than narrow, more open than closed. It does not supply for, much less exclude, the application to the data of narrower conceptualities. Hence, there is no conflict, so far as I can see, between the present proposal and the application to the same material of, for example, sociological analysis.[2] Granted, however, that there is no mutual exclusion of the two approaches, there are several differences between them, and there is one difference which might be immediately specified. The bias of most sociological analysis is toward a view from the outside, whereas the bias of the inquiry into self-definition proposed here is toward a view from the inside. And though the two views are complementary and reciprocally correcting, it seems to me that Collingwood was right to insist that what essentially converts events into actions and so into the proper subject matter of history is a view from the inside. It is "the thought" of the agent, i.e., the whole precipitate of conscious intentionality charging the event, which gives it its internal

---

[2]On the current discussion of sociology and biblical studies, see Robin Scroggs, "The Sociological Interpretation of the New Testament: The Present State of Research," *New Testament Studies* 26 (1980): 164-79.

dimension, weighting it morally, humanly, dramatically.[3]

Recently, Wayne Meeks has offered an account of the social world of the Pauline mission.[4] He urges that in the recent past social scientists have become increasingly sensitive to the problems of conflict between "participant and observer viewpoints."[5] Whatever measure of truth there is in this sanguine generalization, Meeks himself is alert to participant viewpoints and anxious to avoid sociological reductionism. Adopting a stance of "moderate functionalism," he fills out as fully as possible the social context of the mission, describes possible social models for the Pauline communities in their immediate urban environment, and specifies the social functions of Christian rituals and doctrines.

Where this historical work is most clearly tutored by sociology, the questions it can deal with are most clearly limited, and the answers are often necessarily conjectural; for example, the success of Paul's apocalyptic theology lay in its offering his converts "relief from cognitive dissonance" rooted in the "inconsistency of [their] status indicators."[6] Just what question does this answer? We must take a step back. Having noted a structural analogy between the paradoxes highlighted by Paul's central themes and the paradoxical social situations of many in the Pauline communities, Meeks raises the question of a possible causal nexus between the two. Did status inconsistency, including that of Paul himself, impinge on the choice of paradoxical symbols such as cross and resurrection? Do the symbols explain why status-inconsistent persons were drawn to Christianity? Was the Pauline mission thus a welcome refuge to those whose ambiguous social position made them anxious and lonely? Though the answers remain hypotheti-

---

[3]R. G. Collingwood, *The Idea of History*, 215-31.

[4]Wayne A. Meeks, *The First Urban Christians. The Social World of the Apostle Paul*(New Haven: Yale University Press, 1983). Earlier: "The Social Context of Pauline Theology," *Interpretation* 36 (1982): 266-77.

[5]*Urban Christians*, 3.

[6]*Urban Christians*, 173f.

cal, analogies (Qumran, modern millennial movements) promise some guidance in judging their validity. Short of that, Meeks in any case can appeal to the social functions of paradox-laden symbols: to legitimate a new vision of things, to help the displaced make sense of their experience, to enhance group solidarity, and so on.

One cannot fail to be struck, however, by the mismatch in dimension between Paul's symbols and social dislocation among his converts. Even for persons whose social status was definite and secure, the charged symbols of cross and resurrection kept their punch. They primarily addressed something deeper in man than status inconsistency. Moreover, it is doubtful whether the paradox inherent in themes of eschatological reversal correlates structurally with paradoxical social status.[7] To be sure, the concrete dilemmas upon which Paul brought his symbols to bear covered the gamut of everyday problems in the community; they were thereby assimilated to the theme of living out the summoning selfhood of identification with Christ.[8]

Over and above welcome attention to clues for the social description of Pauline Christianity, Meeks's study broaches larger questions, such as why circumcision had been abandoned by the Greek-speaking Christians of Antioch and how it was that, following them, Paul could take the stand that he did on gentile converts and the Law.[9] This indeed is among the issues most basically conditioning "the social world of the Apostle Paul," and Meeks's answer to it is quite unobjectionable: "that the Messiah had died a death cursed by the Law entailed a sharp break in terms of the way in

[7]Paradox in Christian symbolism is a tradition that goes back to Jesus' macarisms, riddles, and parables. The social dislocation of the individual relates to this imagery as a more or less peripheral factor. On the continuity in existential stance between this imagery in the gospels and that of comparable Pauline texts, see J. M. Robinson, *Kerygma und historischer Jesus* (Zurich-Stuttgart: Zwingli, [2]1967) 225-49..

[8]*Urban Christians*, 180f. For some of the concrete forms that this took in Pauline language, see below, 144f.

[9]*Urban Christians*, 167f.

which the people of God would henceforth be constituted and bounded."[10] Two things should nevertheless be noticed: first, the question, while inevitable, is marginal to Meeks's study, a presupposition rather than a focus of interest; second, sociology contributes nothing at all either to the question or to the answer.

By contrast, the present study deals directly and at length with this question about Antioch and about Paul, as well as with related questions, such as why the community gathered in Jerusalem around "Cephas and ...the twelve" (1 Cor 15:5) did not launch a mission to the gentiles. Again, it is a key question for us as to how it was that the variety of views on these topics failed to generate in the earliest Christian leadership (in Peter, in Paul, in James) a consciousness of division and schism.[11]

There appear to be no ready-made sociological categories apt to guide the framing of such questions and the quest of answers to them. Hence, our effort to forge heuristic tools (especially the concepts of "self-definition," "identity," and "development-by-transposition")[12] is designed for exactly this purpose. We are envisaging an area of inquiry that social description and sociological analysis have mostly taken for granted, and understandably so. Finally, just as Meeks hopes that his historical investigation will not be misconceived as anti-theological,[13] I hope that the present historical effort, which I understand to be open in principle to further, more microscopic determination both by social description and sociological analysis, will not be misconceived as anti-sociological.

---

[10]*Urban Christians*, 168. Unlike Meeks (177), however, I would not tie the conclusion (on how the "people of God" would be newly constituted and bounded) so closely and exclusively to the motifs of Galatians 3:13. For my argument, see below, 161-8.

[11]See below, 97-102.

[12]On identity and development, see below, 174f.; 183f.; 186-91.

[13]*Urban Christians*, 7.

Conclusion

No Christian world mission could have been conceived, much less set in motion and sustained against heavy odds, had it not sprung from and accorded with early Christian horizons, values, and purposes, i.e., early Christian self-definition. But where do we find the self-definition that conditioned the possibility of the world mission? The question is real, not rhetorical. Jesus envisaged no world mission nor, originally, did Cephas or James. The explicitly universalist missionary mandate in Matthew (28:19), Mark (16:15), Luke (24:47), and Acts (1:8) and the implicitly universalist mandate in John (20:21f.)may well be the gospel story's single most significant retrojection from later history to Jesus. But if the question about defining and locating the conditions of the world mission is real, the answer is complex. Had the mission not been somehow really rooted in Christ, it would have been Christian only by a courtesy of words. Without Paul it would have had a wholly different history. Without the concurrence of Cephas and James, Paul's race would have risked being run in vain (Gal. 2:2).

III

The Kerygma Revisited

Context and Cutting Edge

A First Approximation

At the center of earliest Christianity's self-definition lay its public proclamation to Israel of salvation to be appropriated by baptism in the name of Jesus of Nazareth. Our most important clue to the earliest moment in Christian self-definition is to be found in this proclamation or kerygma. The task, then, is to recover the kerygma, to understand it, and to press it for what it can reveal of Christianity's new identity and first self-definition.

Though our access to the very earliest kerygma is not direct (that is, we have no transcription of it), we can recover it by inference. The root condition of the kerygma was "the Easter experience." However interpreted, that experience was historically decisive, for nothing else suffices to explain the coming of the kerygma into existence. Conversely, once the Easter experience had affirmed and transvalued the disciples' pre-Easter experience of Jesus, the sufficient condition of the coming to be of the kerygma was fulfilled.

The disciples who made up the core of the first Christian community interpreted their Easter experience as follows: God raised Jesus from the dead (cf., e.g., I Thess 1:10; 1 Cor 6:14; Rom 4:24; 8:11; 10:9; Acts 2:22-24; 3:15; 4:10), so exalting him as Messiah and Lord (e.g., 1 Cor 8:6; 12:3; Rom 10:9; Acts 2:36; 3:20-21).

"God raised Jesus": the event to which this referred was not, could not have been, a brute fact, neutral and uninterpreted, such as a mere resuscitation or revivification of Jesus might have been. Since the event was understood from the start as resurrection in a sense that transcended revivification (namely, as the event of entry into a sphere and mode of life beyond mortality, beyond "this age"), of its very nature it solicited immediate and maximal interpretation. This may be why reconstructions of Easter faith as a slow development by stages toward themes such as exaltation, Messiahship, or Lordship have proved to be unpersuasive.[1] Likewise, the kerygmatic theme of vindication (e.g., Acts 2:22-23; 3:13-15; 4:11) and the appeal to its main scriptural resource — the "Servant" whose suffering was reversed and made intelligible by glorification, and whose suffering and glorification purified the world (Isa 52:13-53:12)—probably went back to the early days of the community (cf. Rom 4:25 and 1 Cor 15:3; Gal 2:20; Rom 8:34).

A new identity and self-definition were correlative to this kerygma. Christian horizons were eschatological and the eschatology in question was "absolute" or "apocalyptic." The event attested by the kerygma — eschatological resurrection realized in the one man, Jesus — could not cohere with any prosaic conception of human history. Resurrection implied a larger eschatological whole. The basic pattern of this eschatology, as it appeared in Judaic apocalyptic,

---

[1]In opposition to the view of Ferdinand Hahn, *The Titles of Jesus in Chrisitianity* (Cleveland: World, 1969) 103-14, 168-72, namely, that Jesus' exaltation as "Lord" and "Christ" did not belong to the earliest Christian understanding of the resurrection, see Wihelm Thüsing. *Erhöhungsvorstellung und Parusieerwartung in der ältesten nachösterlichen Christologie* (Stuttgart: Katholisches Biblewerk, 1970) 26-40.

bore on God's purpose respecting man and his history, a purpose which was revealed in the light of an end-drama ranging the forces of chaos against the divine order and peaking in the triumph of God's reign.[2] The resurrection of one man was not yet fully commensurate with this climax. It was an advance sign, a pattern for the climax to come. The New Testament provides evidence of numerous scenarios designed to fill the interim between this present fulfillment and the still future fulfillment, the scenarios naturally changing as the community grappled with its own unanswered questions about the imminence of the end or, more exactly, about the appointed order of events — "conversion events" (Rom 11:25-27; Acts 3:19-21) — destined for realization prior to the end.

But how did the community understand itself at the outset? It understood itself, first of all, as a community, a community whose allegiance to the risen one made it the beneficiary of his blessings. It was a community of "servants" in communion with their "Lord," destined in virtue of this communion to share in his victory over death. Hence, "Jesus is Lord" (1 Cor 8:6; 12:3; Rom 10:9; Acts 2:36; cf. Rom 14:9) was complemented by "Our Lord, come!" (1 Cor 16:22; cf. Rev 22:20).

This community shaped itself by its bold proclamation, its celebration of the present, its hope for the future. Since it saw itself as Israel restored, it took its cue from the scriptures, making Deuteronomy its messianic charter.[3] In a word, Christianity defined itself by living in its own "myth" — a scheme of absolute eschatology derived in principle and in substantial part from Jesus himself.[4] It called on all Israel

[2]John Gray, *The Biblical Doctrine of the Reign of God* (Edinburgh: T. and T. Clark, 1979) 1-6, 209f., 226-73. It is the merit of J. C. Beker, *Paul the Apostle* (Philadelphia: Fortress, 1980) to give its full importance to this commanding theme in Pauline theology.

[3]Joseph Schmitt, "L' Église de Jérusalem ou la 'Restauration' d'Israël," *Revue des sciences religieuses* 27 (1953): 209-18.

[4]B. F. Meyer, *The Aims of Jesus* (London: SCM, 1979) 202-9.

to enter as rightful heir into this selfsame heritage. The kerygma was thus the call of a community to a people. At stake in the call, from the community's angle of vision, was that people's status as people of God. Only in this framework did the kerygma have its historic intelligibility — a datum so underplayed by kerygma theology that some clarification now by contrast to that theology can hardly be amiss.

Contrast with Kerygma Theology

As New Testament scholarship emerges from the era of kerygma theology, it faces the task of consolidating the gains of that era and making good its losses. The gains have included a heightened appreciation of the New Testament's distinctive confession (e.g., "God through Christ was reconciling the world to himself," 2 Cor 5:19) as the matrix of Christian meaning, personally compelling (for "he loved me and handed himself over for me," Gal 2:20) and productive of a new self-understanding: being "in Christ" is new creation (2 Cor 5:17; Gal 6:15; cf. Rom 4:17). Such gains in the appropriation of the world of early Christian meaning — their full force is seen by contrast to the pedestrian perspectives of the liberal theology that kerygma theology displaced — reflect an intense concern with the existential dimension of faith. The losses related to an existentialist depreciation of the significance of cosmos, society, and history. They were losses inasmuch as earliest Christianity itself had exhibited a keen religious interest in cosmos (not only the whole of mankind and its physical dwelling place but the whole of the spiritual and material creation),society (Israel not as an aggregate of individuals but a people and specifically "the people of God"), and history (events and traditions in their concrete particularity with emphasis on the historic career of Jesus). Kerygma theology's besetting anxiety to limit its vulnerabilities by ruthlessly narrowing the scope of its engagement with the concrete left it without adequate interpretative resources in the face of early Christian concern.

Early Christians were concerned with the impact of the Christ event on the whole cosmos; with Israel as the repository of divine promises; and with the historic career of Jesus, locked as it was in passionate engagement with "all Israel" in its ethnic, geographical, social, and religious concreteness.

Kerygma theology operated on two apparently independent but in fact reciprocally conditioning tracks. Its historical track was typified by hypothetical reconstruction in the fearless style of the history-of-religions school (fl. 1890-1920); its theological track was typified negatively by compliance with Troeltschean relativism[5] and positively by adherence to the existentialism referred to above. Its severely circumscribed theological concerns made possible the brinkmanship of its "radical criticism"; conversely, its daring — almost rakish — historical hypotheses made necessary and inevitable the severely limited scope of its theological concerns. By the middle 1950s both sides of the enterprise had begun to fray. The "new quest" of the historical Jesus was undertaken by kerygma theology itself to cure its sporadically recognized tendency towards "docetism."[6] This has been accompanied by the still more damaging critiques of outsiders.[7] The hypothetical history of christol-

---

[5]Troeltsch's historical relativism is especially evident in his repeated affirmation that history shatters all value systems and in his gradually and painfully acknowledged incapacity to affirm that the Christianity he stood for was "still Christianity," i.e., essentially identical with the Christianity of the New Testament. See Ernst Troeltsch, "What Does 'Essence of Christianity' Mean?" in *Writings on Theology and Religion* (London: Duckworth, 1978) 124-79, esp. 173-5.

[6]E.g., Ernst Käsemann, "Die neue Jesus-frage," in *Jésus aux origines de la christologie*, Gembloux: Duculot, 1975, 47-57, cf. 55-7. Earlier, "The Problem of the Historical Jesus," in *Essays on New Testament Themes*, (London: SCM, 1964) 15-47, cf. 45-7.

[7]For a short survey of the critique in Germany of Bultmann's theological program, see Peter Stuhlmacher, *Vom Verstehen des Neuen Testaments* (Göttingen: Vandenhoeck & Ruprecht, 1979) 185-92. For a sketch of the trajectory of dialectical theology, see Ulrich Wilckens, "Lukas und

ogy favored by the Bultmann school has not been spared.[8] Thus, the role of the gentile Christian community (*heidenchristliche Gemeinde*) as a great creative source for Pauline theology has turned out to be as elusive, not to say fictional, as the theological creativity of its more modest Jewish-Christian counterpart, "the Q community."

We have said that among the gains of kerygma theology was a heightened appreciation of the New Testament's central faith affirmations, such as "God through Christ was reconciling the world to himself" (2 Cor 5:19). But once it was removed from its original semantic context and transposed to the new horizons of kerygma theology, even this confession suffered a sharp loss of meaning; for, every meaning has a context, and a crucial dimension of the Pauline context had been deconstructed. In contrast to kerygma theology, Paul himself had no scruple about affirming Jesus' "meekness and kindness" (2 Cor 10:1) and his utter sinlessness (2 Cor 5:21), nor did he hesitate to affirm Jesus' divinely appointed status as Davidic Messiah (Rom 1:3f.). In Paul's view Jesus became at once God's "slave" (*doulos*) "obedient unto death" (Phil 2:8) and "the servant of the Jews" (*diakonos tēs peritomēs*), realizing God's promises to the patriarchs (Rom 15:8). His "obedience" undid the disobedience of Adam (Rom 5:19). In the Pauline view Jesus went innocently and willingly to his death (1 Cor 11:24f.; Phil 2:7f.; Rom 5:6f.; 2 Cor 5:21) as an expiatory victim (Rom 3:25; 4:25; 5:6-10; 8:3; 1 Cor 15:3; 2 Cor 5:21) out of love for men (Gal 2:20; 1 Cor 8:11; Rom 14:15). Remove this context — that is, excise all reference to the human intentionality that charged his life and death,

Paulus unter dem Aspekt dialektisch-theologisch beeinflusster Exegese," in *Rechtfertigung als Freiheit* (Neukirchen-Vluyn: Neukirchener Verlag, 1974) 192-7.

[8]See Martin Hengel, "Christologie und neutestamentliche Chronologie," in *Neues Testament und Geschichte* (Zurich: Theologischer Verlag, 1972) 43-67; also, "Die Ursprünge der christlichen Mission," *New Testament Studies* 18 (1971-72): 15-38; "Zwischen Jesus und Paulus," *Zeitschrift für Theologie und Kirche* 72 (1975): 151-206.

giving them their depth, their density, their direction, their human historicity — and the sense of "God through Christ was reconciling the world to himself," purged of its Pauline realism, is thinned down to an abstraction. The confession may well retain its high status amid its new surroundings, for it has been assigned a place of priority in kerygma theology's universe of discourse. It does not, however, retain its meaning, for that would require its full historic realism to have been carried over intact into new and spacious horizons. What was needed — and missing — in kerygma theology was a consciousness so differentiated as not only to supersede the past but to affirm thematically this rich historic reality while superseding it. Kerygma theology, on the contrary, abstracted the kerygma as content from the realities that that content intended (real resurrection as much as real death); moreover, it abstracted the kerygma as proclamation from the purpose it had been designed to serve. That purpose, charged with the supposition of divine election, was, first of all, to bring Israel into its appointed destiny as eschatological people of God. In accord with this purpose, the kerygma highlighted God's promises to Israel by announcing their fulfillment.

The risen Christ was seen above all in scriptural terms, as the kerygma repeatedly (e.g., Rom 1:3f.; 4:25; 8:34; cf. Phil 2:6-11) and even explicitly (1 Cor 15:3-5) attests. For Christians the first hermeneutic circle was: Christ in the light of the scriptures, the scriptures in the light of Christ. What gave vitality to this world of meaning was the conviction of fulfillment: the *coming-to-realization* of what had been foreshadowed (1 Cor 10:6;[9] Rom 8:32 = Gen 22:12), promised (Acts 2:16-21, 33), and prophesied (Acts 2:23, 34f.; 3:18, 22); the *coming-to-perfection* of what had been provisional (Matt 5:17;[10] cf. 19:3-12; parr. Mark 10:2-12; Luke 16:18);

[9]See Leonhard Goppelt,"*typos*," TDNT 8, 251f. See also 255 on typological interpretation as "the central and distinctive New Testament way of understanding Scripture."

[10]See Joachim Jeremias, *New Testament Theology I. The Proclamation of Jesus* (New York: Scribners, 1971) 83-5.

the *coming-to-completion*, that is, to full eschatological measure (Matt 23:32), of time (*chronos, kairos, kairoi*), sin (*hamartiai*), suffering (*thlipseis*), and indeed, of the whole drama of cosmos and history. In this manifold of fulfillments Jesus himself was the regulative component, not only as the "first-fruits" of resurrection (1 Cor 15:20) but already as the proclaimer of the reign of God.

For Jesus, too, had presented the nation with a kerygma, one rooted in the scriptures and deliberately reminiscent of the message of the Deutero-Isaian herald (*m^ebaśśēr = euaggelizomenos*) Isa 52:7; cf. Isa 60:6; 61:1) who announced Israel's eschatological restoration. The Easter kerygma of the church was similarly rooted in the scriptures. It took its name "gospel" (*euaggelion*) from the same Deutero-Isaian herald (*euaggelizomenos*) and drew its interpretative categories on the one hand from Jesus and on the other from the prophets (Joel 3:3-5 = LXX 2:28f.; Isa 52-53; 56; 60-61) and Psalms (2; 6; 22; 110; 118; 132) read as interpreting him.

Most important of all, the proclaimers of the kerygma (first, "Cephas and the twelve") conceived themselves and their followers in ecclesial terms, namely, as the first-fruits of restored Israel and so the rightful heir of all those confessions by which Israel had classically defined itself. The early Christian consciousness was by no means the product solely of the Easter experience. It had been initiated and informed by the mission of Jesus; Easter kept it alive by validating and consummating it. Moreover, the proclaiming community presented itself as the locus of fulfillment. It had come into being in response to Jesus' kerygma. It understood itself now as messianic Israel covenanted with her risen Lord, already the beneficiary of what the community conceived as messianic blessings (Acts 2:38; 5:31f.). The failure of kerygma theology to come to terms with this controlling context was part of the price paid for its having misconceived the career of Jesus as an individualistic call to decision, in almost complete abstraction from its Jewishness and from the intra-Jewish historical context of religious competitors for Israel's allegiance (Pharisees, Zealots, Sadducees,

Essenes, baptists.....) We wish to take an entirely different tack.

The Pattern of Election

Across the centuries from the pre-monarchical period (Josh 24) to the post-Exilic restoration (Neh 9) Israel had accumulated a thesaurus of faith confessions expressing the self-awareness of a people that owed its being to a saving act and established its identity by acknowledging that act:

> We were slaves of Pharaoh in Egypt but Yahweh brought us out of Egypt with a strong hand.... (Deut 6:21: cf. 26:8)

The role of response and acknowledgement in making Israel to be what God meant it to be was fully conscious. God's saving act did not alone and of itself make Israel "become what it was." This act called for a proper response, and only in so far as the response was actually forthcoming would Israel come into its appointed heritage and selfhood. For Israel would know itself, would find its identity, only in and through its answer to God. Such was the burden of God's word to the people on the brink of their entry into covenant:

> Now therefore, if you obey my voice
>   and keep my covenant,
> you shall be my own possession among
>   all peoples, for all the earth is mine.
> And you shall be to me a royalty of
>   priests and a holy people.
>
>   Ex 19:5f

Religious identity as the precipitate of historic responses to divine acts filled the oft-told traditions that established Israel's horizons, charged its memory, and formed its sensibility — traditions from the earliest promise of progeny and land through the story of bondage and redemption in Egypt to the wandering in the wilderness and the first effort to force an entry into Canaan. Thus Israel learned the lesson that its real selfhood turned on a proper response to Yahweh. The main function of these traditions was to celebrate the Lord and to elicit Israel's proper response to him. The celebration thanked God for his saving act or begged for his saving act again. In its thousand variations the call for a response showed the evolution of an initially artless sensibility into a fine-tuned discrimination between authentic and inauthentic elements in the nation's answer to God.

In Isaiah the name of this self-defining answer was "faith" (*'ĕmet, 'ĕmûnâ*). Israel's existence hinged on it, for the prophet's word to the king was also a paradigm for his people:

> If you do not stand firm in faith,
>   you shall not stand at all (Isa 7:9).

Such was the covenantal dynamic: a structured transaction comprehending God's saving act, which demanded and defined a proper response, and the response itself which, if proper, would elicit blessings and, if improper, curses and condemnation.

Now, if this were the whole story of the covenantal dynamic, the history of Israel would have been clear and short, and movements like Essenism and Christianity with their claims to embody "true Israel" could not have arisen. But in fact there was a controlling context or framework for the covenantal dynamic, a vital presupposition that not only conditioned the operation of the covenantal dynamic but charged it with transcendent meaning. This was the boundless benevolence in which the covenant originated. Biblical traditions conceived in various ways the process by which Israel became "the people of God" (e.g., Ex 19; Josh 24; Deut 32:10) but Yahweh himself always initiated it. Though all the earth was his, Yahweh chose Israel. Election, then, referred first to Yahweh's predilective initiative; second, to

Israel's resultant vocation to be "chosen." It should be emphasized that election was a vocation; that is, its permanent and unconditional element was God's call. The many biblical traditions relevant to this question are perhaps not perfectly harmonizable, but there is a point at which they converge: the elective call of God was free, gracious, predilective, unconditional, irrevocable. This established the context or framework referred to above, within which the covenantal dynamic would operate as an economy of blessings and curses.

The blessings and curses applied to every generation in Israel, whereas the bearer of the guarantee implied in God's unconditional elective call was not every generation but every properly responding generation or, better still, those in Israel on whose proper response the destiny of Israel would turn. Though any generation in Israel might fall victim to catastrophic judgment, Israel itself would never go under. The biblical story accordingly turned on a double hinge: on the one hand, the predilective love that defined Israel's summoning self; on the other, the actual response of every generation, the recurrent gap between actual and proper response, and the consequent drama of judgment and restoration. But this hold on the unconditional call of Israel was the product of a bitterly painful learning process. The premise that national disasters could not be definitive repeatedly proved liable to false conclusions: "Is not Yahweh in our midst? No evil can come upon us!" (Mic 3:11; cf. Jer 5:12; further, Jer 7:4, 10).

No doubt, the most distinctive single thrust of the prophetic movement was its insistence on the integrity, and so inevitably on the negative aspect, of the covenantal dynamic:

> Only for you have I cared
> out of all the earth's tribes;
> therefore will I punish you
> for all of your crimes
> (Amos 3:2)

Remnant theology through the half-millennium from Amos to Trito-Zechariah consisted in this application of the covenantal dynamic to Israel. But even for Amos there was hope (Amos 5:15) that some might be snatched from the lion's mouth (cf. Amos 3:12). And these few, said the prophets, were the new locus of election and the seed of national restoration. Though the remnant thematic was initially dominated by threat, themes of promise won out in the end, for election (as we have observed) relativized the covenantal economy of blessings and curses. This meant that the gap between actual response and proper response would one day be closed. But it would be closed by God, not Israel. It was not Israel's fidelity but Israel's election that elicited and sustained its passionate hopes for the future: a new reign of David (Amos 9:11f.; Isa 11:1-10; Mic 5:1; Jer 30:9; Ezek 34:23f.; 37:24), a new and paradisal Zion (Isa 2:2-4; 11:6-9; 28:16; 51:3; 54:11), a new heart and a new spirit (Ezek 36:26), a new saving deed (Isa 43:19), a new guarantee (Isa 54:9f.), a new covenant (Jer 31:31-34) — radiant themes and images that transcended all law, even the law requiring boundless love (Deut 6:5).

Neither the primitive Christian proclaimer nor the point and function of his proclamation is intelligible in historical terms apart from this biblical and ecclesial legacy. For, the proclaimer was the spokesman of a community made up of "those who would be saved" (*sōzomenoi*, Acts 2:47; cf. LXX Isa 37:32) at the judgment by calling on the name of the (messianic) Lord (Acts 2:21, from a remnant passage of Joel 3, LXX Joel 2, cf. Acts 2:36; Rom 10:13); and the point and function of his proclamation was to summon Jerusalem and all Israel to its messianic heritage in that selfsame community.

Outside the church there was no kerygma. Apart from the church there was, historically, no sense in any kerygma. Positive response to the kerygma was not simply to go home with a new self-understanding. It was to be baptized (Acts 2:37f.) and so to share in the fulfillment announced by the kerygma; for the kerygma announced the resurrection of

Jesus and the resurrection was the fulfillment of messianic promises to Israel (Rom 1:4; 8:34; cf. 2 Sam 7:11-14; Ps 110:1; also Acts 2:25-31; Ps 16:8-11. An epitome: "...what God promised to our fathers he has fulfilled to us their children by raising Jesus" (Acts 13:32f.). This response— entry into Israel's messianic vanguard, the open remnant of those destined to be saved at the judgment — did not relate to the kerygma in some merely extrinsic way. It was the intrinsically appropriate, intrinsically accurate, response to the kerygma. Messiah and messianic Israel were inseparable. Whatever its potential for being further explored and interpreted, the resurrection was first and foundationally interpreted as the messianic event that vindicated Jesus and changed his disciples into a publicly proclaimed messianic community. It thus set before Israel the new locus of election.

The Root of the Conviction of Election

What had brought the kerygma into being was a radically reorienting experience. The vital and permanent residue of this experience was the consciousness of an appointed task: to bear witness to the supreme fulfillment event of human history. This was the resurrection of Jesus, the capstone of all the fulfillment events that had begun with the Baptist's proclamation in the wilderness. The experience of disciple-ship could be viewed in retrospect as having had its *raison d'être* in a preparation to interpret the Easter experience (cf. Acts 1:21f.). From the start this experience was appropriated not only as a seeing and hearing but as a meeting. The "Easter experience" may accordingly be defined as the sum of those meetings which produced in Cephas and the twelve, in James and Paul, the conviction that by a stunning act of divine vindication Jesus had become the "first" (Acts 26:23) to rise from the dead.

To suppose *a priori* either that the Easter experience could — or that it could not — have generated the beginnings of christology seems to me a fruitless exercise in abstraction.[11] On the concrete *a posteriori* basis of historical inquiry into the career of Jesus and its messianic thematization (the title on the cross: Mark 15:26; parr. Matt 27:37; Luke 23:28; John 19:19-22; the crown of thorns and other symbolic mockeries: Mark 15:17-20; parr. Matt 27:28-31; John 19:2-5; cf. Luke 23:11; the trial before Pilate: Mark 15:2,9; parr. Matt 27:11, 17, 22; Luke 23:2f.; John 18:33, 36f., 39; the trial before the Sanhedrin: Mark 14:58-62; parr. Matt 26:61-64; cf. John 18:35; the confession at Caesarea Philippi: Mark 8:27-30; parr. Matt 16:13-20; Luke 9:18-21; cf. John 1:41f.; 6:68f.), it is evident that the Easter experience was, in fact, the consummation rather than the origin of the interpretation of Jesus as Messiah.[12] For the first disciples the passover of the resurrection was the presupposition not of messianic faith but of messianic *homologia*: the public acknowledgment of Jesus' enthronement as Messiah and Lord (*mēšīhā'* / *christos*; *mārē'-* / *kyrios*).

The "fulfillment" announced by the kerygma was fulfillment far outrunning the to-be-fulfilled; fulfillment, that is, transposed the to-be-fulfilled to a higher register. In historical terms rabbinic *halaka* represented a continuous and fully explicable development of post-Exilic Israel.[13] By contrast, the Lordship of the crucified Messiah was a savage break both with biblical expectations and Jewish dispositions. Only after acknowledging this harsh discontinuity is it possible, in the context of the absolute eschatology of Jesus and of his post-Easter disciples, to find lines of continuity between the "fulfillment" and what it claimed to fulfill. Historical-critical scholarship has often found this task baffling. Thus, kerygma theology tended to consider the claims of "fulfillment" historically artificial and theologically dis-

---

[11]See B. F. Meyer, *The Aims of Jesus*, 175-9.

[12]Meyer, *Aims*, 179-202.

[13]See Rudolf Meyer, "Die Bedeutung des Pharisäismus für Geschichte und Theologie des Judentums," *Theologische Literaturzeitung* 77 (1952): 677-84.

pensable.[14] Independent investigators such as Oscar Cullmann,[15] Ethelbert Stauffer,[16] and Nils Alstrup Dahl[17] found the title "Messiah" to reflect an eschatological conception that had "almost nothing at all" in common with Jesus.[18] Others observed that the earliest church could ground its claim to be "Israel" only by a factitious (e.g., "christological-allegorical")[19] appeal to the scriptures. These views variously reflect the way New Testament fulfillment themes soar over the literal sense of Old Testament texts. Nevertheless, certain claims to continuity— between "Messiah" and Jesus as between "Israel" and the post-Easter community of his disciples—are intelligibly grounded in a conjunction of scriptural meanings and historical acts. Thus, in the earliest Christian usage neither "Messiah" nor "Israel" was merely honorific. Historically grounded in Jesus' self-understanding, "Messiah" epitomized his purpose as the task of building the house of God (Mark 14:58; par. Matt 26:61; Isa 28:16; Matt 16:18.)[20] The earliest community was precisely that house, the vanguard of Israel, just a step ahead of the rest of the people, urgently summoning its brethren to come into their heritage. But this vanguard of Israel had not invented itself by an allegorical

[14]See Rudolf Bultmann, "Prophecy and Fulfillment," in *Essays on Old Testament Hermeneutics* (Richmond: Knox, 1960) 50-75, and "The Significance of the Old Testament for the Christian Faith," in *The Old Testament and Christian Faith*, New York: Harper & Row, 1963, 8-35.

[15]Oscar Cullmann, *The Christology of the New Testament* (London: SCM, 1963) 118-33.

[16]Ethelbert Stauffer, *Jesus and His Story* (London: SCM, 1960) 131f.

[17]N. A. Dahl, "The Crucified Messiah," in *The Crucified Messiah and Other Essays* (Minneapolis: Augsburg, 1974) 10-36.

[18]N. A. Dahl, "The Crucified Messiah," 27.

[19]Johann Maier, *Geschichte der jüdischen Religion* (Berlin-New York: de Gruyter, 1972) 66.

[20]There is a manifold nexus binding Isa 28:16 and Matt 16:17-19, namely, the motifs of Davidic royalty, stone/rock, and faith as access to the remnant of the saved. On the Matthean text see Meyer, *Aims*, 185-97.

reading of the scriptures. It had assembled in response to a call dividing Israel between those destined respectively for restoration or for ruin (Mark 6:10f.; parr. Matt 10:14f.; Luke 9:5); that is, the grounding of the earliest community's self-definition did not turn on a "christological-allegorical" reading of the scriptures but on positive responses to a people-sundering summons to faith (Matt 10:21f., 34-37; par. Luke 12:51-53). Without reference to Jesus' historic career and the purposes that powered it, it is not possible to do justice to the grounding of the post-Easter community's self-understanding.

According to the oracle of Nathan God said to David "I will raise up your heir after you" (2 Sam 7:12) as he had said to Moses "I will raise up for them a prophet like you..." (Deut 18:18). The apostolic preaching presented both these texts (cf. Rom 1:4; Acts 3:22f.) as promises finding fulfillment in the resurrection of Jesus. It follows from the second of them that it was the prophet "raised up" in accord with the scriptures who addressed Israel in the kerygma (Acts 3:22b). In further accord with the scriptures, "anyone who does not listen to that prophet shall be cut off from the people" (Acts 3:23; cf. Deut 18:19; Lev 23:29; 11QTemple 25:12). The new locus of election was genuinely open to all Israel; but to reject it was to repudiate a divine summons — new, climactic, definitive — the response to which defined God's chosen ones (*eklektoi*). The root of the conviction of election was the Easter experience of Jesus' disciples.

Such was the drama of the kerygma and its cutting edge, as earliest Christianity itself understood it. Like the warning of the Baptist and the proclamation of Jesus, the kerygma had for its purpose to call into being God's eschatological people. Negative response turned it into a sword of division separating "my people" from "not my people." Through the kerygma God was enacting a normative economy of reconciliation in Christ. Paul's classically biblical conviction that God's call of Israel was "irrevocable" (Rom 11:28f.) did not contradict this in any way. But — in a prophetic move still to be fully appreciated and exploited by Christian theology today — Paul broke the kerygma's monopoly on access to

222186

salvation by affirming the "secret" that "all Israel" would call on the name of the Lord, once he had come as parousiac "deliverer" to effect the purification of "Jacob" (Rom 11:25f.)

IV

The Christian Hebraioi *of Jerusalem*

Set in concrete historical context, the earliest kerygma, we have said, is an index to Christian identity and to the earliest Christian self-understanding — biblical, ecclesial, and bound at the outset to the land and people of Israel. The last phrase calls for further exploration. The disciples of Jesus were Galileans and a gospel text attributes to Jesus himself the mysterious promise that, risen, he would "go before [=lead?] them into Galilee" (Mark 14:28; par. Matt 26:32). But when "Cephas and the twelve" (1 Cor 15:5) step into the light of post-Easter history, they are settled in Jerusalem (Gal 1:17-19; 2:2-10; Acts 1-15). Why Jerusalem?

Luke answers: because of a command of the risen Jesus (Acts 1:4). But the text recounting this command is redactional rather than traditional and, indeed, is central to Luke's schematic redactional design (cf. Luke 24:47; Acts 1:8). It is inescapable that the text of Acts 1:4 depends on, but does not historically explain, the settlement of the Christian community in Jerusalem.

F. C. Burkitt, in his London lectures on Christian beginnings over fifty years ago, argued that Luke must have been right in locating "the Easter experience" in Jerusalem: "If

LORETTE WILMOT LIBRARY
NAZARETH COLLEGE

the experience of Peter — and it was Peter's experience, no doubt, that was decisive — took place at Jerusalem, then we understand why Peter is found at Jerusalem as soon as we hear of him again. Otherwise it remains a riddle of which no reasonable explanation has ever been given."[1] In the more than half-century since Burkitt's lectures, however, no corroborative analysis of the localization of the Easter appearances in Jerusalem has succeeded in imposing itself.[2] The question "Why Jerusalem?" has remained open. Not long ago Martin Hengel answered it by reference to the community's mission to Israel. "*Whoever wished to address all Israel had to do so in Jerusalem.*"[3] This is doubtless correct. But there was a prior and still more fundamental reason (of which Hengel was explicitly aware, though he did not develop it): the capital city of Jerusalem was the center of the world.

With no tribal associations from early Israelite history, Jerusalem had originally been an unlikely candidate for capital. But this very fact, together with the excellent defensibility of the site, only made it the more attractive to David, the first figure in Hebrew history to claim effective rule over all the tribes. Representing a new and suspect beginning, David's object was to legitimate his kingship, capital, and succession. A virtuoso step in this direction was to bring the ark of the covenant to Jerusalem (2 Sam 6). His son Solomon was to place it in the sanctuary of his temple (1 Kings 8). Mount Zion thus became the throne of Yahweh and embarked on a religious career that has not ended to this day. We shall ask whether a communitarian self-understanding drawing on this tradition might not supply the basic answer to why Jesus' Galilean disciples established themselves in the city of David.

[1]F. C. Burkitt, *Christian Beginnings* (London: London University Press, 1924) 86.

[2]See Hans Conzelmann, "Literaturbericht zu den synoptischen Evangelien," *Theologische Rundschau* 43 (1978): 3-51, cf. 13.

[3]Martin Hengel, "Die Ursprünge der christlichen Mission," 31; "Zwischen Jesus und Paulus," 174.

Peter, John, and James, "the brother of the Lord," were "reputed," according to Paul, "as pillars" (*styloi*, Gal 2:9). Now, the use of "pillars" in the text of Galatians 2 (v. 9: "James and Cephas and John, reputed as pillars") is probably irreducible to isolated metaphor. The positive probability is that "pillars" here derived from a stock of architectural symbols expressing the conception of the community as the house of God.[4] The three were "pillars" of that spiritual and eschatological temple foreshadowed by the temple of Jerusalem or, rather, by its inner sanctuary or shrine (*hēkāl/naos*).

If this is correct, the second chapter of Galatians provides the earliest evidence of the earliest self-understanding of the Jerusalem community. Recognizably rooted in scriptural themes, it nevertheless represents a momentous development beyond the scriptures. For in the scriptures and, above all, in Ezekiel the form of the promise of salvation was "my sanctuary in the midst of them forever" (Ezek 37:36, cf. v. 28). But among the earliest Christians (as among the Essenes, cf., e.g., 1QS 8:5-9; 1QH 6:25-28), the community itself became God's sanctuary. Hence the deep and vital tie in the earliest Christian consciousness between, on the one hand, the treasure of prophecy bearing on Jerusalem, Zion, and the temple and, on the other, the Easter community of the already exalted Messiah.

That the earliest community conceived of itself as the Zion of eschatological prophecy is securely confirmed by the motif of the gathering of the dispersed of Israel in Acts 2:5-11.[5] Isaiah (together with Deutero-Isaiah and Trito-Isaiah), Jeremiah, Joel, Micah, and Zechariah had specified Zion as the place of God's climactic and definitive saving

[4]See C. K. Barrett, "Paul and the 'Pillar' Apostles," in *Studia Paulina* (Haarlem: Bohm, 1953) 1-19, cf. 12-16.

[5]See Antonin Causse, "Le pèlerinage à Jérusalem et la première Pente-côte," *Revue d'Histoire et de Philosophie religieuses* 20 (1940): 120-41; Eberhard Güting, "Der geographische Horizont der sogenannten Völkerliste des Lukas (Acta 2, 9-11)," *Zeitschrift für die neutestamentliche Wissenschaft* 66 (1975): 149-69, cf. 164-9.

act, and Deutero-Isaiah in particular had used "Zion" to signify the community chosen for restoration (e.g., Isa 51:16). The Qumran covenanters, out of the tension between a cultivated consciousness of priestly status and a *de facto* separation from the Jerusalem temple, worked out a communitarian self-understanding according to which the community itself constituted the spiritual and eschatological temple of Isa 28:16, "a house of holiness" (1QS 8:5) and "a holy of holies" (1QS 8:5f., 8), which essentially took the place of the Jerusalem sanctuary. (How the Jerusalem sanctuary ought to have been built is detailed by the Temple Scroll, which also attests the belief of the Essenes that on the day of [eschatological] blessing" God would build a new sanctuary in accord with his covenant with Jacob in Bethel, see 11Q Temple 29:8-10; cf. 5Q13 2:6; Jub 32:16.) Thus, the Essene fellowship — the remnant of Israel (e.g., CD 2:11; cf. 1QM 13:7f.; 14:6-8) — had become the new bearer of election.

Now, the earliest Christian community was characterized by a comparable self-understanding. We have substantial data, however, precisely on its *ties* with the temple (Acts 2:46; 3; 5:19-21, 42; 21:17-26; 22:17-21).[6] With respect to the temple and so by implication to the land and people of Israel, the religious self-affirmation of the Easter community was open in principle to two distinct stances. It could accent continuity or discontinuity. Like the Qumran covenanters it could conceive of itself as having (at least currently) taken the place of the temple, in which case there

---

[6]Like Jesus before them, the *hebraioi* are represented, not as partaking in sacrificial ceremonies — that in the early years they took part in the slaying of the passover lamb, though possible (Joachim Jeremias, "pascha," TDNT V, 902), is uncertain — but as participating in common prayer at the temple, and in teaching there. Within the limits of their distinctive commitments, they bound themselves to the maximum to the pious Israel of their day. Nevertheless, the heart of their cultic life was signified by the ritual "breaking of the bread" (Acts 2:46; cf. 20:7), which introduced celebration of the eucharist in the private homes of the faithful. See Xavier Léon-Dufour, *Le partage du pain eucharistique selon le Nouveau Testament* (Paris: Seuil, 1982) 31-34.

would be effected in the Christian consciousness a displacement of scriptural reference from the literal Jerusalem and literal temple to the new-born community. Or it could conceive of itself as the mediating key, hitherto unknown but now revealed, to the fulfillment of the mass of biblical prophecy on Israel, Jerusalem, Zion, temple, sanctuary. Both these options appear to have found realization and expression. Thus, the process of self-definition,beginning in conscious continuity with Israel at large, came finally to reflect Israel's non-entry into its messianic heritage (cf. the gospels). But discontinuity with Israel found even earlier expression as Greek-speaking Jewish converts, among the first-fruits of the Easter kerygma, established themselves as a distinctive force within the Jerusalem community (Acts 6:1-6) and one unabashedly expressing the consciousness of a break with Israel as epitomized in the Jerusalem temple (Acts 7). For Jewish Christians hailing from "the diaspora of the Greeks" (the *hellēnistai* of Acts) and for native Palestinian Jewish Christians (*hebraioi*) alike, the community of believers had itself been made the sanctuary of the living God. We set aside for the present what the *hellēnistai* made of this. Here we are concerned with the vision of the *hebraioi* and its background.

As God's dwelling place, the community was the first-fruits of messianic salvation; and, as the first-fruits sanctify the whole harvest to come, this community on Zion sanctified all Israel on the point of entry into its heritage. Not the community *in place* of Zion but *on* Zion. Between Zion and the community there was a bond of reciprocal dependence. If it was the community that made Zion the Zion of fulfillment, it was Zion that established the accord between the Scriptures and the community, between the terms of prophecy and those of fulfillment. It was precisely in fulfillment of the scriptures that the Easter community of Jerusalem became the point of assembly for the dispersed of Israel (Acts 2:5-11). In the "new covenant" chapter of Jeremiah "he who scattered Israel" would now "gather" and "keep" him "as a shepherd keeps his flock" (Jer 31:10), and so "they shall come and sing aloud on the height of Zion" (v. 12). At the restoration of Israel people would again say

> Yahweh bless you, O dwelling-place of rightousness, O holy hill! (Jer 31:23).

The dispersed would be gathered "from all the countries to which I have banished them"; they would have "one heart and one way" and the new covenant with them would be "everlasting" (Jer 32:37-40). Jerusalem was destined to become "a name of joy" (Jer 33:9) and would be called "Yahweh is our righteousness" (Jer 32:16). According to Ezekiel, the name of God would be "hallowed" by Israel's being restored in the sight of all the nations, for so the whole world would know "that I am Yahweh" (Ezek 36:23). But this salvation would begin with the gathering of the dispersed. They would be gathered "from all sides" (Ezek 37:21), for Jerusalem was the center of the world (Ezek 5:5; cf. 38:12) — a conviction that had lived in the consciousness of Israel for a thousand years prior to the birth of the Easter community on Zion. Dispersion among the nations in the wake of the northern kingdom's collapse (722) and the fall of Jerusalem (586) had failed to extinguish Israel's sense of election and consequent hope of national restoration. Indeed, it was the catastrophe of dispersion that had converted the coming "day of Yahweh" into a day of salvation, the day on which the dispersion would be reversed. Given the restoration of Israel, moreover, Zion would become the goal of the pilgrimage of the nations (Isa 2:2-4; 18:7; 25:6; 60:1-22; 66:18-23; Jer 3:17, Hag 2:7; Zech 8:20-23; 14:16-19; cf. Isa 14:1f.; 19:23). "Zion, for whom no one cares" (Jer 30:17) would attain its destiny as the peak (Isa 2:2) and sanctuary (e.g., Isa 56:7) of the world.

This tradition (the dimensions of which we have barely indicated) had been mediated to Jesus' followers by words and acts of the master himself. Contrary to a stubborn misconception, Jesus was no "universalist"; nor did he envisage a world mission.[7] The nations were indeed invited to the banquet of salvation, but in the post-historical future, and by their own coming "from east and west" to share it (Matt 8:11; par. Luke 13:29). The wild birds would flock to nest in the branches of the mustard bush (Mark 4:32; parr. Matt 13:32; Luke 13:19) that was to grow out of Jesus' ministry. The "city on a mountain" conspicuous in "the radiance of Yahweh" (Isa 60:1) was — the disciples of Jesus (Matt 5:14; cf. Thomas 32)! Simon was the "rock" (*kêpā'*) on which Jesus, as Messiah, would build the temple of believers (Matt 16:16-19). Above all, the cleansing of the temple must be considered here. No recorded action of Jesus was more laden with symbolic meaning. In its historic immediacy the cleansing aimed at putting an end not only to pre-passover money changing (Mark 11:15; parr. Matt 21:12; John 2:15) and merchandising (Mark 11:15; parr. Matt 21:12; Luke 19:45; John 2:14) in the court of the gentiles and to secular traffic using the court as a short-cut (Mark 11:16), but perhaps to the cult itself — at least for the space of a symbolically significant moment. This, however, detracts nothing from the episode as fulfillment-event (cf. Zech 14:21) and symbol-charged act signifying the future: judgment on empirical Israel (to be related thematically to the cleansing: Matt 23:38; par. Luke 13:35a; cf. Luke 19:41-44) and the restoration of believing Israel (the cleansing as present "sign" — cf. 2 Kings 20:9; Isa 7:11; 38:7; Jer 44:29 — of the future fulfillment of the mass of prophecy on Zion and temple).

Even this, however, fails to yield up the whole secret and whole meaning of the cleansing of the temple (as Mark 11:17, citing Isa 56:7 on the temple as "a house of prayer for

[7]Still the most cogent analysis of the issue is the essay of Bengt Sundkler, "Jesus et les païens," *Revue d' Histoire et de Philosophie religieuses* 16 (1936): 462-99. See also Joachim Jeremias, *Jesus' Promise to the Nations* (London: SCM, 1958). On the non-historicity of the explicitly universalist post-Easter missionary mandate, see Anton Vögtle, "Die ekklesiologischen Auftragsworte des Auferstandenen," in *Das Evangelium und die Evangelien* (Düsseldorff: Patmos, 1971) 243-52.

all peoples," already suggests). But to arrive at this "whole meaning" we must first recall the age-old cosmological image underlying the whole of biblical tradition on the temple. It is the image of the universe as "firmament" (*rāqîaʿ*: "that inverted bowl we call the sky"), "dry land" (*yabbāšâ*), and primeval "deep" (*tĕhôm*) beneath the dry land and above the firmament. The universe is just as it appears. Sun, moon, and stars are set in the firmament and rain is the primeval water seeping through perforations in it. The land is preeminently mountains, their bases sunk in the primeval ocean, their backs emerging above its surface. At the horizon they are pillars supporting the firmament. Numinous and uncanny, the mountains are rivets binding the stories of the universe: sky, land, subterranean sea. The highest mountain is in the center. In its hollow depths lies the netherworld. Directly above is the point of access to him "who sits above the circle of the earth" (Isa 41:22). The point on earth at which the world axis connects heaven, earth, and netherworld is the site of the world sanctuary.[8] Among the patriarchal sagas the dream of Jacob revealed Bethel ("house of El") as this holy place:

> And he dreamed that there was a stairway set up on the earth, its top reaching heaven. And lo, the messengers of God were ascending and descending it: And, lo, Yahweh stood above it: ... And [Jacob] was afraid and said, "How awesome is this place! This is none other than the house of God, and that the gate of heaven!" (Gen 28:12f., 17).

[8]See A. J. Wensinck, *The Ideas of the Western Semites Concerning the Navel of the Earth* (Amsterdam: Muller, 1917) 1-10; E. A. S. Butterworth, *The Tree at the Navel of the Earth* (Berlin: de Gruyter, 1970) 1-5. Shmarjahu Talmon, "*har, gibhʿah*," TDOT III, 437f., has urged that the navel motif is absent from the Hebrew Bible and that *tabbûr* originally meant not "navel" but "high plateau." If this is so, the thematic complex "navel of the earth" will have entered the tradition of Israel in the intertestamental period (see, e.g., LXX Ezek 38:12), complementing the already age-old complex of Zion themes.

Probably as early as the age of Solomon Mount Zion began to be invested with the properties of paradisal myth (Gen 2) and was celebrated as such in the Spring and Autumn cult. The liturgy of "songs of Zion" may well antedate Isaiah.[9] It survives in some of the oldest psalms and is extended in the later psalm literature. "Yahweh reigns!" (Pss 93:1; 96:10; 97:1; 99;1; 146:10; cf. 47:9 [EVV v.8]), "enthroned on the cherubim" (Ps 99:1f.; cf. 47:8), "robed in majesty, girt with power" (Ps 93:1). His reign was his effective re-imposition of rule over the cosmos (Pss 47; 93; 96; 97; 98; cf. 46; 95). From his sanctuary on Zion he secured Israel from its enemies (Pss 20; 46; 47; 48; 93; 97; 98), for he was Lord over all nations on earth (Pss 47; 48; 96; 99). "Of Zion they shall say: 'One and all were born in her'" (Ps 87:5), for everyone, no matter where he was born, would recognize in Zion his real home (Ps 87:7). The psalms often celebrate Zion in mythical terms. Ps 48 refers to "his holy mountain, the fairest of heights," and "joy of all the earth" (v. 3; [EVV v.2]); if the Masoretic text of Ps 46:5 is accurate, it alludes to "the stream whose channels gladden the city of God" (cf. Ezek 47; Joel 4:18 [EVV 3:18]; Zech 14:8. Ps 9 sets "the gates of death" against "the gates of daughter Zion" (vv. 14f. [EVV 13f.]). From Zion, finally, God summons the whole earth "from the rising of the sun to its setting" (Ps 50:1) and his reign conjures up the image of "the princes of the peoples gathered together with the people of the God of Abraham" (Ps 47:10 [EVV v. 9]), for "all the ends of the earth shall remember and turn to Yahweh" (Ps 22:28 [EVV v. 27]; cf. Ps 86:9), bringing their offerings to the temple court (Ps 96:8-10; cf. Ps 68:30 [EVV v. 29]). Little wonder that tradition early and late would find a reference to the navel of the world in the text of Ps 74:12 on God "working salvation in

---

[9]See Hans Wildberger, "Die Völkerwallfahrt zum Zion. Jes II 1-5," *Vetus Testamentum* 7 (1957): 62-81. Günther Wanke, *Die Zionstheologie der Korachiten in ihrem traditionsgeschichtlichen Zusammenhang* (Berlin: Töpelmann, 1966) fails, in my opinion, to demolish Wildberger's argu-

the midst of the earth" ($b^c qereb\ h\bar{a}\,{}'\bar{a}re\d{s}/enmeso\,t\bar{e}s\ g\bar{e}s$).[10]

Isaiah, in any case, drew on established traditions in his description of the world sanctuary and the pilgrimage of the nations (Isa 2:2-4). This vision became a biblical *topos* (Isa, Jer, Trit Isa, Hag, Zech) which in various ways was prolonged in postcanonical literature. But it had never been the sole theme, nor a completely unambiguous theme, on the nations;[11] and especially in the wake of the ruthless Roman suppression of the Jewish revolts (AD 66-73 and 132-136), the theme of Zion, sanctuary of the nations, was swamped by themes of vengeance on the nations and their destruction.

For Jesus, on the contrary, the primeval imagery of the world sanctuary was a vital resource. It should never be forgotten how charged with symbolism his words and acts were. He regularly drew on the near-eastern reservoir of symbols to image the dawn and consummation of salvation. And his public acts, such as his establishing "the twelve" and sending them to Israel, his cures and exorcisms, and his table fellowship with sinners, were parabolic as well as pragmatic; they were acts symbolizing as well as realizing the restoration of Israel. Israel thus occupied the forefront of his field of vision but always, it would seem, set in a cosmic context — hence the imagery of cosmic renewal

mentation. See also Hanns-Martin Lutz, *Yahwe, Jerusalem und die Völker* (Neukirchen-Vluyn: Neukirchener Verlag, 1968). John Gray, *The Biblical Doctrine of the Reign of God* (Edinburgh: T. & T. Clark, 1979) 175, note 34, presents another solution: the text of Isa 2:2-4 is indeed as early as or earlier than Isaiah of Jerusalem, but it is not his composition. It originally belonged to the liturgy of the Autumn festival. A post-Exilic editor inserted it at this point in the text on the basis of kingship themes in Isa 2:6ff.

[10]See, e.g., Didymus of Alexandria, *De Trinitate, Migne* PG 39, 324. This interpretation was taken up in Judaism and became a millenary tradition in Christianity.

[11]See Gerhard von Rad on Isa 60 and Hag 2:6-9, "The City on the Hill" in *The Problem of the Hexateuch and Other Essays* (Edinburgh: Oliver and Boyd, 1966) 231-42.

which readily appeared in words on Israel's restoration (e.g., Mark 2:21f.; parr. Matt 9:16f.; Luke 5:36-38; Thomas 47b).[12] It is this cosmic dimension that comes to light when the temple cleansing is considered against the background sketched above.

The synoptic gospels present several instances of the "I have come" type of saying, which consists of two parts: the formula "I have come" (*ēlthon*/ '*ātēt*) and the specifying infinitive, "to summon," "to complete," etc.[13] Now the single, continuous event made up of Jesus' royal entry into Jerusalem and the cleansing of the temple corresponds, in the mode of parabolic conduct, to the "I have come" series of words. It is an "I have come" action — an action designed to specify the purposes of the agent.[14] The entry implictly

---

[12]See Joachim Jeremias, *The Parables of Jesus* (London: SCM, 1963) 117f.

[13]"I have come" means "it is my intention, my task"; see Joachim Jeremias, "Die älteste Schicht der Menschensohn-logien in den Evangelien," *Zeitschrift fur die neutestamentliche Wissenschaft* 58 (1967): 159-72, cf. 167. This incomplete semantic structure is completed by an infinitive defining the intention or task. In support of the same conclusion, see Eduard Arens, *The ĒLTHON-Sayings in the Synoptic Tradition* (Freiburg: Universitätsverlag, 1976) 253-87. For a critique of Jeremias and Arens, see Jan-Adolf Bühner, *Der Gesandte und sein Weg* (Tübingen: Mohr, 1977) 138-66.

[14]The symbolic acts of the prophets were veiled revelations of God's will for Israel. But Jesus' symbolic acts — in the controlling context of the question put to him implicitly and explicitly from the beginning to the end of his career, namely, "Who are you?" (that is, what role do you claim to perform?) — were a veiled revelation not only of God's will for Israel but of Jesus' own answer to the "Who are you?" question. Like the words "I have come," his symbolic acts (e.g., the choice and sending of the twelve, cures and exorcisms, dining with outcasts), precisely as symbolic acts, expressed his intention or task. In this sense, each symbolic act corresponded to an "I have come" saying. The act itself corresponded to the words "I have come" and the symbolic meaning of the act corresponded to the complementary infinitive. The diverse symbolic acts thus said in effect: It is my task (by cures and exorcisms) "to heal and to free," (by dining with outcasts) "to reintegrate them into God's people," etc.

identified Jesus as the lowly and pacific "king" of Zech 9:9. The symbolic thrust of the cleansing corresponded to the specifying infinitive in an "I have come" saying. And if the cleansing accounts as they now stand in the gospels accentuate the judgment-character of Jesus' symbolic act[15] and so would say "to consign to destruction," the original act bore above all a promise-character, saying: "to purify and renew." Furthermore, in the light of the eschatological context projected by Jesus' whole career, we should accent the symbolism of the temple as the epitome of the universe, the navel and sanctuary not of Israel alone but of the whole world. Jesus' action accordingly said: "I have come to purify and renew not only the temple but Israel, not only Israel but the world."[16] It is possible that the concrete setting of the court of the gentiles supports this significance[17]; in any case, the citation of Isa 56:7

My house shall be called a house of prayer for all peoples

underscores it (Mark 11:17; cf. Matt 21:13; Luke 19:46).

At the center of Jesus' eschatology stood the messianic remnant of Israel, unique beneficiary of salvation. This was the root — the why and the wherefore — of Jesus' consistent

[15]C. K. Barrett, "The House of Prayer and the Den of Thieves" in *Jesus und Paulus* (Göttingen: Vandenhoeck & Ruprecht) 1975, 13-20.

[16]Sundkler, "Jésus," 499, has put the matter succinctly: "As Yahweh in the Old Testament enters the temple, so Jesus purifies the temple and thereby renews the world; for the temple is the center of the cosmos and the mission which Jesus willed is cosmic regeneration." The concrete specification of this symbolism, according to Jesus' esoteric teaching was his coming death for "the many" and his vindication on "the day of the Son of Man" that would bring in the reign of God and the renewal of the world. See Meyer, *Aims*, 202-19. For the temple cult Jesus would substitute, climactically, the expiatory and covenantal offering of his own body and blood.

[17]W. D. Davies, *The Gospel and the Land* (Berkeley: University of California Press, 1974) 349-52.

application to the disciples of the imagery of the city on a mountain (Matt 5:14; cf. Thomas 32), the cosmic rock (Matt 16:18; cf. John 1:42), and the new sanctuary (Mark 14:58; par. Matt 26:61). The disciples were the "flock" (Luke 12:32), destined to be scattered (Mark 14:27; parr. Matt 26:31; cf. John 16:32) and regathered (Mark 14:28; par. Matt 26:32; cf. John 16:17, 22), to whom (as to the "one like a son of man" in Dan 7:13f. or to "the holy ones of the Most High" in Dan 7:22, 27) God intended at the moment of eschatological consummation to "give (the) kingly rule" (Luke 12:32: *basileia* = *malkû*, Dan 7:14a; *malkûta'*, Dan 7:22, 27; cf. Matt 19:28; par. Luke 18:30).

The *hebraioi* gathered around Cephas and the twelve accordingly knew themselves as that sanctuary which Jesus was to build "in three days" (Mark 14:58; par. Matt 26:61; cf. John 2:19). In the light of this identification Israel was on the brink of becoming the city and the mountain and the temple celebrated by the prophets: "holy city" (Isa 52:1), "faithful city" (Isa 1:26; Zech 8:3) "city not forsaken" (Isa 62:12); "holy mountain" (Isa 11:9; Zech 8:3; Joel 4:17 [EVV 3:17]), "mountain of Yahweh's house" (Isa 2:1) where the name of Yahweh of hosts dwells (Isa 18:7); "house of the God of Jacob" (Isa 2:3), the "sanctuary" to be built by him whose name is "the Branch" (Zec 6:12), the spiritual temple (cf. Isa 28:16) crowned by the stone first rejected but then made the copestone of the portal (Ps 118:22).

Here, then, was the fulfillment of the promise of restortion — not a simple return to the past but "a new thing" (Isa 43:19) superior to all paradigms of salvation (cf. Jer 16:13). The splendor of this house was far greater than that of the temple built with hands (cf. Hag 2:9; Mark 14:58). If its present—despite the appearance of the community as a mere sect — was already one of fulfillment, of divine presence and power, of rapid and irrepressible growth, its future was to be the goal of the pilgrimage of the nations, when gentiles would join the restored people of the God of Abraham (Ps 47:10; cf. Isa 56:3-7; Zech 2:15). The program of eschatological Zion was to gain all Israel to its ranks, to greet the day when "the Man" would be revealed (Luke 17:30), to welcome the nations to Zion. For, the day of "the Man" was the day of the Lord; it would put an end to the eschatological ordeal and it would bring God's summons to the nations:

> Assemble yourselves and come, gather together, you survivors of the nations! (Isa 45:20).

This, surely, is the most basic of the reasons why the Galilean nucleus of Jesus' following settled in Jerusalem. They saw themselves not only as the heirs but as the living fulfillment of biblical promise and prophecy on Zion. They and the mountain on which they were established together constituted that Zion by whose light the nations were soon to march (Isa 60:3) and to which every mortal, regardless of where he came from, would say: "all my sources are in you" (Ps 87:7).

V

The Hellēnistai

We find world salvation in the horizons of the Aramaic-speaking church of Jerusalem but we do not find there the enabling conditions of a mission to the world, for this church conceived the salvation of the nations in terms of eschatological myth. But the nations were in fact to come into the legacy of the Jerusalem church not through a post-historical pilgrimage but through a historical world mission. Acts tells us that this took place through the mediation of Greek-speaking Jewish Christians whose perspectives made a mission to non-Jews possible and whose initiative made it actual (Acts 11:20). If we had not been told of the *hellēnistai* we would have had to invent them (as radical scholarship, not content with the data handed it by Acts on Greek-speaking Jews, has, in fact, preferred to re-invent them, as gentiles).

In dealing with the *hellēnistai* known to us from Luke's precious if lacunary sources, we shall focus mainly on what set them apart from the *hebraioi* and on this basis attempt to reconstruct at least some aspects of their ecclesial self-understanding. Our concern is twofold. First, the self-understanding of the *hellēnistai* is of interest in itself as a distinct point of contrast with contemporary and later developments in Christian self-definition. Second, this self-understanding is of peculiar interest as comprehending in itself the enabling conditions of the earliest mission to non-Jews.

It is not impossible that a nucleus of *hellēnistai* had been disciples of Jesus. The positive probability, however, is that, settled in Jerusalem or on pilgrimage there, they were all converts of the Easter kerygma (see Acts 2). What set them apart from other Christians in Jerusalem (as *hellēnistai* from *hebraioi)* was in the first instance a linguistic diversity[1] entailing separate eucharistic services and regular synagogal contact with distinct groups of Jerusalem Jews (cf. the *hellēnistai* of Acts 9:29). It is hardly surprising that out of such separation there should arise practical problems such as the inequity specified in Acts 6:1 (neglect of the Greek-speaking widows in the daily distribution of food). And if the *hellēnistai* were separated from the *hebraioi* by the use of a different language, a different text of the Bible, a different synagogue with its own exegetical traditions, and the intangible but pervasive impact of cultural orientations and styles from the Greek-speaking diaspora, can it be surprising that they should have appropriated in their own way their new faith in the risen Christ? Whatever it was that set them apart from the *hebraioi* at this level, it appears to have found expression in hostility to Torah and temple (Acts 6:14) and in openness to Samaritans (Acts 7:5) and gentiles (Acts 11:20).

What weight should we give to the alleged hostility to Torah and temple expressed in the testimony against Stephen (Acts 6:13f.)? And in answering this question should we draw on the latter's speech (Acts 7:2-53)? Source-critically,

---

[1]For a survey of critical opinion on the sense of "*hebraioi*" and "*hellēnistai*," see E. E. Ellis, "The Circumcision Party and the Early Christian Mission," in *Prophecy and Hermeneutic in Early Christianity* (Tubingen: Mohr, 1978) 116-28. For the most cogent presentation of the distinction in terms of linguistic diversity, see Martin Hengel, "Zwischen Jesus und Paulus," 157-61.

the trial and the speech are distinct, the speech having been inserted into an independent account of the trial (Acts 6:8-15; 7:54-60). Moreover, any estimate of the historical worth of the speech as an index to the views of Stephen and the *hellēnistai* must take account of the speech's unique and hence historically isolated content, its fragmentary state, and its imperfect correlation with its present context. For historians of early Christianity the speech is a mixed blessing, precious for its uniqueness (its view of the temple is paralleled neither in Judaism nor in Samaritanism nor in other known currents of Christianity) but baffling for the same reason. How to relate the speech to early Christian history remains a question.[2]

Despite the difficulties bequeathed to academic history by Acts on the *hellēnistai*, we have here seminal data on "the dynamic element" in earliest Christianity. In an effort to make these data productive we shall draw up a list of the materials in Acts and add to them other New Testament data that might count as derived from the *hellēnistai*; then we shall analyze the whole with a view to retrieving a distinct current of early Christian self-definition.

The data of Acts include the introduction of the *hellēnistai* into the story (6:1-6); Stephen's trial (6:8-15; 7:54-60) and speech (7:1-53); the story of Philip (8:4-40; cf. 21:8); the story of Paul's persecution (8:1-3), conversion (9:1-19), and proclamation of Jesus in the Greek-speaking synagogues of Damascus (9:19-22) and Jerusalem (9:29); the arrival of Christians in Antioch, the first preaching to gentiles, the relations of the Antioch community to that of Jerusalem (11:19-26). All this material probably derived from the *hellēnistai* themselves via an "Antiochene source."[3] Its historic

---

[2]Hengel, "Zwischen Jesus und Paulus," 159f., 186f., 191-93.

[3]Adolf von Harnack, *Die Apostelgeschichte* (Leipzig: Hinrichs, 1908) 169-73; Joachim Jeremias, "Untersuchungen zum Quellenproblem der Apostelgeschichte," *Zeitschrift für die neutestamentliche Wissenschaft* 36 (1937): 205-21, cf. 213-20; Hengel, "Zwischen Jesus und Paulus," 156f.

importance is evident. Despite their lacunary and episodic character, these texts convincingly indicate the *hellēnistai* as the initiators of the mission. The question arises as to how we can make this cardinal, cumulative datum historically intelligible.

Data deriving from the *hellēnistai* preserved in the synoptic tradition are difficult and perhaps impossible to specify with assurance. The translation of oral traditions from Aramaic into Greek was probably effected first by bi-lingual *hellēnistai* and eventually by bi-lingual *hebraioi* as they began to take part in the Greek-speaking sector of the world mission.[4] Here the contribution of the *hellēnistai* probably lay in a materially limited but interpretatively significant editing of oral traditions (e.g., the pre-redactional state of Mark 7:1-23). But to specify any synoptic texts as bearing the marks of pre-world-mission editing by the *hellēnistai* and thus as able to throw light on the launching of the mission is no doubt a hopeless task.

Acts, however, makes it likely that pre-literary gospel traditions were a source for the *hellēnistai* around Stephen; for, according to Acts, Stephen was accused of assuming an anti-Torah, anti-temple stance supported by elements that we learn from elsewhere belonged to the story of Jesus and surfaced at his trial (Mark 14:58; par. Matt 26:61; cf. John 2:19). The two charges against Stephen turned on intolerable claims on behalf of "Jesus the Nazorean": the first, that he would "destroy this place," i.e., the temple; the second, that he would "change the customs that Moses handed down to us" (Acts 6:14). If this is what Stephen was propagating in the Greek-speaking synagogues of Jerusalem, it would account for why from early in Christian history there was a perhaps spontaneous anti-Christian outburst (Acts 7) and an officially sanctioned Jewish persecution of Christians led by Paul of Tarsus (Gal 1:13,23; Phil 3:6; 1 Cor 15:9;

---

[4]On bi-lingual *hebraioi*, see Hengel, "Zwischen Jesus und Paulus," 171f.; on the beginnings of translation of the gospel tradition into Greek, 203f.

cf. Acts 8:3; 9:1-19; 22:4-16; 26:9-18), limited at first to the distinct and distinctly offensive Greek-speaking wing of the community (Acts 8:1).

In the charges against Stephen it is not difficult to recognize at least a garbled version of what Jesus actually taught, so that in the end it was Jesus himself, his sovereignly superior perspectives, purposes, and comportment — now maddeningly renewed by Greek-speaking converts to his cause — that re-triggered the *ressentiment* (cf. *phthonos*, Mark 15:10; par. Matt 27:18) that had always powered the persecution. Whether or not Jesus actually said he would (Mark 14:58) or could (Matt 26:61) destroy the temple sanctuary, there is every probability that an authentic saying of Jesus (cf. John 2:19) stands behind the formulation of the false witnesses both at the trial of Jesus (Mark 14:58; par. Matt 26:61) and in the charge against Stephen (Acts 6:14).[5] Moreover, the *hellēnistai* may have inherited the tradition of his telling the disciples that in the ordeal about to break out not one stone of the temple would be left upon another (Mark 13:2; parr. Matt 24:2; Luke 21:6; cf. Luke 19:44). In short, it is probable that the charges at Stephen's trial reflected his views and that it was proximately and immediately by their way of exploiting the Jesus tradition that Stephen and his followers drew down on themselves a lethal wrath.

Given this clue, it may be well to recall other resources from the Jesus tradition apt to appeal to a Christian group of which we can thus far say only that it seized on Jesus' temple riddle; that under the patronage of Jesus it predicted[6] or already called for a change in "the customs handed down" by Moses; and that it was singularly open,

---

[5]See B. F. Meyer, "The 'Inside' of the Jesus Event," in *Creativity and Method* (Milwaukee: Marquette University Press, 1981) 197-210, cf. 202-7.

[6]The future "will change" (Acts 6:14), which establishes the closest tie between temple and Law, may signify that the "customs" in question here were specifically those that related to temple cult.

when the opportunity presented itself, to "gospelling" (*euaggelizesthai*, Acts 8:4, 12, 25, 35, 40) to Samaritans and gentiles "the reign of God and the name of Jesus Christ" (Acts 8:12), salvation as the fulfillment of the prophecy of the Servant of God (Acts 8:32-35) and the revelation of Jesus as "Lord" (Acts 11:20; cf. 8:16, 22, 24, 26, 39).

Jesus' own teaching had not been meant to annul the Torah but to bring it to its appointed completion in a code of eschatological discipleship (Matt 5:17).[7] To orthodox Judaism, however, anyone who said that this or that verse of the Torah came not from heaven but from Moses "by his own mouth" or that the oral Torah with its *a fortiori* inferences and arguments from analogy was not from heaven, had "despised the word of the Lord" and should be "cut off" from the people (bSanh. 99a Bar.). Now, on both counts Jesus had violated this kind of sensibility on the part of Pharisaic scribes. He had declared that Moses wrote the provision for the dismissal of one's wife "in view of your hardness of heart" (Mark 10:5; par. Matt 19:8), adding: "what God has joined [cf. Gen 2:24] let man not separate" [cf. Deut 24:1ff.]! (Mark 10:9; par. Matt 19:6b). Indeed, he had rejected the casuistry of the scribes, root and branch (Mark 7:9-13; par. Matt 15:4-6; cf. Mark 2:15; parr. Matt 9:10; Luke 5:29; Matt 8:21f.; par. Luke 9:59bf.; Matt 11:16-19; par. Luke 7:31-35). It was remarkable, moreover, that when he referred to the ritual order it was only to assert its ordination to the moral order (Matt 5:24; 23:23; Mark 7:15; par. Matt 15:11). Did Christian *hellēnistai* fasten on such traditions in accord with a tendency, dating from before their entry into the Christian movement, to depreciate the ritual Torah? We have no clear answer; nor do we know how far back in time the first interpretation of Jesus as "declaring all foods clean" (Mark 7:19) goes. Luke's source material attributed the abolition of the distinction between ritually clean and unclean foods to a revelation to Peter (Acts 10:9-35). The traditions of Jesus' words such as

[7]See Joachim Jeremias, *New Testament Theology*, 83-5.

> Nothing that goes into a man from outside can defile him,
> but only what comes out of a man [scil., sins of speech]
> defiles him (Mark 7:15; par. Matt 15:11)

or

> The Law and the prophets were until John, since then the
> gospel of the reign of God is preached! (Luke 16:16; par.
> Matt 11:13)

or

> God made the sabbath for man, not man for the sabbath
> (Mark 2:27)

may have contributed to those convictions of the *hellēnistai*
that provoked the bitter protest "we have heard him say that
Jesus the Nazorean...will change the customs that Moses
handed down to us" (Acts 6:14).

But of themselves the themes that the *hellēnistai* drew
from the Jesus tradition do not account for the distinctive
way in which they were assimilated. A horizon is prior to the
particulars that attest it. We see today from the redactions
of Mark, Luke, and John how diverse currents of gentile
Christianity could recount the story of Jesus' mission, sub-
tly dissolve its original contours and reshape the whole in
accord with their own various perspectives.[8] This process
began with the Easter experience and was inevitably continuous. Transmitters and hearers alike took in the gospel
story by effecting a "fusion of horizons" with it without
regard for the niceties of originally intended meaning. Our
effort to locate the horizon in which the *hellēnistai* interpreted their own faith must go beyond particular texts to
address the question of the resurrection and the affirmation
of the risen "Son of man."

This question, in fact, touches *hebraioi* and *hellēnistai*

---

[8]There is no need to insist on this, relative to the Johannine redaction.
On the Markan and Lukan redactions, see Hans Conzelmann, "Literaturbericht zu den synoptischen Evangelien," *Theologische Rundschau* 37
(1972): 220-72; 43 (1978): 3-5; 321-27. On Mark, 245-57; 22-34. On Luke,
43-51.

alike. The *hebraioi* had deep roots in the past of Jesus' historic mission. Easter was a stunning validation of that past, for it vindicated Jesus' eschatological mission. But Easter was a stunning event, transcending all expectation and demanding a re-orienting interpretation; and here the advantage did not necessarily lie with the *hebraioi*. True, they stood as living guarantors of continuity between the Easter present and the pre-Easter past, including the pre-Easter messianic thematization of Jesus in Jerusalem (Mark 14:62; parr. Matt 26:64; Luke 22:67-70; cf. John 18:37) and, earlier, in the confession of Simon (Mark 8:27-29; parr. Matt 16:13-16; Luke 9:18-20; cf. John 6:68f.; 1:41f.). But Easter itself effected a break with the past by explosively differentiating the eschatological scenario of Jesus himself. In contrast to Jesus' own prophetic vision, his resurrection and the climactically triumphant reign of God diverged *ex eventu*. What had not been foreseen was the single, isolated resurrection of Jesus from the dead, a resurrection dissociated in time from the general resurrection to which it bore advance witness as "sign," a resurrection whose evidences were not manifest to the whole world as an aspect of God's triumph — neither imposed on his judges (cf. Mark 14:62; parr. Matt 26:64; Luke 22:69) nor bestowed on "all the people" (Acts 10:41) but reserved "to us who were chosen by God as witnesses" (Acts 10:41). The eschatological scheme which informed the authentic sayings of Jesus about the future had posited two distinct moments: that of the ordeal (*ho peirasmos*; Aram.: *nisyōnā'*) to be launched by his own suffering and death and comprehending a set of dreadful disasters, and that of the swiftly following ("in three days") resolution of the ordeal by the revelation of "the Man," the pilgrimage of the nations, the judgment, the new temple, the banquet with the patriarchs.[9] There had been no room in this scheme for a single resurrection to take place in historical time nor, consequently, for an interim between the resur-

---

[9]See B. F. Meyer, *The Aims of Jesus*, 202-9.

rection of Jesus and the coming of the reign of God.
Furthermore, we should in all probability posit an unresolved pre-Easter ambiguity respecting the disciples' identification of Jesus with "the Man." Perhaps the best
illustration of ambiguity in a "Son-of-Man"saying is, "Man
[Aram.:*bar 'enāšā'*, which, besides the generic sense "man"
could also have the definite and titular sense "the Man"] is
about to be delivered [by God] into the hands of men"
(Mark 9:31a;[10] parr. Matt 17:22; Luke 9:44b). Even should
the disciples have directly correlated Jesus with "the Man"
and Jesus' ultimate vindication with "the day on which the
Man is revealed" (Luke 17:30; cf. Mark 14:62; parr. Matt
26:64; Luke 22:69), they would still have had no grounds
whatever for expecting an eschatological resurrection of
Jesus prior to or apart from the cosmic coming of the reign
of God. This is the sense in which the Easter event shattered
the eschatological scenario of Jesus and required that the
whole be reconstituted.

The *hebraioi* reconstituted it as far as possible along the
lines laid down by Jesus himself: in the Easter community
on Zion Israel, represented by the first-fruits that sanctified
the whole imminent harvest, had entered into its promised
restoration. It would gather in its brethren and await the
divine ingathering of the nations. The experience of the
outpoured Spirit of God introduced a foundational, all-
permeating newness into the life of the *hebraioi*. For the
rest, the categories of their self-understanding were
grounded in the Jesus tradition: the living sanctuary, key to
the fulfillment of prophecies on Zion and temple; the remnant of the last days; the *qāhāl* (= the convoked people) of
the new covenant.[11] But for a full reconstruction of how the
hebraioi responded to the challenge of reconstituting Jesus'
eschatological scenario, we should have to know, in the first
place, what they did with the theme of the ordeal. For Jesus

[10]See Jeremias, *New Testament Theology*, 281f.

[11]See B. F. Meyer, *The Church in Three Tenses* (Garden City: Doubleday, 1971) 4-12.

the brief, fierce interim between his coming death and his vindication in the reign of God had been essentially characterized by an eschatology of woe epitomized in the destruction of the temple. This eschatology had been not reversed but only relieved by themes of grace such as the promise of the temple built on rock and secure from death (Matt 16:18), the revelation that for the sake of his chosen ones God had already decided to shorten the days of the ordeal (Mark 13:20; par. Matt 24:22), the prayer calling for the coming of God's reign and begging to be saved from apostasy under pressure (Matt 6:9-13 ; par. Luke 11:2-4). But once the disorienting Easter experience had imposed itself on the disciples, did they reaffirm the prophecies of the ordeal? Or did their sense of triumph at this new act of God have a revisionist impact on such prophecies as that "not one stone" of the Jerusalem temple would be "left upon another" (Mark 13:2; parr. Matt 24:2; Luke 21:6)?

The data of the first chapters of Acts, though they offer no ready-made answer to the question, indicate a global conception of the present moment to which doom-laden prophecy was alien and irrelevant. Easter had unexpectedly inserted into the eschatological scheme of things a last segment of time, a moment according Israel the grace of a last (and surely irresistible!) appeal to enter into its rightful heritage of messianic blessings: the forgiveness of sins and the gift of the Spirit (Acts 2:38; 5:31f.). Woes on city and temple gave way to a new scheme of things. The present, the hour appointed for national repentance, was a prelude to "times of refreshment" (cf. 4 Ezra 11:46): the sending of the risen Jesus to Israel as its Messiah (Acts 3:20) and the moment of "universal restoration" promised through the prophets (Acts 3:21).[12]

The Jerusalem *hellēnistai* differed from this vision of things at the two points we have already signaled: their

---

[12]That the text of Acts 3:19-21, like the speech material in Acts generally , is a Lukan composition is clear; it is nonetheless probable that Luke here draws on pre-Lukan tradition (see Jürgen Roloff, *Die Apostelge-schichte* [Göttingen: Vandenhoeck & Ruprecht, 1981] 77f.). For a con-

hostility to temple and Torah (Acts 6:14) and their openness to proselytizing Samaritans (Acts 7:5) and gentiles (Acts 11:20). But we have now moved to the view that the root of these differences must be located not merely in their use of the Jesus tradition but in a prior and more fundamentally explanatory move, e.g., in a projection of horizons by a distinctive appropriation of the Easter event. What interpretation of the Easter event would supply the enabling conditions of the concrete traits we have noticed?

A first approximation might consist in observing that, contrary to the *hebraioi* (whose probable view was optimistically revisionist), the *hellēnistai* interpreted the Easter present as validating Jesus' eschatology of woe on unbelieving Israel: the temple was doomed. Just as the muffling of themes on the ordeal followed among the *hebraioi* from their positive view of the new situation created by the Easter event, the aggressive accentuation of such themes among the *hellēnistai* must have an explanatory setting in their positive view of the novelty of Easter.

A second approximation might accordingly be to posit a radicalizing eschatology by which the *hellēnistai*, unlike the *hebraioi*, conceived the Easter event as transcending the entire old order of things. Henceforward life would be lived in "the age to come." Temple and Torah were obsolete. There would no longer be "Jew" and "Samaritan". . . . This line of reconstruction, to be sure, would be more satisfying if we had clearer indices to the controlling eschatological conceptions of the *hellēnistai*. As it is, the account of Stephen's trial supplies us with one reference to the Son-of-Man theme (Acts 7:56)[13] and in the story of Philip we meet a prophetic interpretation of the Isaian passage on the suffer-

---

trary view, making the text Lukan through and through, and a survey of opinion on this text, see G. Lohfink, "Christologie und Geschichtsbild in Apg 3, 19-21," *Biblische Zeitschrift* 13 (1969): 223-41.

[13]On the translation-Greek that renders *bar/bᵉrā' 'ĕnāš(ā')* with remarkable consistency as *ho huios tou anthrōpou*, and for a plausible view of the sense of this title among the *hellēnistai*, see Hengel, "Zwischen Jesus und Paulus," 202f.

ing Servant (Acts 8:32-35). Though limited and undeveloped, both these allusions to biblical sources are significant, for both sources strike the note of universalism. The salvation of the "many" (= the nations) in which the great Servant text culminates (Isa 53:11; LXX Isa 53:11; cf. 53:12) has as its only antecedent supposition the obedient suffering of the Servant; and the universal dominion of the "one like a son of man" (cf. "all nations, tribes, and languages," LXX Dan 7:14) follows immediately on his ascent to the court of the Ancient of Days (LXX Dan 7:13). The *hellēnistai* need only have identified the Easter event with the reversal of the fate of the Servant (LXX Isa 53:10b-12) and with the ascent of the "one like a son of man" (LXX Dan 7:13) to have understood this event as grounding scripturally an explicit universalism *now*.

The *hebraioi* celebrated restoration; the *hellēnistai*, transcendence. We can make this distinction concrete by concluding our survey with a consideration of two texts conserved by Paul, texts that were not only mediated to him by the *hellēnistai* (as were most, if not all, of the kerygmatic formulas he inherited) but that originated in all likelihood among the *hellēnistai* as their own compositions. Though both probably date from a post-Stephen period, both are products of early Greek-speaking Christianity. They are the fragment underlying Rom 3:25-26 and the hymn preserved in Phil 2:6-11.

That the text of Rom 3:25-26 is at least partly pre-Pauline follows from a convergence of data: the lapidary, hieratic diction, the overloaded and sometimes baffling syntax, and several divergences from Paul's characteristic vocabulary and conceptuality.[14] Like other unannounced citations of traditional material in the Pauline letters (Rom 4:25; 8:34b;

---

[14]*Protithesthai* and *hamartēma* are rare in Paul; *paresis, proginesthai,* and *hilastērion* are Pauline *hapax legomena*; the relative clause *hon proetheto*...suggests a formula; the cultic typology entailed in *hilastērion* is atypical of Paul; there is a syntactical difficulty in intelligibly relating the phrase beginning *dia tēn paresin* with what precedes it.

Phil 2:6), this one begins with a relative pronoun (*hon proetheto*, "whom God displayed," v. 25). A satisfactory literary critique isolates, in my opinion, a pre-Pauline distich:

> *hon proetheto ho theos hilastērion en tō*
> *autou haimati*
> *dia tēn paresin tōn progegonotōn*
> *hamartēmatōn en tę̄ anochę̄ tou theou.*

This may be rendered:

> whom God displayed as the [true]
> propitiatory in his own blood
> for the remission of sins committed in
> [the time of] God's forbearance.[15]

The primary effect of the text is to interpret and highlight Christ's bloody death as a divinely planned eschatological event whose meaning had been limned in advance by the most solemn rite of the Day of Atonement, the sprinkling of blood on the "propitiatory" (Lev 16:14). If in the reservoir of biblical symbolism this golden lid or cover on the ark of the covenant (Heb.: *kapporet*) had signified the presence of God, the locus of revelation, the forgiveness of sins, the very covenant itself, meanings such as these were magnified by transposition to Golgotha where, for all to see, God displayed the fulfillment whose "type" had been hidden in the temple's innermost recess.

But it is a complementary and secondary aspect of the text that engages our present interest: the reduction of the propitiatory — and, by implication, of the whole economy of ritual Torah and temple — to the role of "type." The "true" propitiatory was the crucified Christ. In the perspective of this text the forgiveness of sins had awaited the

---

[15]See below, 84-88.

climactic, definitive, unrepeatable *yom kippur* of Golgotha. Once given this reality, temple and Torah could claim no independent significance. Here the sense of the text converges, at least in approximate fashion, with the accusation against Stephen.

That the Philippians hymn is pre-Pauline follows from its divergence from Paul in language and conceptuality; literary contacts with both the Hebrew and Greek texts of the scriptures as well as other data[16] indicate its provenance among the *hellēnistai*.

I (v. 6) who, being in the form of God,
   did not count equality with God
      something to cling to,
 (v. 7) but emptied himself,
      taking the form of servant.

II (v. 8) Having become like men
   and appearing as a man,
   he humbled himself,
   becoming obedient unto death,
      even death on a cross .

III (v. 9) This is why God raised him high
   and gave him the name over every name,
 (v. 10) that at the name of Jesus every
      knee in heaven and on earth
      and under the earth should bend

[16]Contacts with the Hebrew text: Phil 2:7, *heautone kenōsen* reflects Isa 53:12, *he'ĕrâ lammāwet napšô*; Phil 2:8, *etapeinōsen heauton* reflects Isa 53:7, *na'ăneh*; Phil 2:9 *dio* reflects Isa 53:12, *lākēn*; Phil 2:9 *hyperypsōsen* reflects Isa 52:13 *wĕniśśā' wĕgābâ mĕōd*. Contacts with the Greek text: Phil 2:10f. reflects LXX Isa 45:23. The "other data": that the hymn was composed in Greek is clear from the analysis of Reinhard Deichgräber, *Gotteshymnus und Christushymnus in der frühen Christenheit*, 128-31. Furthermore, the thematic ties between the hymn and the epistle to the Hebrews point decisively in the same direction. See Otfried Hofius, *Der Christushymnus Philipper 2, 6-11* (Tübingen: Mohr, 1976) *passim*, but esp. 16f., 75-92.

(v. 11) and every tongue confess:
>   JESUS CHRIST IS LORD
>   to the glory of God the Father.[17]

The basic thematic sequence is humiliation/exaltation, the transition taking place at v. 9. But, though the theme is thus two-fold — the incarnation (strophe I) and the epitomizing of Jesus' historic existence in his obedience unto death (strophe II) being equally ranged under the humiliation theme — the three strophes correlate with three phases: pre-earthly life (strophe I), earthly life (strophe II), post-earthly life (strophe III). The essential thrust of the hymn is to set the confession *kyrios Iēsous* ("Jesus is Lord!" 1 Cor 12:3) in salvation-historical context. Resurrection, exaltation, installation as Lord were facets of the same event (Rom 10:9; Acts 2:36). The hymn gives the divine "reason why" ("therefore" or "this is why," verse 9) of this event: it was a reward of obedience. That is, it was in response to Jesus' selfless and flawless submission to God that God gave him "the name" by which he is acclaimed as divine Lord. The hymn thus transvalues the scandalous lowliness of Jesus' life and death by conceiving it as obedience, by making this obedience the rigorously coherent follow-through on the pre-existent Son's incarnational kenosis, and finally and climactically, by making kenosis/obedience the key to the dazzling exaltation of Jesus as *kyrios*.

From the general standpoint of the history of religions the hymn's most striking novelty doubtless lies in the motifs of pre-existence and incarnation. In the context of our present inquiry, however, the center of interest is the way in which the hymn takes Jesus' exaltation as *kyrios* to lay claim now to a universal acclamation at the end of time: *every* knee should bend, *every* tongue confess! The exalted Jesus is already the universal Lord. If the final acknowledgment of

---

[17] On the inclusion in the pre-Pauline hymn of vv. 8c, 10b, and 11c, see Hofius, *Der Christushymnus*, 3-17.

this Lordship by the whole universe is reserved for the end,[18] still the decisive turning-point has already come with the enthronement of Jesus as Lord. In the view of the *hellēnistai* who composed this hymn, Easter equivalently sets the stage for the world mission.

The *hebraioi* defined themselves as the avant-garde of the Israel whose conversion they expected. The *hellēnistai* defined themselves by contrast with the Israel destined for judgment. Both were interpreting the Easter–event and drawing on the Jesus tradition. Some of the diversities among the canonical gospels may have roots in this last-named diversity among Jerusalem Christians of the thirties. Diverse accounts of how Jesus stood toward the Torah and on what the final significance of his cleansing of the temple was may be traced to the same era.

In striking contrast to current Jewish conceptions of the destiny of the gentile world and doubtless under the impact of Jesus' own conception of the saving act of God, *hebraioi* and *hellēnistai* alike were unambiguously convinced that the nations were rightful beneficiaries of eschatological salvation. The difference between the two groups was established by a set of conceptions on the part of the *hebraioi* which the *hellēnistai* did not share: e.g., that the unexpectedly isolated vindication and glorification of Jesus created a new situation reducing Jesus' prophecies of the ordeal to provisional status; that the regime of the Torah remained intact as in Jesus' day and with the radicalization he brought to it; that, as to time, the entry of the gentiles into messianic salvation was to be signaled by "the day of the Man" in accord with Jesus' own view; that, as to mode, this would take place by the eschatological pilgrimage depicted in the scriptures, again in accord with Jesus; that the mission of his followers was consequently limited, as in his own lifetime, to the house of Israel. Given these conceptions, the disparity between the already determined inclusion of the gentiles in

[18]See Hofius, *Der Christushymnus*, 41-55.

God's saving act and, on the other hand, their continuing isolation from messianic Israel was not felt to be enigmatic nor incongruous. But in the absence of this set of conceptions and in the face of contrary convictions — that the vindication of Jesus confirmed the doom of the temple; that his expiatory death rendered the temple cult superfluous; that it was the destined reality of which this cult had been but a type; that the glorification of Jesus positively demanded universal acknowledgment and celebration — the world's non-entry into messianic salvation was precisely an incongruity calling for resolution.

Thus, the distinctive horizons projected by the *hellēnistai* progressively opened towards an explicit universalism, not in the mode of hellenistic humanism but in that of realized eschatology. The Servant, now glorified, was seen to have served "many" well (LXX Isa 53:11; cf. the "many nations" of 52:15); now "all nations, tribes, and languages" (LXX Dan 7:14) would serve him, the Son of man installed at God's right hand (Acts 7:56; cf. Ps 110:1). The history of man's sin and God's forbearance — the ever accumulating debt and the patiently postponed settling of accounts — had come to an end on Golgotha (Rom 3:25f.). The millenary horizon projected by the theme of Yahweh and his people now gave way to a horizon projected by the theme of God, Christ, and humankind ("every knee" and "every tongue," Phil 2:10f.). If the *hebraioi* were the link of the earliest community with the past of Jesus, the *hellēnistai* by their self-understanding made themselves the link with the future: not as the vanguard of Israel but as the vanguard of a purified mankind.

APPENDIX

The Pre-Pauline Formula in Rom 3:25-26a

In the preceding chapter we proposed that there was a pre-Pauline distich to be isolated in Rom 3:25-26a; moreover, we drew on it as part of our effort to recover and understand the theological views of the *hellēnistai.* Though we indicated in a general way what lines of argument supported the reconstruction of the pre-Pauline text, we cannot claim to have laid out the relevant evidence in anything like satisfactory fashion. This would have so interrupted the train of thought as to undermine rather than illuminate it. Still, a more adequate statement of the evidence is clearly enough called for, and this is what we intend to undertake here.

Bultmann[1] and Käsemann[2] proposed that a pre-Pauline formula was to be found in Rom 3:24-26, beginning with *dikaioumenoi* ("justified") in v. 24 and ending with *en tē*

[1]Rudolf Bultmann, *Theology of the New Testament*, vol. 1, (New York: Scribners, 1951) 46.

[2]Ernst Käsemann, "Zum Verständnis von Römer 3, 24-26," in *Exegetische Versuche und Besinnungen*, vol. 1, (Göttingen: Vandenhoeck & Ruprecht, 1960) 96-100.

anochē̦ tou theou ("in the forbearance of God") in v. 26, modified by two Pauline additions: *dōrean tē̦ autou chariti* ("by his grace as a gift") and *dia pisteōs* ("by faith"). Lohse[3] accepted the proposal of a pre-Pauline formula, but argued cogently on the basis of word frequencies that it began only with v. 25: *hon proetheto*... ("whom God displayed..."). Within these limits there remained still unsatisfactorily resolved the twofold question of how to construe *dia* with the accusative *paresin* in v. 25 and how to construe *dia tēn paresin* with the words that precede it.

Neither Bultmann nor Lohse took up this question in detail, but Käsemann did, in his Romans commentary. He understood *dia* with the accusative in v. 25 to signify final cause: "with a view to,"[4] though in his actual translation he settled on "so that": "(This happened) to show his righteousness, *so that* by divine clemency the transgressions committed earlier would be remitted."[5] When the text so construed is reduced to its barest elements, the sequence of correlated purposes — (a) Golgotha happened (b) "to show God's righteousness" (c) so that sins would be remitted — expresses a deep but simple idea in oddly convoluted fashion.

An alternative solution would be to read *dia* with the accusative as signifying instrumental cause: "whom God displayed...to show his righteousness 'by the remission of men's former sins.'"[6] This sense is indeed simpler and clearer; but *dia* with the accusative expressing instrumental cause is weakly attested (cf. Rev 12:11; 13:14) or, at best, too rare to commend itself except as a last resort.

---

[3]Eduard Lohse, *Märtyrer und Gottesknecht* (Göttingen: Vandenhoeck & Ruprecht, ²1963) 149f.

[4]Ernst Käsemann, *An die Römer* (Tübingen: Mohr, 1973) 93.

[5]*An die Römer*, 85.

[6]J. A. Fitzmyer, "The Letter to the Romans," in *The Jerome Biblical Commentary*, 2 vols., (Englewood Cliffs: Prentiss-Hall, 1968) vol. 2, 302.

Wengst[7] has offered a better solution, one that breaks with the supposition that *dia tēn paresin* need continue syntactically the phrase *eis endeixin tēs dikaiosynēs autou* ("to show his righteousness"). Removing, as a Pauline addition, *dia pisteos* ("by faith"), Wengst proposed that in the pre-Pauline text the finite verb of the main clause is continued by a series of prepositional phrases:

God displayed (or designated) (Christ Jesus) as a means of expiation

means:	by his blood,
goal:	to show his righteousness,
cause:	for the sake of the remission of former sins,
ground:	out of God's clemency.

This elegantly neat solution to the syntactical problem, however, is probably not definitive, for it fails to do justice to the choice of the words *proetheto* ("displayed") and *progegonotōn* ("former" or "formerly committed"). The choice of *protithesthai* in v. 25 remains relatively opaque until it is seen in the light of the deliberate contrast between the *kapporet/hilastērion* ("propitiatory") hidden in the holy of holies and its antitype, the *kapporet/hilastērion* of Golgotha. Thus, *protithesthai* = "to display (publicly)" and *hilastērion* = "propitiatory" are reciprocally illuminating *hapax legomena* in Paul. But if *hilastērion* alludes to the "propitiatory" (and so is irreducible to the abstract "means of expiation," as Wengst would render it), the following *en tō autou haimati* can no longer be plausibly read as the first of four coordinated prepositional modifiers of the finite verb, but in all probability should be taken simply as the modifier of *hilastērion*; and *autou*, exemplifying the commonplace hellenistic neglect of the reflexive particularly in the genitive, highlights a distinctive note of this, the "true," propitiatory: "whom God displayed as the [true] propitiatory in his *own* blood."

[7]Klaus Wengst, *Christologische Formeln und Lieder des Urchristentums* (Gütersloh: Mohn, ²1973) 87-90.

Again, the point or function of *progegonotōn* in v. 25 remains opaque until it is seen in the light of the following *en tē anochē tou theou* ("in God's forbearance"). In accord with the implicit playing off of the *kapporet/hilastērion* of the Mosaic covenant against the *kapporet/hilastērion* of Golgotha, *progegonotōn* thematizes the "past," not in superfluous, non-functional fashion, but to set up a complementary specification — *en tē anochē tou theou* = "in (the time of) God's forbearance" — making the past of the Mosaic covenant merely attest God's "forbearance" or "patience" prior to his eschatological action on sin. This view is supported by the use, elsewhere in Romans, of God's *anochē* = forbearance (Rom 2:4) or *makrothymia* = patience (Rom 2:4; 9:22).

But even if Wengst's way of construing the text fails to hold up in every particular, the syntactical coordination of propositional phrases modifying the finite verb nevertheless does seem to hold the solution to our problem. For there appears to be a solution that simultaneously keeps the intentionally charged sense of *hilastērion* ("propitiatory"), keeps the usual sense of *dia* with the accusative ("because of" as signifying either *goal*, i.e., "for the sake of," "with a view to," or *ground*, i.e., "in virtue of," owing to"), and intelligibly relates *dia tēn paresin*, etc. to what precedes. This solution would interpret "to show his righteousness" as a comment on "whom God displayed...," the comment being left syntactically uncontinued; it would understand *dia tēn paresin*, etc. to modify and continue not this comment but the finite verb of the main clause ("whom God displayed as the [true] propitiatory in his own blood...for [the sake of] the remission of sins"). Hence the following layout of the text. The first line contains the main clause; each of the following lines begins with a prepositional phrase modifying the finite verb:

(1) whom God displayed as the [true] propitiatory, [operative] through faith, in his own blood,

(2) to show his righteousness,

(3) for the remission of sins committed formerly in [the time of] God's forbearance,
(4) to show his righteousness at the present time. . . .

I take the two comments "[operative] through faith" and "to show his righteousness," to be Pauline additions, for three reasons: they are syntactically uncontinued, isolated; they are conceptually distinct from their immediate surroundings; they are thematically related to one another (Rom 1:17; 3:22; 9:30-10:4). If they are removed, we are left with a pre-Pauline distich:

> whom God displayed as the [true] propitiatory in his own blood
> for the remission of sins committed formerly in [the time of] God's forbearance.

The main thrust of the text is the interpretation of Christ's bloody death as a divinely planned eschatological antitype. But it further implies that the forgiveness of sins had had to await the unique and unrepeatable *kippûrîm* ("day of atonement") that was Golgotha. Once given this reality, temple and Torah could claim no independent significance. This is the signature of the *hellēnistai.*

In virtue of the Pauline additions and context, this perspective on Golgotha has been absorbed into the thematic scheme that dominates Romans: the eschatological revelation of "the righteousness of God" (Rom 1:17; 3:21, 22, 26; 10:3 bis; cf. 3:5) made effective for man by his acceptance of this revelation, his submission to this righteousness — in short, "by faith" (Rom 1:17; 3:22, 26, 27-31, etc.; cf. 10:2-4).

VI

Antioch and Jerusalem
The Pivotal Decision

Two Schematic Traditions

The classical Christian conception of the launching of the world mission found expression in two schematic traditions: the sending of the Apostles and the call of Paul.

The concrete form of the first scheme, portrayed in the Synoptic gospels and Acts and especially in Matthew (Matt 28:18-20; cf. Acts 1:8; Luke 24:46-49; [Final] Mark 16:15f.), was the explicitly universalist missionary mandate of the risen Jesus to the inner circle of his disciples. Though the theme of the world mission had already penetrated the gospel tradition (see Mark 13:10; 14:9),[1] formulas rooting the explicitly universalist mission in the words of the risen Jesus were probably composed rather late, perhaps only after the failed Jewish revolt of 66-73 A.D. As they stand

[1]See Joachim Jeremias, *Jesus' Promise to the Nations* (London: SCM, 1958).

they are probably the work of final redactors.[2]

What was the function of this schematization? In general terms it was self-definitional, designed to objectify as normative the world-wide horizons, missionary self-understanding, and missionary policy of the Greek-speaking church. Whereas it ostensibly accounted for the coming-to-be of this self-definition, it actually depended on this self-definition's having already come to full maturity. The two elements that found late, schematic expression were the explicit universalism of the missionary mandate and the limitation of this mandate to "the twelve" (cf. 1 Cor 15:5) or, as Matthew was careful to put it, to "the eleven disciples" (Matt 28:16; cf. Luke 24:35; 45-47). But, as Paul, our most reliable witness to the consciousness of the earliest church, indicates, others besides the twelve had been commissioned by the risen Jesus and with them made up the firmly defined circle of "Apostles"[3] (see, first, Paul's reference to "those who were Apostles before me," Gal 1:17; second, his reference to Cephas, the Twelve, James, and "all the Apostles" in 1 Cor 15:3-7).

The schematic tradition on the call of Paul, stylized first in accord with Paul's own mature consciousness (see esp. Gal 1:11-17; 1 Cor 15:8-10; Phil 3:4-11), then with the developing consciousness of his diverse theological heirs (Col 1:24-26; Eph 3:1-10; Acts 9:1-21; 22:3-21; 26:9-18; 1 Tim 1:12-17; 2:7; 2 Tim 1:11f.), originated (as, indeed, all the traditions affirmed) in the "revelation" (Gal 1:16; cf. Matt 16:18)[4] that precipitated Paul's about-face from persecutor to champion of the Christian cause. Paul understood the point of this call to be to proclaim Christ "among the

---

[2]See Heinrich Kasting, *Die Anfänge der urchristlichen Mission* (Munich: Kaiser, 1969) 34-45.

[3]Kasting, *Die Anfange*, 61-81.

[4]See D. J. Chapman, "St. Paul and the Revelation to St. Peter. Matt. XVI. 17," *Revue Bénédictine* 29 (1912): 133-47, cf. 140-7.

gentiles" (Gal 1:16)[5] and the later tradition resolved an inherent ambiguity by interpreting it to mean that the call of Paul and his vocation to preach to the gentiles were simultaneous (cf. Col 1:25-28; Eph 3:1-10; Acts 9:15; 22:15, 21; 26:17-20; 1 Tim 2:7). Did Paul in fact inaugurate his vocation as a solitary herald of the gospel in the Nabataean kingdom (compare Gal 1:17 with 2 Cor 11:32)?[6] The matter is not clear. There is a tradition in Acts, however, according to which he was commissioned together with Barnabas by the church of Antioch (Acts 13:1-3). Finally, at the time of his first extant letter (1 Thess) he conceived of his apostolic commission as a personal, unique, world-wide missionary mandate (1 Thess 2:3-7; cf. Gal 2:2, 7-9) to "Greeks and barbarians, the wise and the simple" (Rom 1:14; cf. 1:5; 11:13; 15:15-28).

These charged traditions — the sending of the Apostles and the call of Paul — were generated and developed partly in dependence, partly in independence, of one another. In their final form they are awkwardly harmonizable. Neither could find this final form except through the long transforming experience of the mission itself. Our effort will be to get behind these self-definitional schemes, so imposing in their full, final expression, in quest of their historical origins. This is an act of "deconstruction," but only in the sense that in their mature form the two great traditions of the sending of the Apostles and the call of Paul are endproducts that invite historical clarification. In neither case is the original generative matrix, the consciousness of a sending by the risen Christ, put in doubt. This motif is impressively attested by texts on the appearances of the risen Jesus (1 Cor 15:3-8; Gal 1:16; cf. 1 Thess 2:4; 1 Cor 1:17; 9:16;

[5]On the two aspects of one event, namely, the revelation of God's Son and the call to the apostolate, see Heinrich Schlier, *Der Brief an die Galater* (Göttingen: Vandenhoeck & Ruprecht, 1971) 56.

[6]For a recent "yes," see F. F. Bruce, "Further Thoughts on Paul's Autobiography (Galatians 1:11-2:14)," in *Jesus und Paulus* (Göttingen: Vandenhoeck & Ruprecht, 1975) 23. See also Meeks, *Urban Christians*, 10.

Rom 1:1, 5, 14; 15:5f.; also Matt 28:18-20; Acts 1:8; [Luke 24:46-49]; [Final] Mark 16:15.; John 20:22f.) and appears, moreover, to have belonged to the very center of gravity of "the Easter experience of the disciples." Our effort in each case will be to set such consciousness in historical context and to trace the unfolding of its meaning.

"The Jew First, Then the Greek"

Among the *hellēnistai* the eschatological scheme of "temple" and "pilgrimage of the nations" never took root. Eschatological schemes of thought yielded rather to an eschatological initiative: "some men of Cyprus and Cyrene, coming to Antioch, spoke to the Greeks, too, preaching the Lord Jesus" (Acts 11:20). This initiative, we have argued, reflected a new self-definition. But the lag of several years between the founding of the Antioch community of Jewish and gentile Christians in the thirties and its sponsorship of a mission along the western border of the Roman province of *Syria* and *Cilicia campestris*[7] in the forties (Acts 13:1-3) indicates that time was needed for this communitarian self-definition to take fully conscious shape. Nevertheless, the ongoing initiative that first founded the Antioch community and then led to its sponsorship of a mission to Cyprus and south-central Asia Minor stands as a paradigm of the continuity between communitarian self-understanding and communitarian policy. To become what it already was — the vanguard of a saved mankind — the mixed community of Antioch *had* to launch its mission. The summoning self of the community was missionary.

As Acts 13-14 represents it, the mission of Barnabas and Paul typically began as the evangelization in a given locality of "Israelites and God-fearers" (Acts 13:16; cf. 17:2, 10, 17; 18:6), but was often swiftly converted into a mission to

[7]See Martin Hengel, "Die Ursprünge der christlichen Mission," 18 and note 15.

gentiles there (Acts 13:46; cf. 18:6). The programmatic sub-schema epitomized in Paul's phrase "the Jew first, then the Greek" (not, of course, in this concise Pauline formulation, but in its substance) figured in both the great missionary traditions: the sending of the Apostles (relate Mark 7:27 to Mark 13:10; 14:9; relate Matt 15:27 and 22:1-10 to Matt 10:5; 15:24; 28:16-18; similarly, relate Luke 14:16-24 to Luke 24:46-49 and Acts 1:8; relate John 12:20-24 to John 20:21-23) and the call of the Apostle of the gentiles (Eph 3:4-6; Acts 26:20; cf. Acts 13-14). Was this merely a reflective schematizing, after the fact, of what had taken place in spontaneous, random fashion? Or does this sub-schema mean that the mission to the gentiles had been explicitly predicated on the failure of the mission to the Jews? What is its origin and what, if anything, does it reveal about the launching of the world mission?

One of its aspects, in any case, is unproblematic. "The Jew first, then the Greek" reflects an unambiguous conviction of Israel's salvation-historical prerogative. By biblical definition the eschatological community is "Israel." If the gentiles were to attain to salvation, this would be by salvation-historical inheritance (*klēronomia*, Acts 20:32; cf. *synklēronoma*, Eph 3:6), a participation (*symmetocha*, Eph 3:6) in Israel's appointed lot (*klēros*, Col 1:12) — and this even when gentiles were depicted as enjoying salvation in place of Jews (e.g., with the patriarchs, Matt 8:11f.; par. Luke 13:28f.).

But does this signify, as Paul would seem to indicate (Rom 11:11; cf. Acts 13:46), that the world mission was contingent on Israel's rejection of the kerygma? The answer would seem to be this: when Paul asserted that Israel's refusal of belief brought salvation to the gentiles, he was giving simultaneous expression to two schemes of thought. Both of them reflected his biblically tutored view of God's governance of the world: first, that of the sovereign resourcefulness by which God made the evil acts of men serve his own good purposes (cf. the structuring of Rom

9-11 by the themes announced in Rom 9:6 and 11:11);[8] second, that of "eschatological measure," according to which the places at the banquet of salvation, if not filled by Israel, would be filled by gentiles (also *plēroma* in Rom 11:12, 25, and the parable of the great supper, which in both Matt 22:1-10 and par. Luke 14:16-24 has been converted into a reflection on the gentile mission and ends with the motif of the filled hall or house). Paul does not say that, had there been no rejection of the gospel by the Jews, there could have been no mission to the gentiles. Rather, he says that God has in fact made good the refusal of the Jews by bringing in the gentiles, so stirring the Jews to jealousy (Rom 11:11) in order, in the end, to save "all Israel" (Rom 11:26). Israel's refusal was not a condition of possibility (that without which the world mission could not have taken place at all) but a condition of actuality (that without which it would not have taken place in the way it actually did).

It is obvious, then, that "the Jew first, then the Greek" was more than a mere schematization, after the fact, of what had originally been a random enterprise. It expressed an understanding of the Christian present as the fulfillment of eschatological prophecy. To be sure, the idea of Israel's refusal of salvation was utterly foreign to the great biblical schemes, such as the eschatological pilgrimage of the nations, that envisaged the salvation of the gentiles in the wake of the salvation of Israel. As the early Christians were well aware, the actual events of the mission of Jesus (repudiated by Israel but vindicated by God) and of his disciples (knowing themselves to be the messianic community of the last days

---

[8]Rom 9:6 implicitly poses the question, "Has the word of God failed?" Chapter nine says: no, for the word of God is addressed not to the physical but to the election-historical children of Abraham. Chapter ten says: no, it was Israel that failed, namely, by preferring to "the righteousness of God" a righteousness of its own devising. Chapter eleven says: no, for he saved a remnant. Rom 11:11 then sets up the final progression of thought. Just as God turned the refusal of Israel into the salvation of the gentiles, so he will turn the salvation of "the full number" of gentiles into the salvation of "all Israel."

but reduced within Israel to the status of a dissident minority subject to periodical crackdowns) were painfully discontinuous with classical prophecy. "The remnant of Israel" represented the one scheme of prophetic thought to which this situation was amenable; hence, it was a cherished category of the earliest Christian self-understanding.[9] The conscious ordering of missionary policy epitomized by "the Jew first, then the Greek" discloses a like effort to make the life of the church accord with the linear structure of biblical eschatology: first the salvation of Israel, then the salvation of the nations. But in the actuality of history, contrary to the buoyant expectations of the Easter *hebraioi*, it was not to be the *salvation* of Israel first but only the *offer* to Israel, the *mission* to Israel, first. And if, in fact, the mission then turned to the gentile world (in the best of times mildly hostile toward and contemptuous of the *curti judaei*),[10] was this not only just? Was it not history's *lex talionis*, a divinely endorsed counterbalance to the refusal of the Jews? The gentile mission followed the mission to Israel not only in fact but by right and, among the *hellēnistai*, in the full consciousness that this was by right.

Jacob Jervell has presented a noteworthy critique of the view that in Luke's presentation the mission to the gentiles had as its decisive supposition the refusal of the gospel by the Jews.[11] The view that Jervell rejected, based mainly on three texts (Acts 3:46; 18:6; 28:28), overlooked the positive significance both in itself and in relation to the mission to gentiles of Luke's repeated notices on mass conversions of Jews (Acts 2:41[47]; 4:4; 5:14; 6:1, 7; 9:42; 12:24; 13:43; 14:1;

---

[9]See B. F. Meyer, *The Church in Three Tenses*, 4-12; on how this was rooted in the work of the historical Jesus, see Meyer, *The Aims of Jesus*, 210-15.

[10]Horace, *Satires*, Book I, Satire 9, line 70.

[11]Jacob Jervell, "Das gespaltene Israel und die Heidenvolker," *Studia Theologica* 19 (1965): 68-96. (See Bibliography for English translation.) For a useful critique of Jervell's treatment, see Stephen G. Wilson, *The Gentiles and the Gentile Mission in Luke-Acts* (Cambridge: Cambridge University Press, 1973) 220-37.

17:10ff.; [19:20] 21:20). To specify this positive significance, Jervell exploited the allusion in the speech of James (Acts 15:16-18) to LXX Amos 9:11 (cf. Jer 12:15):

> After this I shall return
> and rebuild the fallen tabernacle of David;
> from its ruins I shall rebuild it
> and set it up again
> so that the rest of mankind may seek the Lord,
> all the nations over whom my name is invoked...

First, God restores Israel; then, in dependence on this restoration event, the gentiles seek the Lord. In the context of Acts the Cornelius episode signals an already realized restoration of Israel as portrayed in the preceding chapters. In James's view the conversion of the gentiles is the fulfillment of promises to Israel.

This scheme is recurrent in Acts. First, the word is offered to the Jews, who split into camps of believers and unbelievers. By their faith the believers constitute restored Israel, heir of the covenant and promises. Now and only now may gentiles find salvation, precisely by assimilation to restored Israel. Thus, the continuity of salvation history is maintained.

Jervell maintains that, inasmuch as this schema is operative throughout Acts, even including the final scene of Paul's meeting with the Jews of Rome (see Acts 28:24f.), it belongs to the redactor's own theology. This is true; but it should be added that it is an inherited, not an original, theological schema. Rooted in the Law and the prophets, it represents a scheme of thought that, though it first came to expression among the *hellēnistai* of Antioch as theologically controlled missionary policy, could be adopted in turn by *hebraioi* such as James (Acts 15:16-18), once gentile believers presented themselves as an established fact.

Whether the schema "the Jew first, then the Greek" goes back as far as the first Antiochene mission to Cyprus and Asia Minor depends, to be sure, on the historical worth of Acts 13-14. A reasonable resolution of such problems calls for a critical treatment of Acts; this, however, is distinct from the spuriously critical, wholesale depreciation of Acts as a source of historical data. The discrepancy in Paul's missionary status between Acts 13-14 (cf. 14:12) and the later journeys in Acts, where he is the hero of the world mission, is an index favoring historicity.[12] It is accordingly probable that we have in Acts 13-14 evidence attesting the schema "the Jew first, then the Greek" in the missionary theology not simply of Paul, nor of Barnabas and Paul, but of the Antioch community. It is pre-Pauline theology in the sense that it antedates the Pauline letters and originates in a community of which Paul was but one of several leaders.

It should be emphasized that "the Jew first, then the Greek" was a matter not merely of missionary tactics but of missionary theology. It expressed an ecclesial priority to which Paul — if, as is possible, he had soon after his call abortively initiated a career as Apostle of gentiles — submitted himself and his vocation. It effectively laid down the lines of future missionary thought and action. Once again the *hellēnistai*, leaders of the Antioch community in this early period, proved to be the dynamic and seminal element of early Christianity. It was neither the word of the risen Jesus to the twelve nor the dramatic call of Paul that established the theological and historic order of the primitive Christian mission. It was a policy correlative to the Antioch community's self-definition, generated and sponsored by the largely anonymous, extraordinarily assured, open, active, pneumatic, city-oriented, Greek-speaking Jewish Christian heirs of Stephen.

A Partial But Crucial Fusion of Horizons

For the *hellēnistai* the eschaton had been inaugurated by the enthronement of the crucified Messiah at God's right hand.

---

[12]It should be added that Gal 1:21 is rather in accord than in discord with Acts 13-14. See Hengel, "Ursprünge," 18; Roloff, *Apostelge-schichte*, 194f.

The economy of temple and Torah had thus been brought to an end, not unmasked as a deliberately fraudulent revelation (as some later gnostics would assert),[13] but revealed in its role of "type" foreshadowing a reality to come. The scriptures had attested that the dawning eschaton would be the signal for God's own act of restoring Israel in the sight of the nations (see, for example Ezek 36:23). And God's mercy on Israel would signal the salvation of the gentiles:

> God be merciful to us and bless us,
>   cause his face to shine on us,
> that men may know thy way on earth,
>   thy salvation among all nations.
> Let the nations, O God, give thanks to thee,
>   let all the nations give thee thanks
>   (LXX Ps 66:1-3).
>
> Turn to me and you shall be saved,
>   you who hail from the end of the earth!
>   (LXX Isa 45:22).

"On that day" (Isa 19:19) the gentiles would be saved, and with the resurrection of Jesus "that day" had dawned.

In accord with the resultant missionary perspectives and policies of the Antioch community, it was taken for granted that gentiles would "come in" to present fellowship and future glory without "coming in" to a religious economy already obsolete. We know nothing of whether the Christian *hebraioi* of Jerusalem received any gentile converts nor whether, if they did, such gentiles were circumcised. Quite apart from the narrow issue of historicity, the story of the conversion of Cornelius (Acts 10-11) dramatizes a disparity between standard Jerusalem expectations and the coming of salvation to gentiles. Probably — but only probably, for

---

[13]The extreme form of this thesis was proposed by Marcion. The Valentinians considered Old Testament revelation to be a mixture of truth and deception. To reject the whole body of Hebrew scripture as fallacious and deliberately misleading was a common gnostic attitude.

the story in Acts does not entertain this precise issue and does not resolve it — the circumcision of gentile converts would have accorded with the Jerusalem community's self-understanding as the remnant. By contrast, Antioch's table-fellowship among Jewish and gentile Christians attested the community's abandonment of food laws and implied its correlative abandonment of circumcision and the ritual Torah in accord with that community's self-understanding not as restoring but as transcending historical Israel.

In schematic terms we may say of early Christian history that policy was mediated by self-understanding and self-understanding by the gospel. But in fact these mediations took place accompanied by the baggage of undifferentiated horizons, inheritances, suppositions, values, preferences. This is why it is unreasonable to conclude, abruptly and without qualification, from two self-understandings to two gospels. In the history we are about to reflect upon, the most compelling phenomenon is the process by which the "pillars" of the Jerusalem community, on the basis of one lived experience of salvation, one gospel, and one church, began the painful process of differentiating, in accord with priorities intrinsic to the gospel, the diverse demands that lay on them. It was on the basis of a common gospel that the pillars of Jerusalem and the missionaries of Antioch could bridge diverse self-understandings and agree on one policy for the gentile mission.

In this policy agreement lay a convergence of achievements. On the side of the Antiochene leaders it was an achievement of insight and will, insight into God's act in Christ and a will, equal to that insight, to realize by a pioneer missionary act the promise of salvation for the nations. On the side of the Jerusalem pillars the achievement was likewise one of insight and will, insight into the Antiochene initiative as sponsored and abetted by the Spirit of God, and the firm will to acknowledge it as such. Both before and after this policy decision there were Christian *hebraioi* recalcitrantly critical of the Torah-free mission. Why? Because in their view it devalued the covenant. In the course of the long and ever more bitter conflict between

"Jew" and "Greek" from the Maccabaean Wars to Hadrian's decree making the circumcising of an adult a capital crime, circumcision had become for Jew and Greek alike the symbol of the Jewish cause. For the Jew it had not only "the emotional significance of a partisan badge against a hostile and hated oppressor";[14] it was also the "seal" of his membership in the covenant. For the Greek, however, and even for one well disposed to the Jewish doctrine of the one living God, circumcision usually prevented his becoming a proselyte. He viewed the operation "not merely as humiliating and ridiculous in itself, but as the sign of the deliberate adoption of the 'barbarian' cause against the Greek."[15]

It is a testimony to the vital element of transcendence in their faith that the pillars of Jerusalem could see through and beyond this cultural division. For, it is false to say that the "fronts" of Antioch and Jerusalem simply "remained," that there was "no clarification" of the theological issues, no "compromise" and no revision of position.[16] James, Cephas, and John evidently did come to a clarification of issues; they did, in fact, compromise with the policies of Antioch and, if this was not a flat revision of position, it was an epoch-making differentiation of religious consciousness. It attested the openness of the community gathered around the twelve to an initiative of the Spirit that met the test of their own pneumatic experience. This stance is epitomized in an awe-struck inference: "Then to the gentiles too God has granted life-giving repentance!" (cf. Acts 11:18). The effect of this acknowledgement was to seal the authentic character of gentile Christianity. It thus opened up a new future, cutting Christian fortunes free of their moorings in a Jewish sect.

---

[14]Gregory Dix, *Jew and Greek*, 34.

[15]Gregory Dix, *Jew and Greek*, 34.

[16]Rudolf Meyer, *"peritemno,"* TDNT 6, 83. For a far superior account of the ecclesial relationships revealed both by the Council and by the Antioch incident, see Bengt Holmberg, *Paul and Power* (Lund: Gleerup, 1978) 22-34.

If consent to the Torah-free mission on the part of the leaders of the *hebraioi* played this crucial role in Christian history, we should pause to examine the "irreducibly transcendent element" in their faith. It had a triple root. In part it derived from Jesus' words on salvation for the nations and from the "dangerous memory" of his sovereign comportment toward temple, Torah, and religious *élite*; in part from acknowledgement of the risen Christ as the focal point of eschatological fulfillment (*marana tha!*), utterly transcending the prefabricated themes of biblical and Judaic expectation; in part, finally, from the Torah-transcendent character of the Easter experience of salvation, which acquitted the sinner and bestowed on him the Spirit of God. Without reference to this element of transcendence irreducibly rooted in the faith of the *hebraioi*, there would be no historical accounting for the words: "the acknowledged pillars, James, Cephas, and John, gave me and Barnabas the right hand of fellowship. . ." (Gal 2:9).

In these few paragraphs we have touched on the most important points relevant to ecclesial decision in favor of the mission. It turned on an initiative of the *hellēnistai*; it represented the explicit approval of the *hebraioi* gathered around the Jerusalem "pillars"; it was by all odds the cardinal policy decision of the first-century church. We have explored the self-understanding from which the initiative of the *hellēnistai* sprang and we have alluded to the self-understanding from which the approval of the *hebraioi* emerged. These things stand as acquisitions regardless of how the details of early Christianity's pivotal decision be reconstructed. This is not to belittle current efforts to revise Pauline chronology and reconstruct the sequence and significance of the agreements and tensions between Paul and the pillars of Jerusalem. Nevertheless, there is a historical ascertainment at once more accessible and more fundamental than the necessarily provisional untangling of the skein of historical detail. This is the ascertainment of a constructive dialectic between two Christian self-definitions. Historically, the most important feature of this dialectic was

Jerusalem's agreement with the Torah-free mission to the gentiles, first, in principle (Gal 2:9; cf. Acts 15:7-11), then, some time after the clash with Paul in Antioch (Gal 2:11-21), in the participation of Cephas himself in the mission to the gentile world.[17]

Conclusion

The classical Christian conception of the launching of the world mission was embodied in two schematic traditions: the sending of the Apostles (Matt 28:18-20; Mark 16:15f.; Luke 24:46-49; Acts 1:8; John 20:22f.) and the call of Paul (Gal 1:16; 2:7; 1 Cor 15:8-10; cf. 1 Thess 2:4; 1 Cor 1:17; 9:16; Rom 1:1, 5, 14). Behind these traditions stood a complex and dramatic dialectic of self-definitions. In Jerusalemite self-definition the Christian community was the "remnant" bringing historical Israel to eschatological restoration. In Antiochene self-definition the community transcended an Israel that had lost, not its privileged status as called to be God's people, but its status as properly responding at the present time to that call. The actual working out of Paul's vocation as Apostle of the gentiles hinged on the dialectic of Jerusalemite and Antiochene self-definition. In the actuality of history Paul's career came effectively to fruition in an initiative shared with Barnabas and set in motion by the community of Antioch. The concrete policies of this initiative (the priority of the appeal to diaspora Jews, the non-imposition of circumcision on gentiles) accorded with the Antioch community's horizons and self-understanding. The criticism of the latter policy urged by conservative Christian *hebraioi* in Jerusalem precipitated a crisis. The crisis was resolved by what in retrospect was the pivotal decision of early Christian history. It attested an epoch-making differentiation of religious consciousness on the part of the Jeru-

[17]See Ferdinand Hahn, *Mission in the New Testament* (London: SCM, 1965) 48-54.

salem pillars. It signaled the victory, in principle, of Paul, Barnabas, Antioch. Its impact was momentously epitomized by the subsequent missionary career of Cephas.

Paul's career took wing and attained its full dimensions only after the Antioch incident (Gal 2:11-14), which put an end to his special ties with that community. Henceforward his work would be wholly independent and world-wide.[18] Moreover, it would accord with the new salvation-historical scenario referred to in Rom 11:25f.: the entry into salvation of the "full number" of the gentiles would condition the salvation of "all Israel." This did not subvert the principle, "the Jew first, then the Greek," but it broadened the applica-

---

[18]Did Paul carry out his own world-missionary enterprise by exploiting the network of synagogues in the "diaspora of the Greeks?" The answer in all probability is yes, as most scholars from Harnack to the present day have maintained. This view alone seems to do real justice to 1 Cor 9:19f. and 2 Cor 11:24. See, for example, Peter Stuhlmacher, *Das paulinische Evangelium I*, (Göttingen: Vandenhoeck & Ruprecht, 1968) 99.

Possibly, but not certainly, relevant to this question is the view of A. T. Kraabel, "The Disappearance of the 'God-Fearers,'" *Numen* 28 (1981):113-26, according to which the God-fearers of Acts were a fictional device of Lukan theology. This broad conclusion is derived from slim premises, namely, (a) lack of reference to the God-fearers among archaeological data of synagogues from the Christian era, and (b) Kraabel's view of Acts as "theology in narrative form—rather than an historical record."

A final piece of evidence to be pondered is Rom 10:14-21. Paul certainly includes himself among those whom God has sent as heralds of the gospel (Rom 10:18). But the logic of the passage as a whole as well as the particularity of v. 18 inescapably suggest, if they do not require, that the Jews of the diaspora be understood as included among those to whom these heralds are sent. (For an expressly speculative alternative view, according to which no special missionary provision would have been made for diaspora Jews, see E. P. Sanders, *Paul, the Law, and the Jewish People*, 188-190.)

On how Paul's independent missionary work fit into the larger context of the whole Christian mission in the gentile world, see Holmberg, *Paul and Power*, 69-72.

tion of the principle to the divine plan as a whole (Rom 1:16; cf. 9:4f.). The present moment was concentrated on the salvation of the gentiles. The Apostle of the gentiles had come into his own.

VII

Theology for the World Mission

Orientation

The foremost figure in the story of the Christian self-definitions that diversely developed under pressure of the world-missionary movement was Paul of Tarsus. Torah-free Christianity was not Paul's invention (it characterized Antioch before Paul settled there) nor was it limited in the Mediterranean basin to Paul's own missionary communities. Rome, for example, attests Torah-free Christianity by the tensions that obtained there between the "strong" and the "weak" (Rom 14:1-15:13).[1] Not all missionaries and missionary churches were at one on the proper kind or

---

[1]The beginnings of Christianity in Rome are opaque. It may well be that it was not in the first instance missionaries but simply Christian converts, Jewish and gentile, who brought Christianity to "the city." By the time of Paul's letter to the Romans the Christians there had registered the marks of Jewish Christian leadership and tradition. See the recent treatment of Raymond E. Brown, "The Roman Church near the End of

degree of freedom from the Torah.[2] When all is said and
done, however, it remains that no one contributed more
incisively than Paul to the dominant post-Pauline gentile
Christian self-definition that emerged from the Mediterranean mission. The mediating positions of Cephas (Gal 2:9-
14; Acts 15:7-11; cf. Acts 8:14-17; 10:34f., 47; 11:17) and of
James (Gal 2:9-12; Acts 15:14-21), though critically important in their own time to the birth and early life of gentile
christianity, proved finally to be transitory.

So much is common opinion.[3] There are two questions,
however, which are important to our reconstruction of the
ties between the world mission and various Christian self-
definitions, and on which the community of scholarly opinion breaks down.

We have already had occasion to deal with aspects of the
first question, namely: *in what relationships of authority
and influence, of agreement and disagreement, did Paul
stand to other Christians, and in what relationships did they
stand to him?* Of the many topics that the question evokes,
we shall touch on only two.

the First Christian Generation," in Raymond E. Brown and John P.
Meier, *Antioch and Rome* (New York: Paulist, 1983) 105-127. The
"strong" were those who understood themselves to be bound by no food
laws; the "weak" were those who felt obliged to observe at least some of
these laws. On the practical problems that arose from the presence of
both in one community, see (apart from Romans 14-15) 1 Cor 8:7-13.

[2]This reflects divisions, first of all, among the Christian *hebraioi*. For
the views of the right wing, see Acts 15:1; for those of the center, Acts
15:14-21; for those of the left wing, Gal 2:12a. Again, among the *hellēnistai* not all were of one mind. The Antioch community followed the
Jacobite decree (Acts 15:29); Paul and his communities did not.

[3]The solidly probable view that Peter was the first-century church's
most effective mediator by no means contradicts the above statement on
the incisive long-range influence of Paul. On the historic importance of
the mediating views epitomized by Peter, see Brown and Meier, *Antioch
and Rome, passim.*

The more important of them is unquestionably the "partial but crucial fusion of horizons" that allowed the Jerusalem pillars to affirm the gospel proclaimed by Paul and Barnabas in the diaspora of the Greeks. This helps to isolate the element of radical Jerusalemite opposition to Paul both at the time of the "council" in Jerusalem and throughout his missionary career. Radical opposition did not derive from the center among the *hebraioi* (represented by James) nor from their left wing (represented by Cephas and John), but from a right wing made up of those *hebraioi* who insisted that gentiles be circumcised as a condition of entry into the church (Gal 5:2, 12; 6:13; Phil 3:2; cf. Acts 15:1).

The second matter evoked by the question of Paul's intra-Christian relationships is the issue of continuity and discontinuity between Antioch and Paul. In short, how isolated was Paul? German scholarship from the mid-nineteenth century to World War II characteristically isolated Paul as a lone hero doing battle against all comers — Jews, pagans, and fellow-Christians. This scholarship registered the pull of a tacit but magnetic thesis: the true church hove into view only twice in history, in the age of Paul and in the age of Luther. Ferdinand Christian Baur (1792-1860), Adolf von Harnack (1851-1930), and Walter Bauer (1877-1960) mounted the most distinctive efforts in the century from 1834 to 1934 to reconstruct the unfolding of early Christian history. They confronted historical data as critical observers, willing to bring to expression an unaltered "participant viewpoint" only in the case of Paul. F. C. Baur and Walter Bauer especially were sceptical of other sources. In Baur's reconstruction, Paul had only a negative or antithetical relation to Jewish Christianity under the leadership of Peter.[4] This view impinged on Harnack, too, for whom the leitmotif of Paul's Christian career was "opposition to the

<hr/>

[4]Albrecht Ritschl was an early critic of Baur's positing of a flat antithesis between Peter and Paul. F. C. Burkitt, *Christian Beginnings* (London: London University Press, 1924) 57, note 1, quotes volume 1 of *The Beginnings of Christianity* (London, 1920) as follows: "'It is one of the

legalistic righteousness of the pharisees, i.e., to the official religion of the Old Testament."[5] (Whereas Baur had attributed positive significance to the Old Testament, Harnack was a life-long Marcionite, soldiering on in the tradition of Hegel and Schleiermacher.)[6] For his part, Walter Bauer concerned himself immediately with the second century; he nevertheless allied himself with Baur and Harnack in allotting Paul a role of splendid isolation. For all Paul's flexible and undogmatic tolerance,[7] he was the lone heresiarch of the apostolic age.[8] And when late-second-century orthodoxy laid claim to him, the price that the Apostle of the gentiles had to pay for this was "the complete surrender of his personality and historical particularity."[9] The line from Baur to Bauer is still vigorously represented in Germany. There is nevertheless a growing current of international and ecumenical scholarship today bent on greater balance and plausibility on this issue, not by denying the originality of Paul's personal thought and work, but by acknowledging — alongside his call/conversion — the historic importance of his years in Antioch and rootage in Antiochene tradition.

Our second question asks: *how should we conceive of the*

---

mistakes of the Tübingen School that it did not recognize that Peter, not only in Acts but also in the Pauline Epistles, is on the Hellenistic, not the Hebrew side' (*Beginnings*, vol. i 312). This admirable sentence may be taken to mark the end of a long controversy." Nevertheless, there are still defenders (e.g., Martin Hengel, C. K. Barrett) of the view that behind the subversion of Paul's work in Corinth and elsewhere lurked the figure of Peter.

[5]Adolf Harnack, *Outlines of the History of Dogma* (New York: Funk & Wagnalls, 1893) 21.

[6]See A. H. J. Gunneweg, *Understanding the Old Testament* (Philadelphia: Westminster, 1978) for the attitudes toward biblical Israel of Hegel (119, 152f.), Schleiermacher (153-156), and Harnack (39, 119).

[7]Walter Bauer, *Orthodoxy and Heresy in Earliest Christianity* (Philadelphia: Fortress, 1971) 234f.

[8]This was from the perspective of the Judaists, who excommunicated Paul; see *Orthodoxy and Heresy*, 236.

[9]*Orthodoxy and Heresy*, 227.

relation between Paul's mission and his soteriology? This, too, is a large and many-sided question. We shall break it down into three parts.

Part one will bear on the sense in which Paul's theology was "missionary." In the relatively brief era of kerygma theology, the decisive contextual determinant of Pauline theology was thought to be the issue of man, of man standing before God. By accenting the concrete contextual reality of the Pauline mission, however, scholars in recent decades (e.g., Georg Eicholz,[10] N. A. Dahl[11]) have exposed the abstract, ahistorical character of this view. We shall offer here a survey of the textual data on the missionary context of Paul's thought. This will admittedly leave unresolved the question of whether it was Paul's commitment to the gentile mission that generated his distinctive soteriological theses (e.g., that the Law no longer binds, that Christ is the end of the Law, that his converts were not "under law" but "under grace"). But eventually — once we shall have treated the particulars of Pauline soteriology — we shall deal with the question of whether it was the mission itself that commanded the leading traits of Paul's thought.

Just what Paul's soteriological vision of things consisted in is not a matter of indifference to the present inquiry. Hitherto, we have been intent on connecting the origin of the mission with the self-definition that made it possible and helped to launch it. Now we are intent on correlating the mission with the self-definition that emerged from it and, even more, with the emergent realization of a single Christian identity, which had been and would continue to be variously incarnated in many self-definitions. If our inquiry were to skip over the soteriological particulars into which Paul translated his faith, life, and thought, it would lose touch with the historical Paul and his mission; worse, it

---

[10]Georg Eichholz, *Die Theologie des Paulus im Umriss* (Neukirchen-Vluyn: Neukirchener Verlag, ²1977).

[11]N. A. Dahl, *Studies in Paul. Theology for the Early Christian Mission* (Minneapolis: Augsburg, 1977).

would fail to disclose the ground of Paul's own capacity to differentiate between "the gospel," on which he built everything, and the de-Judaized Christian self-definition of which he was the champion, but which he also relativized in the name of the gospel. It is therefore indispensable that we attempt a retrieval of Pauline soteriology: its structure, its themes, its "sequence," its internal relations. This is part two of the question on Paul's mission and his soteriology, and it will be the burden of chapter eight, "A Soteriology Valid for All."

The third and last part of the question will inquire after the generative matrix of Pauline soteriology. Is it true, as many scholars today maintain, that Paul's call to the world mission determined the contours of his soteriology? Our negative answer to this question and the presentation of a positive alternative is the substance of chapter nine, "The Matrix of Pauline Soteriology."

A Missionary Theology

Paul's theology[12] was world-missionary theology designed to initiate the missionary churches of the Empire and particularly his own churches into the source and goal and distinctive character of their common life "in Christ," to teach them how to appropriate their new relationships to "God our Father and the Lord Jesus Christ" (1 Cor 1:3; 2 Cor 1:2; Rom 1:7; Phil 1:2; Phm 3) and in this light to know what relationships were proper to one another as well as to understand how they stood with reference to Jews and Greeks, to the past and to the future. This is the first sense in which Paul's theology was "missionary": it was thought out and articulated in the service of a basic self-orientation in faith on the part of young missionary churches.

But Paul's theology was missionary also in the sense that his theological thinking and missionary labor conditioned

[12]I derive "Paul's theology" from what I take to be his own compositions: 1 Thess, 1 Cor, 2 Cor, Gal, Phil, Phm, Rom.

one another. If the theology served the mission, the mission entered as an intrinsically conditioning factor into the theology, the sharply drawn lines of Paul's thought and expression reflecting multiple-front debates and battles (waged directly with his own congregations, but indirectly with the counter-missionaries that competed for their allegiance) — battles in which he lived out his life until, like Cephas among others, he fell victim to the volatile and casually brutal politics of the Empire (cf. 1 Clem 5:7).

Finally, his theology was missionary in the sense that the mission was itself a theme of first rank in Paul's conception of the dawning eschaton. Just as slave or servant (*doulos*) was the correlative of Lord (*kyrios*), so the servant's task — the world mission (Gal 1:10, 16; 2 Cor 4:5; cf. 1 Cor 3:5; 2 Cor 3:6; 6:4) — was the correlative of the Lord's reign (1 Cor 3:21b-23; 15:22-24). "The same Lord is Lord of all" (Rom 10:12); hence, he was to be acknowledged by all, namely, by their call on him to save them (Rom 10:12f.).

> But how are they to call on one in whom they have not believed? And how are they to believe in one of whom they have never heard? And how are they to hear without a herald? And how can men herald unless they are sent? (Rom 10:14f.).

Therefore, God and the Christ whom he had enthroned as *kyrios* of Jew and Greek (Rom 10:12) were necessarily senders, sending their Apostles and servants to circumcised and uncircumcised alike. The logic of universal Lordship entailed the world mission. Through his Apostles God was enacting throughout the world the reconciliation he had accomplished through Christ (2 Cor 5:18-20). This mission defined the sense and constituted the content of the interim between Christ's resurrection and parousia. It had been set in motion by the resurrection (1 Cor 15:3-10; Rom 1:4f.) and it had the parousia for both end and goal (Rom 11:25; cf. 15:19).[13] Gentiles delivered from the judgment — to which

---

[13]See Martin Hengel, "Die Ursprünge der christlichen Mission," 18-22.

the mission looked (1 Thess 1:10; 1 Cor 3:10-15; Rom 5:9f.; cf. 2 Cor 5:18-20; Phil 1:6) and which would follow upon the parousia (cf. 1 Thess 1:10; 2 Cor 5:10; Rom 2:16) — were to be Paul's priestly offering to God on that day (Rom 15:16). This ministry of a new life and new dispensation (2 Cor 3:6) converted the climactic end of history into a vast "liturgy in the Spirit."[14]

In obedient response to the call of God and Christ (Gal 1:1, 10-12, 15; cf. 1 Cor 1:1, 17; Rom 1:1) — a call that held him like a compelling destiny (1 Cor 9:16; cf. 4:9), structuring his purposes (Gal 1:16; 1 Cor 9:1f.; Rom 15:20) and energizing their fulfillment (1 Thess 1:5; 1 Cor 2:4f.; 3:10a; 15:10; 2 Cor 5:18-20; Rom 15:15b-19) — Paul undertook as his central task the breaking of the news of salvation (cf. 1 Cor 1:17) to the gentile world (Gal 1:16; 2:7-9; Rom 1:5, 13-15; 11:13; 15:15-28; cf. 1 Thess 2:4; Phil 1:12). Of his missionary allies some had the distinctive status of Christ's "Apostles" (1 Thess 2:6; Gal 1:17; 1 Cor 4:9; 9:5; 12:28f.; 15:7, 9; Rom 16:7); others were his "servants" (1 Cor 3:5; 4:1; 2 Cor 3:6; 4:5; 6:4; Rom 16:1). His own staff of "co-workers" (1 Thess 3:2; 1 Cor 3:9; 2 Cor 1:24; 8:23; Rom 16:3, 9, 21; Phm 1; 24) or "fellow soldiers" (Phil 2:25; Phm 2) participated, through Paul's apostolic commission, in an eschatological event: God breaking his silence to the world with a powerful if disconcerting (1 Cor 1:17f.) appeal (2 Cor 5:19f.), the world answering fatefully with yes or no (1 Cor 1:18; 2 Cor 2:15f.; 4:3). The conduct of all these missionaries was to be radically heteronomous, for they were "envoys on Christ's behalf," God himself addressing the world through them (2 Cor 5:20). "When you heard from us the word of God," Paul wrote to the Thessalonians, "you accepted it,

---

[14]Still worth reading: the article of A.-M. Denis, "La fonction apostolique et la liturgie nouvelle en esprit," *Revue d'Histoire et de Philosophie religieuses* 42 (1958): 401-36; 616-56; cf. 403-8 and 650f. on Rom 15:16. But this should be complemented by the article of Aus in the following note as well as by the philologically exact and theologically deft exegesis of Heinrich Schlier, "Die 'Liturgie' des apostolischen Evangeliums (Röm 15, 14-21)," in *Das Ende der Zeit* (Freiburg: Herder, 1971), 169-83.

not as the word of men, but as what it truly is, the word of God" (1 Thess 2:13). And this last word of God to the world was the counterpart of his first: "Let there be light!" (cf. 2 Cor 4:6). It was a creative word (cf. 2 Cor 5:17) flooding with light not the chaos about to become cosmos but the hearts of men (2 Cor 4:6) about to see "the splendor of the gospel of Christ's glory" (2 Cor 4:4). The mission mediated a new creation, at once transposing and fulfilling the age-old dream of the nations' pilgrimage (Rom 15:19b).[15]

Such was Paul's grandiose conception of the world mission and of the source (Christ's death and resurrection), goal (parousia, judgment, reign of God), and character (deliverance and reconciliation through a newly created common life) of the salvation that the mission offered to the world. The mission was both the telling of the story and was itself part of the story. It belonged to the climax defined by the story's structuring as a movement of reversal from estrangement and enmity to reconciliation, from condemnation to acquittal, from bondage to deliverance, from a teleology of death to a teleology of life.

This leads us directly to our next topic: the structure, themes, "sequence," and inner relationships of Pauline soteriology.

---

[15]For a full treatment of the inner nexus among Rom 11:25 ("the full number [*to plērōma*] of the gentiles"), Rom 15:19 ("I have completed [*peplērōkenai*] the preaching of the gospel in a circular sweep from Jerusalem as far as Illyricum"), and Rom 15:24, 29 (Paul's plans to come to Rome and to make Rome a base for a further missionary journey to Spain), see Roger Aus, "Paul's Travel Plans to Spain and the 'Full Number of the Gentiles' of Rom. XI 25," *Novum Testamentum* 21 (1979): 232-62.

VIII

A Soteriology Valid for All

Abstractly, one might describe the controlling structure of Paul's soteriology as one of "problem and solution." If a man is drowning, however, it is ludicrously inadequate to say that he has a problem and, if rescued, that that was the solution. The paradigmatic image of salvation is, rather, the miracle: curing the incurable, reversing the irreversible, retrieving the hopelessly lost. Nevertheless, we shall use the admittedly inadequate abstract terms "problem and solution" so as not to prejudice from the outset by some particular choice such as "condemnation and acquittal" or "bondage and deliverance" or "enmity and reconciliation" the question of what in Paul's view most exactly or profoundly designated the heart of man's predicament and its resolution in Christ.

It seems clear in any case that for Paul "the gospel" was the proclamation of Christ's universal Lordship, itself embodying God's deed on behalf of every human being in the death and resurrection of his Son;[1] that Paul's theology was his effort to make the gospel maximally intelligible to himself and his churches; that, inasmuch as such efforts are necessarily discursive, Paul's theology had a structure; that

[1]On the Pauline use of "gospel," see Peter Stuhlmacher, *Das paulinische Evangelium I*, 56-108; Georg Eichholz, *Die Theologie des Paulus im Umriss* (Neukirchen-Vluyn: Neukirchener Verlag, [2]1977), 14-16, 33-8.

the formula "problem and solution" may be called on to describe that structure; that the exegetical task is to work out a satisfactory understanding of the thematic resources and expository strategies that Paul has drawn on to communicate to his readers his view of the human problem and its divine solution; that it is of historical interest to seek to locate the generative matrix of Paul's thinking and so to reconstruct the genetic order of his theology; and, finally, that in this way we may arrive at a differentiated view of the contribution of Paul's theology to early Christian self-definition and at the role of the world mission in shaping it.

It is important to draw, and to maintain, the distinction between two kinds of task. To recover the intended sense of an author's text by defining his themes and the strategy of their exposition is an exegetical task. To reconstruct the process by which he came into possession of his themes and to probe purposes that we may establish by inference (though he did not himself intend to communicate them) is a historical task. Each of these is relevant to the other. In this chapter we shall give an account of Pauline soteriology. Without reference to its concrete particulars we could hardly depict the Christian self-definition destined to emerge from the Pauline mission. Hence, we shall deal with the major motifs of this soteriology: transgression and expiation, bondage and redemption, enmity and reconciliation, sin and justification, death and the bestowal of new life. Characteristic Pauline themes, such as law and grace, Adam and Christ, which bridge and illuminate all these antitheses, will appear in the course of the exposition.

What follows is necessarily a summary of results, not a full account of the particularity of texts. If I thought that there were radical, comprehensive developments in Paul's soteriology within the period covered by the letters, I would not offer the following summary, but would attempt to trace his thought from text to text chronologically. In my opinion, however, the proponents of radical developments (e.g., in Paul's individual and general eschatology) have failed to make their case. Moreover, they have often betrayed a constricting "process" bias against synchronic hermeneutic structures. Such structures do exist. The purist's refusal to let an author's *opera omnia* serve as a context for interpreting his individual works forecloses interpretative possibilities. It has also generated many a "trajectory" either demonstrably illusory or sheltered from all possibility of being verified or invalidated. The letters, to be sure, exhibit striking differences of tone in accord with the diversity of the audiences and situations to which they are addressed. There are equally striking variations in Paul's conceptualizing of issues and in his formulation of arguments. Still, the specifically soteriological arguments appear to support rather fixed positions. In short, the variations reflect Paul's conceptual and rhetorical resourcefulness rather than change in his central soteriological tenets. Even those who think me mistaken on this issue of development may find something of value in the following summary, namely, more coherent soteriological sense than they had previously found credible in Paul.

The letter to the Romans gives us Paul's apocalyptic conception of history. There are two dynamisms in history: the Adamic dynamism of sin and death, set in motion by Adam's disobedience, and the Christic dynamism of righteousness and life, set in motion by the promise to Abraham. The Law is set in the line of Adamic dynamism. Christ's death and resurrection is the reversal of Adam's disobedience, the fulfillment of the promise, the end of the Law, and the signal for the world mission. The mission is the condition of the parousia and of the salvation of all Israel. Apart from this scheme of thought, the discrete soteriological motifs in Galatians, Philippians, and the Corinthian correspondence seem not to add up to a coherent whole. With it, all these same motifs fall into place. We cannot flatly exclude the possibility that Paul arrived at this coherent framework only late in his career — produced to order, as it were, for the composition of Romans, yet clarifying and illuminating retrospectively his earlier thought on righteousness (e.g., Phil 3:9) or the Law (e.g., Gal 3:19; 1 Cor 15:56; 2 Cor 3:6f.). It seems to me incomparably more probable, however, that with the possible exception of the "secret" of Rom 11:25-27, Paul was in possession of his view of history throughout the period from which the letters date.

Transgression and Expiation

Paul had inherited faith-formulations that (usually though not invariably by allusion to Isa 53) affirmed the death of Christ as expiatory, i.e., designed to purify from sin by winning forgiveness (e.g., 1 Cor 11:24; 15:3; Gal 1:4; Rom 3:25; 4:25; 8:3). He never abandoned this inheritance. The forgiveness of sins — too frequently and superficially supposed to be marginal in Pauline thought — finds repeated expression in his citation of such formulas. The citations are solemn rather than perfunctory, witness the above largely formulaic texts. They are integral to the Pauline perspective on the human problem and its solution, witness the pivotal placement of Rom 3:25f. and the climactic placement of Rom. 8:3. Far from dropping out of sight, the expiation theme is, if anything, more fully and formally expressed in his last letter than anywhere else in his correspondence (Rom 3:25f.; 4:25; 8:3; cf. 14:15b).

The two main grounds for scholarship's often having undervalued this aspect of Pauline soteriology are, first, that it usually finds expression in Paul through inherited materials and, second, that it is consciously blended into other schemes of thought (redemption, justification, Lordship, and so on). But neither singly nor together do these data ground the judgment that expiation has little or no role in Paul's thought.[2] This becomes clear from analysis of *why* Paul fails to isolate themes of expiation for independent treatment. The analysis calls for a preliminary consideration of "bondage."

[2]Owing at least in part to the great influence of Bultmann (*Theology of the New Testament I*, 295f.), this has become a mistaken point of convergence for a substantial segment of international New Testament scholarship. In recent years, however, it has been vigorously opposed; see the

In Pauline thought human bondage is not endowed with hellenistic impersonality. It is fate-like, yet irreducible to fate. It is not religiously neutral. It is not dreadful independently, of itself. It is dreadful as stabilizing and entrenching a state of broken communion with God. It is dreadful because it makes transgression chronically recurrent and condemnation inevitable. This is bondage to an overwhelming legacy and environment of sin and to a lethal pattern of sinning (Rom 6:20). And, as a leading Pauline motif on the role of the Law in history will make clear, sin is not mere disorder. The Law, Paul argues, reveals sin in its real character as a wrath-provoking affront to God. Since this is precisely the aspect of sin to which expiation is correlative, expiation in Paul's view belongs indispensably to the solution to the human problem.

We should insist on this point. A fundamental aspect of the human predicament is the sequence transgression-condemnation (to death). In Paul this usually finds expression in connection with the expiation that repairs transgression (e.g., 1 Cor 15:3; 2 Cor 5:19; Gal 1:4); in Romans it is given fuller treatment (Rom 1-3; 4:15; 5:12; 6:23, etc.). Here the Law is assigned a penultimate, peneschatological function: to turn iniquity into transgression, i.e., into conscious violation of the will of God (Rom 4:15; 5:13, 20; 7:7-13; cf. 6:4). In the face of progressively more conscious offence, the forbearance of God (Rom 2:4; 3:25f.) first holds, but eventually yields to the wrath of God (Rom 1:18; 2:5, 8; 3:5; 4:15). Still, this is just the moment when, true to his covenant promises, God acts to save. In the actuality of history this saving act was to display his Son on Golgotha as the true propitiatory in his own blood... (Rom 3:25). Thus, redemption (*apolytrosis*, 3:24) and expiation (cf. *hilasterion*, 3:25) are mutually defining. What should be

formulation of Peter Stuhlmacher: the expiatory death of Jesus is for Paul *the condition of the possibility of his theology of justification and the cross* (my emphasis). "Achtzehn Thesen zur paulinischen Kreuzestheologie," in *Versöhnung, Gestez und Gerechtigkeit* (Göttingen: Vandenhoeck & Ruprecht, 1981), 195.

noted is the contribution of the trajectory, transgression-wrath-condemnation, to the specifically religious character of the human predicament, and the contribution of the trajectory transgression-expiation-acquittal to the specifically religious character of its resolution.

It remains a fact that the theme of expiation is almost wholly confined to the citation of pre-Pauline formulas. Why is the thrust of Pauline thought not to single out expiation for independent treatment, but — just the opposite — to integrate it with other elements of "problem and solution"? There is a presupposition and a compelling reason for this. The presupposition is that transgression is not repaired by the sinner's own repentance, but calls for an expiatory act that surpasses the whole cultic order of Israel (Rom 3:25f.). The compelling reason for the integration of expiatory with other motifs is that expiation and forgiveness would be futile gestures unless the spell of sin, its hold on man and power over him, were broken. If "offence to God" makes the predicament of man religious, "bondage to offence" makes it insoluble. By itself expiation would be unavailing, just as by itself bondage would be religiously neutral. A first characteristic of Paul's thought to come to light, then, is a kind of organic density. His thematic schemes are not merely juxtaposed; they overlap and interlock. We shall have occasion to return to this observation.

Bondage, Redemption, and Freedom

Turning now to the bondage theme, we have one main point to make: it is that the antithesis to bondage is not only "freedom" (*eleutheria*, see 2 Cor 3:17; Gal 2:4; 5:1, 13; Rom 6:18-22; 8:2, 21) but "redemption" (see 1 Cor 6:20; 7:23; Gal 3:13; 4:5; cf. Rom 8:23). Paul interpreted freedom in a distinctive way. It was the freedom of men ransomed at "a price" (1 Cor 6:20; 7:23), acquired by God as Israel of old had been acquired to be "his own possession" (Ex 19:5). So now the redeemed were to "live no longer for themselves" but for their Lord "who died and was raised for them"(2 Cor 5:15). Freedom was subsumed under kyriology. Paul did not assess it in the modern manner as thoroughgoing autonomy. This he flatly rejected: "You are not your own"(1 Cor 6:19; cf. 2 Cor 5:15; Rom 6:11, 13, 17-22; 14:7-9).

It does not follow, however, that Paul rendered freedom null and void. Man's freedom was doing what he wanted. The perspective in which Paul held this truth (and the crucial premise of the great passage on bondage in Romans 7) was that in the depths of his being man wanted and had always wanted — the good (Rom 7:19). What he wanted was not to be a god, knowing good and evil. It was to be himself, one with himself, able to act in accord with his inmost self. But this was nothing other than his being-toward-God ("in my inmost self I joyfully concur with the law of God," [Rom 7:22]). Shackled, this longing was pathetic (Rom 7:14-24). Redemption threw off the shackles. Freedom was "freedom from," from fear (Rom 8:15), from the Law (Gal 3-4; Rom 6:14; 10:4), and so, in Pauline logic (see 1 Cor 15:56; Rom 5:20f.; 6:15-18, 22f.), from the dominion of sin (Rom 6:14) and of death (Rom 6:16, 22f.). It was also "freedom for," for service (Gal 5:13), for the deep human fulfillment (see Rom 7:14-24) that was living and dying "to the Lord" (Rom 14:8; cf. Gal 2:20), for entry into sonship (Gal 3:26; 4:5-7; Rom 8:14-17, 21-23, 29), and, finally, for "sanctification and its goal, eternal life" (Rom 6:22).

Such is the structure of the bondage-and-freedom theme. It is betokened by the semantic reversibility of the verb *douleuein* ("to serve," "to perform the duties of a slave"): "You *rendered slaves' service (edouleusate)* to beings that by nature are not gods. . . " (Gal 4:8; cf. *douleuein* in Gal 4:25; Rom 6:6) versus "Now we are discharged from the law, dead to what held us captive, so that we *selflessly serve (douleuein)* in accord with the newness of the Spirit, not the obsoleteness of the letter" (Rom 7:6; cf. *douleuein* in Gal 5:13; Rom 12:11; 14:18). The second of these two usages shows that freedom put an end not to allegiance but to what had sapped it. Freedom at its best was allegiance unhin-

dered. It found its real identity in order and thereby escaped
the range of bondages, from caprice to fanaticism, begotten
of unqualified autonomy. Freedom was doing what one
deeply wanted, not doing whatever one chanced to want.
For Paul it was a perversion to turn the freedom won by
Christ into "an opportunity for the flesh" (Gal 5:13), for
freedom was not indifferently disposed to the authentic and
the inauthentic. Freedom and authenticity ("what is good
and pleasing and perfect," Rom 12:2) interpreted and supported each other. They met in release from the "letter"
(Rom 7:6), joy in the Spirit (Rom 14:17), service in the cause
of Christ (Rom 14:18).

Let this stand as a summary approximation of Paul's
view, leaving aside for the moment the origin of human
bondage and the locus of its grip on man.

Enmity and Reconciliation

Sin in biblical terms was both iniquity (*'āwôn*) and rebellion (*peša'*). The ancient Israelite traced back to sin the
enigmas of the world and of his own existence, everything
that pained, burdened, baffled him. To this legacy, we have
already recalled, Paul added his thesis on the hermeneutic
function of the Law: to bring iniquity to full consciousness
as transgression or rebellion. The result in man went beyond
estrangement to a state of hostility toward God (Rom 5:10).
This predicament was met by a one-sided initiative: God in
Christ "reconciling the world to himself" (2 Cor 5:18f.).

Reconciliation (cf. the *katallassein* family of words)
comes to thematic expression in two texts: 2 Cor 5:11-21
and Rom 5:1-11 (cf. 11:15). Both are peak passages, but we
shall limit our comments to the first of them.

The text, which appears in the broad context of Paul's
apologia and instruction on the office of Apostle (2 Cor
2:14-7:4), is made up of three parts (2 Cor 5:11-14a; 14b-17;
18-21). Taking its point of departure from a preceding
reference to the judgment (2 Cor 5:10), part one (vv. 11-14a)
returns to the "Apostle" theme by evoking "the fear of the

Lord" who will judge him, as a spur of his apostolic "appeal to men" (v. 11). This is followed by a principle of discrimination between inauthentic and authentic Apostles (v. 12). What did they put stock in? Outward show (*prosōpon* = appearance) or inward worth (*kardia* = heart)? That Paul had opted for the latter was clear from his life: if he was "beside himself" (ecstatic), it was for God; if in his right mind, for the church (v. 13). What impelled him? The love of Christ (v. 14a). And the key to this was his having reached an all-orienting foundational judgment, which opens part two (14b-17): "one died for all; therefore, all died" (14b).

This compact enthymeme gives rise to a brilliant stream of theological consciousness, as charged as a succession of symbols, yet finely structured. The "foundational judgment" was an inference: if one died for all, all died (v. 14b).[3] Further inferences follow: if in the death of one for all, all died, then "all" were henceforward to live "not for themselves" but for him "who died and was raised for them" (v. 15). Next Paul points to an epistemological consequence that he has made his own; that is, he answers the question — obviously relevant to the discernment of true and false Apostles — of how one ought to judge. Once the turn of the ages had come ("one died for all; therefore, all died" v. 14b), the standards of judgment proper to natural man (*kata sarka*) were obsolete, though they had indeed determined the way in which Paul himself once judged Christ (v. 16). Finally, this stream of thought climaxes in the theme of new creation: the old order was finished, all was new. "To be in

---

[3]The category of thought operative here is that of "representation," by which those represented participate in the act/fate of the one appointed to represent them. Such is Paul's view of human solidarity whether with Adam or with Christ. In both cases there is a human appropriation: men share the sin-and-death heritage of Adam "inasmuch as all men sinned," *eph' ho pantes hēmarton* (Rom 5:12), whereas the reconciliation-and-life heritage of Christ is available "to whoever commits himself [to the gospel] in faith," *panti to pisteuonti* (Rom 1:16). See the discussion of Morna D. Hooker, "Interchange in Christ," *Journal of Theological Studies* 22 (1971): 349-61. See also below, note 10.

Christ is new creation" (v. 17).

This thematically over-determined sequence has burst the casing of the ostensible topic (discernment among claims to apostleship). But, still at the level of the new creation theme, it returns in part three (vv. 18-21) to "Apostle" by defining his role in God's act of reconciling the world to himself. The text reads as follows:

(18) But all this comes from God,
    who through Christ reconciled us to himself
    and gave us the ministry of reconciliation;

(19) for it was God who in Christ was
    reconciling the world to himself,
    not counting their transgressions
      against them,
    and who founded in us the message of
      reconciliation.[4]

(20) So we are envoys on Christ's behalf, God himself
    making his appeal through us.[5]

[4]*Hōs hoti*: "'for' it was God...";cf. Bauer-Arndt-Gingrich, under *hoti*, 1, d, beta, and Blass-Debrunner-Funk, paragraph 396, for discussion. My translation follows the lead of the Vulgate's *quoniam quidem*. Favoring the rendering "it was God who in Christ" over the attractive alternative "God was in Christ" (cf. Col 2:9) is the observation that *theos* without the article is predicative. Even so, Otfried Hofius argues that for the kind of translation adopted here an article before *katalassōn* is indispensable. See "'Gott hat unter uns aufgerichtet das Wort von der Versöhnung' (2 Kor 5:19)," *Zeitschrift für die neutestamentliche Wissenschaft* 71 (1980) 7, note 19. If this is cogent, the better translation would be: "God was in Christ — reconciling the world to himself." "Who founded in us": the word "founded" (a) may well be contrasted, by allusion to LXX Ps 77:5, to the "founding" of the Law in Israel; (b) refers, with maximum probability, to God's revelation to the Apostles of his risen Son. Hofius makes both points, 11-16; see also his essay, "Erwägungen zur Gestalt und Herkunft des paulinischen Versöhnungsgedankens," *Zeitschrift für Theologie und Kirche* 77 (1980): 191f.

[5]*Hōs* followed by the genitive absolute need not have conditional force; see Bauer-Arndt-Gingrich under *hōs*, III, 1, b. Neither "as if" (NEB) nor "as it were"(NAB) seems to cohere well with the thrust of the immediately preceding verses.

> on Christ's behalf, we beseech:
> Be reconciled with God!

(21) For our sake he made him to sin
who knew no sin,
that, in him, we might become the
righteousness of God.

"Apostleship" defines the literary context of the text, and the text defines the ultimate context of apostleship. This ultimate context was the climactic and definitive act of God. It was the act *of God*, for if these things were true — that "one died for all" so that all should "live for him" (vv. 14f.) and that "to be in Christ is new creation" (v. 17) — they were true inasmuch as God himself was at work in this death of one for all and consequent death of all, and in this act of creating anew whoever was "in Christ." True, God acted "through Christ" (v. 18). But his act had ineffable immediacy. It was God in Christ who was reconciling the world to himself (v. 19a) and God who by the revelation of his risen Son "founded" in the Apostles the message of reconciliation (v. 19c). V. 19 thus supplies the ground and explanation of the preceding summary statement (v. 18).

The phrase "not counting their transgressions against them" (v. 19b) is designed to unpack the word "reconciling." The first moment whether of "reconciliation" or of "justification" was the lifting of condemnation, an act terminologically distinct from but materially identical with the forgiveness of sins (Rom 3:25c; cf. 4:5-8; 1 Cor 15:17), and grounded (as the parallel text of Rom 5:10 establishes, and as 2 Cor 5:21 confirms) in the expiatory death of Christ.[6] The

---

[6]Joseph A. Fitzmyer, "Reconciliation in Pauline Theology," in *To Advance the Gospel* (New York: Crossroad, 1981),162-85, makes the point that the concept "reconciliation" does not derive from a cultic context and is not an intrinsically cultic theme (164-75). That is true. But Fitzmyer goes further, dissociating the theme of reconciliation from that of expiation in the Pauline texts (Rom 5:10; 2 Cor 5:18-21), and that is

pattern is significant; Paul places Christ's expiatory death at
the root of salvation in all its modalites: justification (Rom
3:21-26; 4:22-25); reconciliation (= release from "enmity"
and rescue from "the wrath," Rom 5:6-11), and the whole
panoply of "life" (= the lifting of condemnation, the gift of
the Spirit, freedom from sin and death and "the flesh," Rom
8:1-4).

V. 20 begins as a reprise of vv. 18c and 19c; it culminates in
a dramatic summary of the apostolic appeal: Be reconciled!
The first motif of the whole passage, God's authorship of
salvation, recurs in v. 21. What did he do to reconcile the
world to himself? "He made him to be sin" (*hamartia* =
'āšām = a sin-offering, cf. Lev 4:24; the allusion here is to
LXX Isa 53:10; cf. Rom 8:3)[7] "who knew no sin," and did so
"for our sake," that "in him" (i.e., by solidarity with him
who was God's righteousness in person, cf. 1 Cor 1:30), "we

---

erroneous. Rom 5:9f. belongs to a pivotal passage (5:1-11) designed to set
up an *a fortiori* argument: if we have been made righteous and have been
reconciled to God by the bloody death of his Son (ch. 1-4), so the more
surely shall we be saved by his risen life for which we, too, are destined
(ch. 5-8). The first limb of this argument includes a deliberate reprise of
Rom 3:21-26, where "blood" is explicitly an expiation motif. (Reference
to covenant sacrifice, as in 1 Cor 11:25, is neither implied nor intimated
by Rom 5:9f.). Again, Hofius, "Erwägungen zur Gestalt," 186-94, has
established beyond cavil the internal thematic ties in 2 Cor 5:18-21.
Justification is a central component in reconciliation (on this Fitzmyer's
views are unobjectionable), and for Paul Christ's expiatory death indispensably grounds both (contrary to Fitzmyer). Finally, Hofius argues
persuasively ("Erwägungen zur Gestalt," 194-99) that Deutero-Isaian
texts, emphatically including the great expiation passage of Isa 52:13-
53:12, are a key source of the Pauline theme of reconciliation and its
proclamation.

[7]Parallel to 2 Cor 5:21 ("he made him to be sin" are Gal 3:13 (Christ
became a curse for us)— and Rom 8:3 (God condemned sin in the flesh,
namely, of his own Son). Though many are content to leave these
statements in their unvarnished form (e.g., Karl Kertelge, "*Rechtfertigung" bei Paulus* (Münster: Aschendorff, 1967), 101-6; Hooker, "Interchange in Christ"), any *real opposition* between Father and Son would

might become the righteousness of God." It now appears that the text's conspicuous alternation of motifs — God's act (18ab, 19ab, 21) and its apostolic proclamation (18c, 19c, 20) — is structurally calculated. V. 21, returning to "God's act,"completes a chiasmus that opened with v. 19 (*a*=19ab; *b*=19c; *b*=20; *a*=21); and the text ends on a climactic note: grace divinizing what had been an alienated world.[8]

Inasmuch as this extraordinarily charged passage (2 Cor 5:11-21) evokes a series of themes prominent in Pauline

breast the main current of Pauline soteriology as an unassimilable foreign body. This holds, whatever exegesis be adopted. To avoid any such meaning — as unacceptable to Paul as to later tradition — many from the time of Augustine on have preferred to resolve Pauline metaphor into non-metaphorical terms, comparing 2 Cor 5:21 with Rom 8:3. According to this text, God sent his Son in the likeness of sinful flesh (=in the same flesh as that of sinful humanity, cf. *homoiōma* in Rom 6:5; see Bauer-Arndt-Gingrich under *homoiōma*, 1) to expiate sin (epexegetical *kai* followed by *peri* with *hamartia*; see Bauer-Arndt-Gingrich under *peri* 1, g); he "condemned" (not by passing nor by executing a sentence, but by triumphing over [cf., among recent critics, Lyonnet, "Pauline Soteriology" in *Introduction to the New Testament* (Tournai: Desclée, 1965), 862f.]) sin, namely "in the flesh" of his crucified and glorified Son. The references to *hamartia* in both Rom 8:3 (three occurrences) and 2 Cor 5:21 (two occurrences) feature a clear play of antithesis. Both, moreover, allude to Isa 53. In Rom 8:3 the allusion is to LXX Isa 53:10 (see Joachim Jeremias, *The Servant of God*, 97, note 442); in 2 Cor 5:21 the two phrases on sin, played off against one another, both allude to Isa 53: *ton mē gnonta hamartian* alludes to Isa 53:9b (Jeremias, *Servant*, 97, note 441) and *hyper hēmōn hamartian epoiesēn* alludes, like Rom 8:3, to LXX Isa 53:10. On *hamartia* in place of *peri hamartias*, cf. Ex 29:14, 36; Lev 4:21, 24f., 33f.; 5:12. On the history of the exegesis of 2 Cor 5:21, see Léopold Sabourin, "Christ Made 'Sin' (2 Cor 5:21)" in *Sin, Redemption, and Sacrifice* (Rome: Biblical Institute Press, 1970), 187-296.

[8]On the chiasmus, see Hofius, "'Gott hat unter uns aufgerichtet...'" 3-9. On persuasive literary grounds this settles the question of how v. 21 is related to what precedes it. It confirms, in short, that the expiatory death of Christ belongs foundationally to the Pauline theme of reconciliation. "World" in v. 19 is the human world. The "we" of v. 21 — now no longer the apostolic "we" of vv. 19-20 — are all those in whom the reconciliation of the world is actually enacted.

soteriology — Christ's death " for all," their death and new life (vv. 14 f.), the obsolete character of life (here, specifically, of knowing) "according to the flesh" (v. 16), being "in Christ" and hence a new creation (v. 17), reconciliation (vv. 18-20), justification (v. 19b), and expiation (v. 21; cf. vv. 14f.) — it offers an occasion for asking how all these themes are correlated and whether there is a hierarchy among them. Still, we must decline this discussion until our survey is complete.

Condemnation and Justification

The entire family of words and ideas to which "justification" belongs had its biblical *Sitz im Leben* in the customary processes of judgment. Given the covenantal structure of the faith of Israel (cf., e.g., Ex 19:3-6), nothing was more natural than to make the process of maintaining order and justice in society the model for understanding Yahweh and his "way." He was Israel's covenantal Lord and judge. From this came a flood of biblical texts having a juridical cast. His acts were judgments (*mišpāṭîm*), just or righteous decisions (*ṣĕdāqôt*).

> The Rock, his work is perfect,
>   for all his ways are justice
>   (*mišpāṭ*),
> A God of faithfulness (*'ĕmûnâ*) and
>   without wrongdoing,
>   righteous (*ṣaddîq*) and upright
>   (*yāšār*) is he (Deut 32:4).

Juridical language early, permanently, and profoundly textured the religious consciousness of Israel, penetrating not just the Torah but the whole biblical tradition. It is no surprise that the pseudepigrapha and the Qumran texts are uninhibitedly eloquent in their exploitation of this language. Perhaps it is somewhat more surprising that the same language appears in the letters of Paul, addressed as they were to predominantly gentile congregations. But how else was Paul to come to terms with adversaries of his view on the Law? And in what other terms was he to rethink for himself and others their common biblical inheritance?

Before we turn to the Pauline texts, we should recall two aspects of the Bible's juridico-religious tradition: the themes of God as judge and God as savior.

On the first theme, recall that the division of men into two classes, the righteous and the wicked, was a pillar of the biblical world. The judgment of God first of all *established* the moral order (the righteous were those who were righteous in his eyes and the wicked those who were wicked in his eyes) and, second, *vindicated* it (in the end the righteous would be blessed and the wicked ruined). The righteous were those who served, feared, loved the Lord, the wicked those who refused to (Deut 6:5, 24f.; Mal 3:18).

> And righteousness (*ṣĕdāqâ*) will be ours if, in the sight of Yahweh our God, we carefully keep the whole of this commandment ["you shall love the Lord your God with all your heart..." Deut 6:5] as he has commanded us (Deut 6:25).

Righteousness was both the state of "clean hands and a pure heart" and its vindication (Ps 24:4f.). For, since God was a just judge (*šōpēṭ ṣaddîq*, Ps 7:12 EVV 11), he would reward the righteous and punish the wicked. The righteous pleaded for these judgments:

> Hear, o heaven [prayed Solomon], take action and judge your servants. Condemn the wicked man, bringing his conduct down on his own head, but acquit the righteous man, rewarding him according to his righteousness (1 Kgs 8:32).

If Yahweh acquitted (*hiṣdîq*) the righteous or innocent (*ṣaddîq*), by the same token he condemned (*hiršîaʿ*) the wicked (*rāšāʿ*) and, though slow to anger (*ʾerek ʾappayim*), would "absolutely not clear" the guilty (Nahum 1:3; cf. Ex 23:7).

Thus, he dealt with men in accordance with truth. On this basis the unjustly afflicted repeatedly called on God as avenger of the innocent (Pss 5:11; 7:10-12; 10:12-15 etc.) and Job cried out against condemnation (Job 10:2).

Our second theme, that of God as savior, again presents itself to us in a juridical idiom. Let an Isaian text illustrate. Set in the covenantal and so juridical context of God's wrath against transgressors in Jerusalem and of his will to cleanse and restore the city, it is filled with this language:

> I will restore your judges as at first
> and your counsellors as in the
> beginning;
> after that, you shall be called
> "city of righteousness (*ṣedeq*),"
> "faithful city."
> Zion shall be redeemed (*tippādeh*) by
> justice (*mišpāṭ*), and her repentant
> ones by righteousness (*ṣĕdāqâ*)...
> (Isa 1:26f.).

The "justice" (*mišpāṭ*) in question was God's decisive and gracious act in favor of Jerusalem; "righteousness" (*ṣĕdāqâ*) stands in synonymous parallelism with it. Thus, the "righteousness" of Yahweh (Deut 33:21; cf. *ṣidqôt YHWH*: his "righteous acts" in Jgs 5:11; 1 Sam 12:7; cf. Mic 6:5; Isa 1:27; 45:24f.)[9] was a ground of hope: he was able and willing to save and restore his people.

But perhaps this is said too easily and quickly. In terms of religious and theological coherence, there was a radical problem with such themes of restoration. It lay in the chronic sinfulness of Israel. Moral sobriety so characterized

---

[9]"The righteousness of God" was probably less than a widely used, well established formula in pre-Christian tradition. Whether it became a technical term in Jewish-Christian pre-Pauline tradition depends especially on whether "to show his righteousness" in Rom 3:25 is Paul's own composition (see Appendix 84-88, especially) or was inherited by Paul as part of the baptismal text he cited.

the theme of God as just judge that the prophet who clung to this alone could discern nothing but disaster for Israel. There were prophets, however, who in the face of ills that justice could not cure but only aggravate, wrongs that justice could not right except by destroying God's people, broke through the limits of the justice category and changed the ring of its vocabulary. God's interventions (*mišpāṭîm, ṣĕdāqôt*) were not those of an arbiter only but of a savior. They turned on his covenant-love (*ḥesed*) and spontaneous graciousness (also *ḥesed*), his count-on-ability (*'ĕmet*) and tender compassion (*rāḥămîm*).

If these extravagant themes transcended the sphere of rational arrangements typical of the juridical order, they remained nonetheless within the framework of election and covenant. Like the covenant itself, Yahweh's promises were founded on his self-explaining and otherwise finally inexplicable predilective love for his people. On this improbable and mysterious premise, promises of restoration and their fulfillment had covenantal logic. By an order-establishing intervention (*mišpāṭ*), God showed his righteousness (*ṣĕdāqâ*), his graciousness and faithfulness (*ḥesed wĕ'ĕmet*). Guilt notwithstanding, Israel found salvation:

> What God is like thee, removing guilt
>> and passing over transgression for the remnant of his inheritance?
> He is not one to stay angry forever,
>> for he delights in covenant-love;
> he will again have compassion on us,
>> trampling our guilt underfoot.
> Thou wilt cast all our sins
>> into the depths of the sea
>> (*Mic* 7:18f.).

Such were among the resources on which Paul drew to formulate, biblically and juridically, what had happened in Christ's death and resurrection.

Once gained to the Christian cause, Paul came to the view, uncommon in Palestinian Judaism but held by the

Baptist and Jesus before him, that in the face of imminent consummation the conventional division of "righteous" and "wicked" was irrelevant, that all in Israel and not merely notorious "sinners" were liable to condemnation. Like Stephen and the *hellēnistai*, Paul acknowledged the urgent imperative of real acquittal, real righteousness, in the eyes of God; and in the light of Easter faith, he, too, considered the standing cultic and other resources of Israel to be utterly impotent respecting this need. The inherited soteriological formulas of *hebraioi* (1 Cor 15:3-5) and *hellēnistai* (Rom 3:25f.) alike would command Paul's repudiation of conventional righteousness and his striking transformation of this age-old theme.

The Pauline formulation would bring the tension between the Bible's God-as-judge texts (he "absolutely shall not clear" the guilty, Nahum 1:3) and its God-as-savior texts (he delights in covenant-love and will cast our sins into the sea, Mic 7:18f.) to a stunning climax. In the death of Christ "for us" God showed "his righteousness" (covenant-love keeping its promises, Rom 3:25f.) and this amounted to clearing the guilty, acquitting the wicked, reconciling the hostile (Rom 4:5; 5:6-11; cf. 3:21f., 26).

The central problem met by the revelation of God's saving righteousness was, then, a state of sin from which no one could emerge on his own. To count oneself among the righteous was illusion. The righteous were indeed those who were righteous in God's sight — and

> None is righteous, no, not one
> (Rom 3:10, paraphrasing Pss 14 and 53).

To count oneself among the righteous was to cultivate a righteousness of one's own devising. Such had been Paul's experience: to have "a righteousness of my own derived from law" (Phil 3:9); it was equally that of his fellow countrymen: "not knowing the righteousness of God, and intent on setting up a righteousness of their own, they did not submit to the righteousness of God" (Rom 10:3). As the pagans' capital sin was that they did not see fit "to recognize

God" (*ton theon echein en epignōsei*, Rom 1:28), the Jews, though intent on God, were likewise "without discernment" (*ou kata epignōsin*, Rom 10:2). The object of this primordial not-knowing was "the righteousness of God": his gratuitous saving act, probably not only as fulfillment but as promise and fulfillment. Correlative to their not knowing the righteousness of God, which envisaged the salvation of the whole world (Rom 1:16f.; 3:21f., 26), was their cultivation of a righteousness of their own (derived from the Law, as in Phil 3:9); and this lay at the root of their refusal to submit to the righteousness of God as it was finally and concretely revealed in the Christ event.

The key to this line of thought was Paul's view of the dissociation of righteousness from the Law. God's purpose in giving the Law had never been to mediate righteousness. As the scriptural paradigm of Abraham showed, God accredited righteousness in view of man's acceptance in faith of the promise of universal salvation. If there was nevertheless a righteousness derived from Law (cf. Phil 3:9), it was Israel, not God, that "set up" (*stēnai*, Rom 10:3) this righteousness; thus, it was a righteousness of their own (Rom 10:3). It was "their own," moreover, as the fruit of their own "doing," their efforts to observe the Law (cf. Phil 3:9). The righteousness that God himself set up, on the other hand, was accessible to Israel by faith in God's promise, and once the promise was fulfilled and this good news was broadcast not only to Israel but to the whole world, righteousness was accessible to all without distinction by faith in the promise fulfilled. The progression of thought in Rom 10:3 from the first to the second occurrence of "the righteousness of God" accordingly moves from one to another moment: from the failure to discern the righteousness of God as attested in advance by "the law and the prophets" (Rom 3:21) to the failure to acknowledge its actual appearance in Christ.

Unrecognized and unacknowledged by Israel, the human problem was unrighteousness with no exit, illusory righteousness papering over real estrangement. The solution was a divine initiative that "redeemed" (*exagorazein*, Gal 3:13; 4:5; cf. 1 Cor 6:19f.; 7:23) those condemned and accursed by the Law, "acquitted" (*dikaioun*, Rom 3:26; 5:9) sinners by the expiatory shedding of blood, and "reconciled" (*katallassein*, 2 Cor 5:18-20; Rom 5:10) with God an alienated humanity. By soteriological re-definition — God the savior was now depicted as the acquitter of the ungodly (Rom 4:5) and the saved as those who, while still enemies, yet had been reconciled (Rom 5:9f.)[10] — Paul brought the tension between the saving righteousness of God and the infallible truth of God's judgment to the last possible turn of the screw. It reversed the oath of Exodus, "I will not acquit the wicked" — not, to be sure, in the sense that Paul's "acquittal of the ungodly" (*justificatio impii*) implied God's disregard of the moral order or man's discharge from it. The point was that there were more things in this aquittal than were dreamt of in the Exodus oath. Acquittal *transformed* the unrighteous (*adikos*), making him righteous (*dikaios*).

Righteous and unrighteous, as Paul used the terms, were contradictory states. One could not simultaneously be both. The unrighteous became righteous by accepting Christ as his savior — precisely what had happened in "the Easter

---

[10]Prior to the human act of acceptance named "faith," God in Christ already realized for all mankind a saving act of expiation (Rom 3:23-26, *pantes* + *hilastērion*), redemption (Gal 3:13f.; v. 13: Jews; v. 14: gentiles), reconciliation (2 Cor 5:19, *kosmon katallassōn*), justification (Rom 3:23f., *pantes...dikaioumenoi*; Rom 5:15-19), gift of eschatological life (1 Cor 15:22) and glory (1 Cor 15:49: universality implicit from "men of dust — man of dust" vs. "heavenly men — man of heaven" in v. 48). The texts on the universality of justification, life, and glory have posed acute exegetical problems, the solution of which would appear to lie in taking these texts to refer to the reality not of determinate events of justification, etc., but of salvation-historical teleology or finality. (See Bernard Lonergan's definition of finality as the "dynamic orientation towards a completeness that becomes determinate *only in the process of completion*," *Insight*, 444, my emphasis.) Paul refers not to a logical but to a real future, not to a rhetorical but to a real universality, and, finally, not to determinate events but to the teleology or finality of God's act in Christ. This view is distinct from but allied with those of C. K. Barrett, *From First Adam to Last* (London: Black, 1962), 73, and of Karl Kertelge, "*Rechtfertigung*," 144-7.

experience of the disciples" from Cephas to Paul.[11] The name of this acceptance was "faith" (*pistis*). Thus, faith became an alternative to the Law. But since the righteousness to which faith gave access differed, as real from illusory, from the righteousness that Israel had set up as its own (Rom 10:3), faith was not an alternative in the sense of another route to the same goal. It was another route to a different goal, namely, to righteousness in the sight of God. The only real righteousness, and so the only righteousness that counted, was mediated by the faith-acceptance of God's act in Christ. That observance of the Law was an achievement, Paul never doubted. That it mediated the one thing necessary — righteousness in the sight of God — he simply denied. It follows that Paul's way of conceiving the situation of man in the sight of God stood in unyielding contradiction to the way of Judaism.[12]

This issue is not adequately classified under "Paul's view of the Law." The role of the Law, as an expository *topos* of Pauline theology,[13] is part of a larger scheme of salvation-historical reflection. Righteousness by faith began with Abraham (Gal 3:6-18; Rom 4) and was already then the justification of the ungodly (Rom 4:5). How is it that God assigned "faith" the power to mediate this righteousness? From the fact that faith was man's yes to God's redemptive scheme. The object of faith on Abraham's part was the same

[11]See Peter Stuhlmacher, "Jesu Auferweckung und die Gerechtigkeitsanschauung der vorpaulinischen Missionsgemeinden," in *Versöhnung, Gesetz und Gerechtigkeit,* 71f.; Otfried Hofius, "Erwägungen zur Gestalt," 191f.

[12]There is, moreover, no way to justify exegetically a supposed Pauline view proposing distinct economies of salvation for Jews and for gentiles, respectively (as maintained by Krister Stendahl, "Paul Among Jews and Gentiles," in *Paul Among Jews and Gentiles and Other Essays*[Philadelphia: Fortress, 1976], 1-77).

[13]Some recent works on Paul and the Law, which, however distinct, converge in rejecting the adequacy of Bultmann's anthropological analysis (the only thing worse than breaking the Law is observing it) and the accuracy of his thesis on Jewish legalism (religion is legal observances,

as the object of faith on the part of Cephas and the twelve, James and Paul; but Abraham put faith in God's promise and the Apostles in the promise fulfilled. What had been promised? That in Abraham "all the nations" would be blessed (Gal 3:8), receiving God's Spirit through faith (Gal 3:14); that Abraham would be "father of many nations" (Rom 4:17); that his offspring — believers (Rom 4:9-12) as numerous as the stars or the sand (Rom 4:18) — would inherit the world (Rom 4:13). Now, if the fulfillment of the promise were to come about through the Law, it could not come about at all, for law gave rise only to wrath (Rom 4:15). But if not by law, then by faith; and as Abraham's own faith conditioned the beginning of the fulfillment, the faith of the gentiles belonged to its consummation.

That real righteousness was by faith was therefore no arbitrary arrangement. It did not isolate faith as in and of itself peculiarly privileged. The primacy of faith lay in this, that it was man's self-involving yes to God's scheme of salvation. First as promise, finally as fulfillment, this scheme spanned the ages from Abraham to Christ and the Apostles. Rather than undercutting a salvation-historical appropriation of the biblical tradition, "justification by

which ground man's "boast" before God): E. P. Sanders, *Paul and Palestinian Judaism* (Philadelphia: Fortress, 1977), 474-502; Heikki Räi-sänen, "Legalism and Salvation by the Law," in *Die Paulinische Literatur und Theologie* (Arhus: Aros, 1980), 63-83, and E. P. Sanders, *Paul, the Law, and the Jewish People*, 65-91. Convergent in rejecting the adequacy of Bultmann's anthropological analysis and in affirming the christological starting point and perspective for Paul's reflections on the Law: Andrea van Dülmen, *Die Theologie des Gesetzes bei Paulus* (Stuttgart: Katholisches Bibelwerk, 1968); Ulrich Wilckens, "Was heisst bei Paulus: 'Aus Werken des Gesetzes wird kein Mensch gerecht?'" (1969), in *Recht-fertigung als Freiheit* (Neukirchen-Vluyn: Neukirchener Verlag, 1974), 77-109; Peter Stuhlmacher, "'Das Ende des Gesetzes,'" (1970); "Acht-zehn Thesen zur paulinischen Kreuzestheologie," 194-7 (1975); "Zur paulinischen Christologie" (1977); "Die Gerechtigkeitsanschauung des Apostels Paulus," 99-108, 111-14 (1981), all in *Versöhnung, Gesetz und Gerechtigkeit.*

faith" pointed to and highlighted the history of salvation. The thrust of "by faith, not works of the law" was to fix attention on the work of God: the promise to Abraham, its fulfillment in the atonement (1 Cor 15:3; 2 Cor 5:21; Rom 3:25), the redemption (1 Cor 6:19f.; 7:23; Gal 3:13), the reconciliation (Rom 5:6-11) that entailed a world mission (2 Cor 5:18-20). This fulfillment "showed" (Rom 3:21, 25f.) God's righteousness. It showed "that he himself is righteous" — he fulfills his promise — "and that he makes righteous whoever has faith in Jesus" (Rom 3:26) — the concrete content of the promise (Rom 4:17f., 23-25).

From Death to Life

This making righteous was life to the dead (Rom 4:17-19, 24f.; cf. Gal 3:21). In 1 Cor 15 and still more elaborately in Romans, Paul defined the human predicament as "death," this word signifying not only physical but eschatological death (= damnation, cf. Rom 1:32; 6:16, 21, 23; 7:5; also 5:12, 15, 17, 21). If the problem of man was death, the solution was life (Rom 5:17f.; 8:10), new life (Rom 6:4; cf. 7:6; 12:2), eternal life (Rom 5:21; 6:22f.; cf. 2:7), life defined as acquittal (Rom 5:18) and as God's free gift (Rom 6:23), life mediated by righteousness (Rom 8:10) and associated both with "reign" (Rom 5:17, 21) connoting rescue, reversal, triumph (as in Dan 7:18, 22, 27) and with "peace" (Rom 8:6), the epitome of eschatological blessing (Isa 2:4; 9:5-7; 11:6-9; Zech 9:9f.). In earlier letters this charged use of "life" and "death" had appeared only sporadically (death: 2 Cor 3:7; 7:10; life: 2 Cor 2:16; 3:6; 4:12; Gal 3:21; 6:8); now Paul drew on it to designate in comprehensive fashion what was at stake in faith and unfaith.

The theme of life and death was bound up with Christ's death and resurrection. His own risen life was the condition of Christ's conferring acquittal (Rom 4:25), the capacity for living a new life (Rom 6:4, 11), and the hope of resurrection (Rom 6:5). If man was held captive by sin and death, he was acquitted ("no more condemnation") by being "in Christ

Jesus" (Rom 8:1) and was set free by the Spirit, a new principle of life (Rom 8:2).

"Death" as the name of the state and destiny from which man was saved and "life" as the name of salvation appear mainly in Romans 5-8. This reflects Paul's structuring of the exposition in Romans 1-8 as a *qal wāḥômer* (*a fortiori*) argument: if we have been "reconciled to God by the death of his Son," so the more surely shall we be "saved" by the risen life we are called to share in (Rom 5:10). All eight chapters deal with God's saving act. The first four chapters are set under the heading of man's entry into righteousness, the first moment in the appropriation of this act. Righteousness then serves as the ground and guarantee of a second moment: final salvation (Rom 8:28-30), immortal life to the mortal body (Rom 8:11), which is its "redemption" (Rom 8:23), and the "glory" (Rom 8:18, 21, 30) of those whom God loves with the love he has for his Son (Rom 8:31-39; cf. 8:29).

Two reasons for Paul's reserving the themes of death and life for the part of his exposition that deals with the climactic second moment in salvation are the following. First, the text of Habakkuk 2:4, which serves as a scriptural heading for the argument of the letter, suggests it. "He who through faith is righteous [Rom 1-4] shall have life [Rom 5-8]." Second, themes of death and life are especially associated with the Adam-Christ typology. Death came into the world through the sin of Adam (Rom 5:12; cf. Wis 2:24; 4 Ezra 3:7, 21f., etc.), whereas the role of the last Adam — first-born of many (Rom 8:29) — was to initiate the everlasting life of a new mankind. If, then, the Adam-Christ scheme belongs just where it is (a point to which we shall presently return), so do the themes of eschatological death and eschatological life.

There are real differences of function, which make understandable the differences of thematic content, between the exposition of the human predicament in Rom 1:18 — 3:20 and that in Rom 5:12 — 7:25. The point of the first exposition is to establish the universality of the need met by "redemption ... in Christ Jesus" (Rom 3:24). Jew and

Greek alike were liable to condemnation at the world judgment (Rom 2:3-11). The scriptures put both "under the power of sin," and since scriptural condemnations addressed "those under the law," it followed that every mouth, including the mouth of the Jew, was stopped (Rom 3:19).[14]

The exposition of the human dilemma in Rom 5:12 — 7:25 is not limited to the single purpose of establishing the universal need of redemption. Its positive functions remain

---

[14]Both current views — that Rom 1:18-3:20 fits in nicely with the rest of Paul (recently, Günter Klein, "Sündenverständnis und theologia crucis bei Paulus" in *Theologia Crucis-Signum Crucis* (Tübingen: Mohr, 1979), 249-82, cf. 253-61) and that it does not fit in at all (recently, E. P. Sanders, *Paul, the Law, and the Jewish People*, 23, 123-35) — overlook the moving standpoint from which Paul presents his argument in Rom 1-4. The phases of the argument are irreducible to parts of a single final view. Specifically, the function of Rom 1:18-3:20 is to make the point that all stand condemned, for all have sinned. To this end it was sufficient that Paul, who had probably given this exposé many times in the synagogues of the northern Mediterranean basin, exploit his agreements with Judaism to the effect that sin is transgression of the moral law, that the judgment of God rightly falls on sinners, that what counts here is not hearing the Law but doing it, etc. To be sure, Paul goes far beyond Judaism in this opening passage, not only in individual statements (e.g., in the parenthetical statement that God will judge the secrets of men "in Christ Jesus," 2:16, or in the proleptic statement that no human being will be made righteous in the sight of God by works of the Law, 3:20), but, above all, by the thrust of the passage as a whole: all mankind, including Israel, stands ineluctably condemned before God. Nevertheless, Paul for the most part speaks the *language* of Judaism here, knowing that once he had made his point on the whole human race standing convicted and condemned, he can progress to a solution (Rom 3:21ff.) that will establish a new state of the question. The text of Rom 1:18-3:20 is not meant, then, to give expression, already, to the most distinctive traits of Paul's soteriology (e.g., on the Law); it is meant to take his readership a crucial step forward toward that soteriology. Recognition of the text's rhetorical character both as a locutionary act making a single point and as a performative act moving its audience from common ground to new ground, relativizes what has been a major distraction: the issue of minute conceptual coherence with a distinctive soteriology still to be detailed.

to be clarified, and a large part of that clarification comes from the text's organization.

The first verses of Rom 5 forward the argument by spelling out the consequences of justification: rejoicing (5:2, 3, 11) in hope of glory (5:2-5); peace and reconciliation and access to grace (5:1f., 10f.); God's love for us (5:5, 8) poured out in the hearts of those who receive the gift of the Spirit (5:5); and definitive salvation on the day of judgment (5:9f.). These same themes find fuller expression in ch. 8, thus establishing a thematic *inclusio*. This *inclusio* is essentially an affirmation of the present ("since we are made righteous by faith") designed to lay claim on the future ("we rejoice in our hope of sharing the glory of God," Rom 5:1f.). The connection between present and future, grounded proximately in the dynamism inherent in justification itself (5:1, 9f.) and ultimately in God's love (5:8), is framed (as we have remarked) as a *qal wāḥômer* argument, of which the final conclusion is a crescendo of assurances: the pneumatology of Rom 8:1-27, the divine economy "for those who love him" (Rom 8:28-30), lastly, God's love for us, which, since it is a love "in Christ Jesus our Lord," is irrevocable (Rom 8:31-39).

Rom 5:1-11 and 8:1-39 must consequently guide the reading of the passages they frame (5:12-7:25). Now, within the framed section 5:12-21 presents itself as the proximate basis of ch. 6 and 7. That is, the Adam-Christ typology provides the key terms — trespass (*paraptōma*) vs. free gift (*charisma*), condemnation (*katakrima*) vs. justification (*dikaiōma*), death (*thanatos*) vs. life (*zōē*) — through which Paul, grasping the beginning and the end, now takes hold of history as a totality. The beginning spawned the dilemma (sin and death); the end brought the promised solution (acquittal and life). As Adam initiated a humanity trapped in sin, Christ initiated a renewed humanity, free at last to realize the good it had always wanted (cf. Rom 7:15-20). In this protological and eschatological vision human history emerges as the deliberate validation of a primeval dilemma. It is finally undone by the solution that brings history to an end.

Of itself the Adam-Christ schema is a typology celebrating peripeteia and victory. In context, it provides the *a priori* condition of the possibility of "peace with God . . . access to . . . grace" (Rom 5:1f.). Given the general expository strategy of Romans as a movement from "He who through faith is righteous" to "shall have life," the Adam-Christ schema could appear nowhere other than where it is. Whereas its Adamic component introduces the motif of obstacles still to be overcome (sin in ch. 6, the Law in ch. 7), its Christic component promotes the controlling *qal wāḥômer* argument. The typology is unique insofar as type and antitype correlate respectively with "human dilemma" and "divine resolution." Hence, both limbs of the schema — the type and the antitype — have a significance independent of typology as such. Adamic dynamism gave final biblical form to Paul's conception of the human dilemma. It thereby specified the condition of the possibility of the Law's historic role as he conceived it, a thrust already felt in 5:13, and again in 5:20f.

Perhaps in opposition to an alternative Judaic schematization of history,[15] Paul refused to mitigate the sin of pre-Torah man or to qualify in any way sin's universal issuance in death. Death reigned even over those "from Adam to Moses" whose sin was not "transgression." History was unrelieved subjection to the Adamic dynamism of sin and death. The Torah, coming onto the scene to multiply sin, is thus firmly integrated into this dark vision. Far from being the final principle of religious discernment, the Torah only revealed the darker reaches of the dilemma, a drama spiraling to ruin. The most original and offensive feature of Paul's entire retrieval of the history of sin and salvation was this

[15]The "perhaps" reflects the lateness of the rabbinic attestation of the threefold division of human history: (1) from Adam to Moses, two thousand years of chaos (*tohû wābohû*); (2) from Moses to the Messiah, two thousand years of Torah; (3) two thousand years of the Messiah (bSanhedrin 97b; Abodah zarah 9b; jMeg. 70d; cf. Epist. Barnabas 15:4). See Joseph A. Fitzmyer, "Paul and the Law," in *To Advance the Gospel*, 186-201, esp. 188 and 199, note 8.

positioning of the Torah in the line of Adamic impact.

The purpose of this positioning was to reserve the mediation of righteousness to God the promiser and promise-fulfiller. On the promiser: the object of the promise to Abraham was precisely the gift of righteousness to the world (Gal 3:8). "Is the law against the promises of God? Certainly not!" (Gal 3:21). True, the Law would have been against the promises if the Law had been meant to mediate righteousness. But that is excluded, for it would require that the Law be able to "make alive," to breathe life into the dead, something no law can possibly do (Gal 3:21). Conclusion: the Law is positioned not to mediate righteousness but—just the opposite—to attest that the mediation of righteousness is to lie elsewhere. On the promise-fulfiller: God fulfilled his promise of righteousness by authoring the redemptive and expiatory death of his Son for all men (Rom 3:23-26). "But if righteousness were by the law, then Christ died to no purpose" (Gal 2:21). The conclusion is the same: it cannot have been the intention of God that the Law mediate righteousness. Rather, the Law was to dramatize in its own way that this mediation was reserved to the correlatives, God's promise, man's faith.

Such was the purpose of the Law's being assigned a role in the line of the Adamic dynamism. The condition of this role, however, was extrinsic to the Law. It lay in the solidarity of man with Adam. "Flesh" (*sarx*) names man as subject to the Adamic dynamism of sin and death. "God has done what the law, weakened by the flesh, was not able to do," namely, "to condemn (= triumph over) sin in the flesh" (Rom 8:3). This was a victory in which the Law had no share, for it could do nothing to change the condition of man. The impotence of the Law was reducible to the impotence of man, and this was flesh: his subjection to sin and death. Such was his legacy from Adam (Rom 5:19), but it was a legacy that he validated by his own transgressions (Rom 5:12;[16] 6:23). In

[16]On Rom 5:12 (*eph' hō pantes hēmarton*, "inasmuch as all men sinned") see Stanislas Lyonnet, "Le sens de *eph' ho* en Rom 5, 12 et l'exégèse des pères grecs," *Biblica* 36 (1955): 436-56.

solidarity with Adam, he was "sold under sin" (Rom 7:14), but as validating this condition he was "without excuse" (Rom 1:20; 2:1). Human resolve offered no way out. Nothing short of making man over again would do.

New Creation

Jeremiah and Ezekiel had been the first to come to this heightening of the issue of man and sharpening of focus on his misery and glory as a client of God (Jer 31:33f.; Ezek 36:26f.). The hope of these prophets centered on a new relationship (covenant) with God, predicated on escape from the crassness of the human heart —

> the heart is of all things the most
> crooked, it is beyond remedy
> (Jer 17:9) —

and from the faithlessness of the human spirit, an escape from sin in virtue of having a new heart and a new spirit and in this sense of being a new man. In the very opening oracles of Deutero-Isaiah were established the great themes of the Creator Lord (Isa 40:12-14, 22, 28; 42:5), sole Lord (Isa 40:12-14, 25f.) of the whole earth (Isa 40:15-17), effective Lord of events (Isa 40:22-24; 44:2-4), of an ordered cosmos and ordered history ("I did not say ... 'Seek me in chaos,' " Isa 45:19). Past fulfillment, even the exodus, was soon to be outshone. Yahweh was about to do "a new thing" (Isa 43:19; cf. 42:9; 48:6, "new things, hidden things"), namely to accomplish a new exodus and to restore his people. But the prophet's perspective was world-wide. As a "covenant to the people (of the whole world)," Israel would mediate salvation to them, blind and in bondage as they were (Isa 42:6f.). Trito-Isaiah thematized the antithesis "former" vs. "new" (Isa 42:9; 43:19; 48:6) as the act of creating new heavens and a new earth (Isa 65:17f.) — majestic rhetoric for the restoration of God's people in Jerusalem.

This complex of themes took hold, fixed like a fish-hook

in the soul of post-Exilic Israel. According to the Qumran vision of the relation of the present to the future (1QS 4:15-26), two spirits ruled all generations. How things went for each man depended on what portion (*naḥălâ*) he had in the spheres of these spirits. The struggle between the two was fierce (*qin 'at rîb*). But God had ordained an end to perversity and at the time of his visitation (*bĕmô'ēd pĕqûdâ*) he would destroy it forever. Then truth would be definitely established; God would purify man and "all the glory of Adam (*kôl kĕbôd 'ādām*) shall be theirs."[17] The Qumran conception of the new creation (cf. 1QS 4:25, "the making of the new," *'aśot ḥădāšâ*, see Isa 43:19; cf. 1QH 13:11f.) was alive with prophetic themes from Jeremiah, Ezekiel, and Deutero-Isaiah. Moreover, there was already a re-making of man (cf. *yāṣartâ*) in the divine act of cleansing him of his sins and bringing him into the holy community (1QH 3:19-21; cf. 1QH 11:10-14).

In the Palestinian pseudepigrapha the accent fell rather on the cosmological concept of a necessarily still future making of new heavens and a new earth (EthEnoch 72:1 ["new creation"]; 45:4; 91:16; 106:13 [cites Isa 43:19]; Syr-Bar 32:6 [new creation begins in eschatological tribulation]; 54:2; 4 Ezra 7:75). In the Greek-speaking diaspora the future re-making of man was reaffirmed (Jub 5:12; cf. 23:26-31); and in parallel with Qumran and anticipating the rabbis, the novella *Joseph and Aseneth* attests the notion of entry into the covenant as a new creation (49:18-50:3; 61:2-7, Batiffol edition). In Qumran, Joseph and Aseneth, and rabbinic tradition,[18] then, the new creation (*bĕriyya ḥadaśa* in a few

[17]For a discussion of 1QS 4:15-26 see A. R. C. Leaney, *The rule of Qumran and its Meaning* (Philadelphia: Westminster, 1966), 154-61.

[18]See Erik Sjöberg, "Wiedergeburt und Neuschöpfung im palastinischen Judentum," *Studia Theologica* 4 (1950): 44-85; "Neuschöpfung in den Toten-Meer-Rollen," *Studia Theologica* 9 (1955): 131-6; Gerhard Schneider, "Die Idee der Neuschöpfung beim Apostel Paulus und ihr religionsgeschichtlicher Hintergrund," *Trierer theologische Zeitschrift* 68 (1959): 250-70; cf. 260-64; Peter Stuhlmacher, "Erwägungen zum

rabbinic texts)[19] was brought to bear in the present on the moment of beginning a new relationship to God. In all of them, to be sure, language inherited from the prophets and more immediately borrowed from apocalyptic was now made to designate a present transforming of the human person. Such transformation is at least akin to proleptically realized eschatology. Yet present realization remains at best a distant analogy to the future. And if the application of new creation motifs to present conversion exploits apocalyptic in consciously critical fashion, it also purges the borrowed motifs of their originally intended ontological thrust.[20]

The most telling contrast between Paul and these parallels is situated at just this level. In 2 Cor 5:17, as we have seen, existence "in Christ" is equated with "new creation." It is clear from parallels and quasi-parallels in Paul under the headings "in Christ" and "body of Christ" (e.g., Gal 3:28; 1 Cor 6:17-19; 10:17; 12:12-30; Rom 12:2-8), the gift of the Spirit (e.g., Gal 3:2-5, 14; 2 Cor 3:6; 5:5; Rom 8:29f.), and "new creation" (Gal 6:15f.; cf. Gal 3:21, 28; 1 Cor 15:45; 2 Cor 3:6; 4:6; Rom 8:29f.), that this is meant to signify not only a new purpose but *a new mode of being.* In the text of 2 Cor 5:17, new creation is indeed associated with Paul's conversion (cf. 2 Cor 5:14-16), but it is irreducible to notions of conversion and covenant. To be "in Christ" in and by the Spirit given by faith (Gal 3:2-5, 14) or baptism (1 Cor 12:13; cf. 2 Cor 3:18b) is "to be conformed to the image of [God's] Son" (Rom 8:29), "transformed from glory to glory into his likeness" (2 Cor 3:18). It is to co-suffer (*sympaschein*, Rom 8:17) with Christ, in a process of "growing conformity" (*symmorphizein* in pres. pass. partic., Phil 3:10) with his

ontologischen Charakter der *kainē ktisis* bei Paulus," *Evangelische Theologie* 27 (1967): 1-35, cf. 12-20.

[19]The technical term is Amoraic, but its emergence had been prepared well in advance. For the texts see Billerbeck II, 421f.; III, 845-7.

[20]See Stuhlmacher, "Erwägungen zum ontologischen Charakter," 15 (on the selective and critical way in which the rabbis accepted apocalyptic traditions, with consequent and proportionate loss of their ontological thrust).

death, to be co-crucified (*systauroun*, Gal 2:19; Rom 6:6)
with him, made co-natural (*symphytos*, Rom 6:5) with him
in a death like his, carrying his death in one's own body (2
Cor 4:10; cf. Gal 6:17). It is to be co-buried (*synthaptein*,
Rom 6:4) with him, to be his co-heir (*sygklēronomos*, Rom
8:17) to glory and to be co-glorified (*syndoxazein*, Rom
8:17) with him — in short, to be "co(n)formed" (*synmor-phos*, Rom 8:29) to the image of God's Son. The principle of
Christian existence is accordingly an ontically real, bap-
tismal (Rom 6:3-6) and eucharistic (1 Cor 10:16-21), inser-
tion into the pattern of Christ, his sufferings (Phil 3:10; 2
Cor 1:5-7; Gal 6:17), his death (2 Cor 4:10; Gal 2:19; Rom
6:5f.), his resurrection (1 Cor 15:21, 49; Rom 6:5, 8), his very
being as image and glory and Son of God (1 Cor 11:7; 2 Cor
3:18; 5:21 [cf. 1 Cor 1:30]; Rom 8:29).

Consequently, one must speak of an "old self" prior to
this entry into participation in Christ, a self now "crucified,"
so that one henceforward is "dead to sin" but "alive to God"
(Rom 6:5-11; cf. Gal 2:17-20). To be "in Christ" is not to be
alone but to be with others who are in him, to constitute
with them an organic unity and, with them, to transcend
divisions, conflicts, bondages: "There is neither 'Jew' nor
'Greek,' there is neither slave nor free, there is no 'male and
female' [Gen 1:27], for you are all one in Christ Jesus" (Gal
3:28). Inasmuch as this passage on "putting on Christ" (cf.
Gal 3:27) and being "in Christ Jesus" provides the closest
parallel to the "new creation" text of Gal 6:15,

> Neither circumcision nor uncircumcision
> counts, only new creation,

we have here an analogy with 2 Cor 5:17, where "new
creation" defines being "in Christ." Moreover, "new creation" in Gal 6 transposes easily into the election-historical
title "the Israel of God" (Gal 6:16).[21] This means that in the

---

[21]Stuhlmacher, "Erwagungen zum onotologischen Charakter," 3-8. Also,
see above, 17, note 6.

heir to election — originally the remnant of Israel gathered by Jesus,[22] now this remnant gone "forth out of Jerusalem" and "out of Mount Zion" (Isa 37:32) to the world — was realized both the age-old election of Israel and the eschatological refashioning of humanity. The harvest of the world mission was both God's own people and a new mankind.

Paul never failed to qualify such statements, however, first by rooting them in their source, the grace of the risen Christ, to exclude every human boast, and, second, by tempering them with insistence on a twofold "not yet": (a) the paranetic injunction to "become what thou art" or, in Pauline language, "pattern yourselves no longer on this age but be transformed by the newness of your spirit" (Rom 12:2), and (b) the still to be divinely accomplished consummation, when participation in Christ would be brought to perfection.

The new mankind — neither circumcision nor uncircumcision — was what it was uniquely by a participation in Christ (cf. 2 Cor 5:17) that sublated[23] national, class, and sexual distinctions (Gal 3:28), and this participation was still but a beginning.

> Just as through a man there came death,
> so all the more surely through a man
>   *there shall come* the resurrection of
>   the dead;
> just as by solidarity with Adam all men die,
> so all the more surely by solidarity
>   with Christ *shall all be made to live*
>   (1 Cor 15:21f.).

---

[22]B. F. Meyer, *The Aims of Jesus*, 210-15.

[23]The word renders Hegel's *aufheben/Aufhebung* and signifies the manner in which realities on one level of being or activity are preserved but transcended by promotion to a higher level of being or activity. In the distinctive use of the term adopted here from Bernard Lonergan, sublation does not destroy, but completes and enhances what is sublated. See *Insight*, 421f. and "The Subject," 80.

Thus it is written:
The first man, Adam, "became a living
    soul";
the last Adam has become a life-giving
    spirit. . . .
The first man was "from the earth, of
    dust,"
the second man is of heaven.
Men of dust are patterned on the man of
    dust,
heavenly men, on the man of heaven;
for just as we have borne the image of
    the man of dust,
so the more surely *shall we bear* the
image of the heavenly man, as well
    (1 Cor 15:45, 47-49).

These are among the scores of passages that banish doubt
about the still future-oriented dynamism of present participation "in Christ." Meantime, those in Christ lived by hope:
"if we have hoped in Christ for this life only, we are the most
pitiable people of all" (1 Cor 15:19); in this life "I face death
every day" (1 Cor 15:31); the condition of existence today
was still "this mortal being" (1 Cor 15:53b, 54b); "men of
dust" were still "patterned on the man of dust" (1 Cor 15:48).
The Christian present was a time of affliction and hope (2
Cor 1:4-7). Its hallmark was the desire "to know" Christ, to
experience and understand and affirm "Christ and the
power flowing from his resurrection." This was "to know
the fellowship of his sufferings in growing conformity with
his death" (Phil 3:10).

Pauline Soteriology: Sequence; Dialectic; Internal Relations

There was a three-step Pauline sequence in soteriology:
(a) God's expiatory (Gal 1:4; 1 Cor 15:3; 2 Cor 5:21; Rom

3:25) and redemptive (Gal 3:13; 1 Cor 6:19; 7:23; cf. 1 Thess 5:10)[24] act in Christ, shaping an economy of universal justification (Rom 5:19)[25] and reconciliation (2 Cor 5:18-20), (b) enacted in the world (2 Cor 5:18-20) through a divinely appointed "ministry of the Spirit" or "of righteousness" (2 Cor 3:8f.), i.e., through the proclamation to the world, by men "speaking on behalf of Christ" (2 Cor 2:17; 5:18-20), of "the gospel" (1 Thess 2:2-9; Gal 1:11; 2:2-9; 1 Cor 15:1; Rom 1:16) entrusted to them (1 Thess 2:4, Gal 2:7; 1 Cor 9:16f.; cf. Gal 1:12), and (c) acceptance of this same gospel by "faith" (1 Thess 1:8; 3:1-10; 1 Cor 15:14, 17; Gal 2:16, 20; 3:2-5, 7-26; Phil 3:9; Rom 1:5, 17; 3:25f., 27-31; 4:5; 5:1f.; 9:30-32) mediating the efficacy of God's act in Christ (Rom 3:22, 25; cf. 2 Cor 5:18-20), righteousness (e.g., Gal 2:16; 3:8; Rom 1:17; 3:25f.; 4:9), the gift of the Spirit (Gal 3:2-5, 14), sonship to Abraham (Gal 3:7; cf. Rom 4:11f.) and to God (Gal 3:26), fulfillment of the promises to Abraham (Rom 4:16), and freedom from the Law (Gal 3:24f.).

This three-step sequence generated in those who made the response of faith *a dialectical existence*, already rooted in

[24]That "redemption" in Paul signifies not only liberation but also acquisition is entirely biblical. See the twofold use of *pādā* and the parallel use of the *polel* form of *kūn* in 2 Sam 7:23f.; par. 1 Chron 7:21f.: "What other nation on earth is like thy people Israel, whom God redeemed to be his own people (*lipdôt-lô lᵉʻ ām*) . . . driving out nations and gods before thy people, whom thou didst redeem (*pādîtā*) for thyself from Egypt? And thou didst establish (*wattĕkōnēn*) for thyself thy people Israel to be thy people forever; and thou, o Lord didst become their God." See the synonymous parallelism of "redeem" (*gāʼal*) and "acquire" (*qānā*) in Ps 74:2. For a fuller treatment, see Lyonnet, *Sin, Redemption, and Sacrifice*, 104-19. Inasmuch as God's eschatological act of redemption was placed "through Christ" and "in Christ" (2 Cor 5:18f.), redemption signified the acquisition of the redeemed "through Christ" (as prototypal Son, the first-born of many, 2 Cor 3:18; 5:21; Rom 8:29) and "in Christ" as Lord (1 Thess 5:10; 2 Cor 5:15; Rom 14:7-9; cf. 6:11-22). The Pauline theme of redemption/acquisition thus correlates with the motif of Jesus' death as covenantal sacrifice (1 Cor 11:25; cf. Mark 14:24; parr. Matt 26:28; Luke 22:20; see Meyer, *Aims*, 219; 311, note 131).

[25]See above, note 10.

"new creation," already en route to final transformation:

> ...we shall all be changed
> in an instant, in the twinkling of an
>   eye, at the last trumpet blast,
> for the trumpet will blast,
> and the dead will be raised immune from
>   decay,
> and we shall be changed (1 Cor 15:51f.).

In the meantime the man of faith lived under a new law, "the law of the Spirit of life" (Rom 8:2; cf. Gal 6:2; 1 Cor 9:21) challenging (*synechein*, 2 Cor 5:14) and energizing (*energein*, Gal 5:6) and encouraging (*parakalein*, 2 Cor 1:4; 7:6f.) him to set his mind, "not on the flesh," which is death, but "on the things of the Spirit" (Rom 8:5).

If the theme of the "new mankind" is among the peaks in Paul's decisively christological soteriology (1 Cor 15:45; 2 Cor 5:17-21; Rom 8:29f.), its characteristic dialectic of present and future establishes a sub-dialectic within the present. For this is a present that, as Paul attested by his life as well as by his instruction, was, on the one hand, subject to limits (1 Cor 10:29-33; 12:4-30), to pain (2 Cor 4:10f.; 11:24-27), sorrow (2 Cor 2:1-7; Phil 2:27; Rom 9:2), anxiety (2 Cor 11:28f.), humiliation (2 Cor 11:24; 12:21; Phil 4:12), privation (1 Cor 4:11f.; Phil 4:12), failure (Gal 1:6; 3:1-4; 4:11, 15, 20; 2 Cor 12:20), and desertion (Gal 2:13); on the other hand, it was filled with "the joy that comes from the Holy Spirit" (1 Thess 1:6; cf. 3:9; Gal 5:22), a deep-set joy that endured despite afflictions (2 Cor 7:4) and was accompanied by peace (Gal 5:22; Rom 14:17; 15:13) "beyond understanding," which stood guard over the heart and mind (Phil 4:7), a gift of God (cf. "grace and peace" in 1 Thess 1:1; 1 Cor 1:3; 2 Cor 1:2; Gal 1:3; Phil 1:2; Rom 1:7) bestowed by the Spirit (Gal 5:22 ; Rom 14:17; cf. 8:6). There is more than a chance resemblance between this Pauline conception of the present lot of the new mankind, a conception of life freely synchronized with and locked into the pattern of Christ's paschal mysteries, and, on the other hand, the cutting edge of contemporary intentionality analysis on the basic human fulfillment to be found in what Bernard Lonergan calls "the state of being-in-love with God." For the latter state is profoundly attuned to the deepest yearnings of the human heart:

> It constitutes a basic fulfilment of man's being. Because it is such a fulfilment, it is the source of a great peace, the peace that the world cannot give. It is a wellspring of joy that can endure despite the sorrow of failure, humiliation, privation, pain, desertion. Because it is such a fulfilment, it removes the temptation of all that is shallow, hollow, empty, and degrading....[26]

We conclude this sketch by relating it to a fusion of theological horizons still taking shape in New Testament scholarship today. Its salient feature at present is insistence on doing exegetical and theological justice to (a) *the act of God* in Pauline soteriology ("the righteousness of God" as God's act; the expiatory dimension of the Christ event; the distinctiveness of the Christian thematic in both cases, together with the hermeneutical indispensability to both of Old Testament tradition) and to (b) *the complementarity of Paul's soteriological schemes* (e.g., righteousness, reconciliation, being "in Christ," etc.). To underline the ecumenical aspect of this still crystallizing fusion of horizons, I shall footnote the particulars by reference to the work of both Catholic and Protestant scholars, limiting the coverage, however, to Lyonnet and Kertelge on the one side, Stuhlmacher and Wilckens, on the other.[27]

---

[26]Bernard Lonergan, "Theology and Man's Future" in *A Second Collection* (New York: Herder & Herder, 1974), 145f.

[27]A caveat: these four scholars are notably independent and their works are variously related to the propositions that I have chosen to underline. I have noticed many differences of opinion among them even where they are, by and large, allied, and other differences of detail have doubtless escaped my notice. Many of Lyonnet's studies date from earlier than those of the others and were produced in independence of the discusssion inaugurated by Käsemann's 1961 essay on the righteousness of God.

Pauline soteriology was designed to acknowledge and exalt the act of God both as the cause of man's real and radical transition from one state (sinful, estranged, captive) to another (righteous, reconciled, free) and as the continuing source of the second state. Critical retrieval in the present century[28] of "the righteousness of God" in Romans as *the act of God* began with J. H. Ropes's 1903 essay, "'Righteousness' and 'the Righteousness of God' in the Old Testament and in St. Paul"; it has been presented anew with a variety of qualifying accents,[29] attacked,[30] and vigorously and successfully defended since.[31] The significance of this achievement lies partly in the simultaneous affirmation of

[28]For a brief but deft history of the conception of "the righteousness of God" and of Paul's use of it, see Ulrich Wilckens, *Der Brief an die Römer I* (Neukirchen-Vluyn: Neukirchener Verlag, 1978), 212-22; Karl Kertelge, "*Dikaiosyne*" in *Exegetisches Wörterbuch zum Neuen Testament* (Stuttgart: Kohlhammer, 1980), col. 787-93.

[29]Ernst Käsemann, "'The Righteousness of God' in Paul" (ET of essay that first appeared in 1961) in *New Testament Questions of Today* (London: SCM, 1969), 168-82; Christian Müller, *Gottes Gerechtigkeit und Gottes Volk* (Göttingen: Vandenhoeck & Ruprecht, 1964); Peter Stuhlmacher, *Gottes Gerechtigkeit bei Paulus* (Göttingen: Vandenhoeck & Ruprecht, 1965): Karl Kertelge, "*Rechtfertigung" bei Paulus* (Münster: Aschendorff, 1967); Hans Heinrich Schmid, *Gerechtigkeit als Weltordnung* (Tübingen: Mohr, 1968).

[30]Rudolf Bultmann, "DIKAIOSYNE THEOU," *Journal of Biblical Literature* 83 (1964): 12-16; Günter Klein, "Gottesgerechtigkeit als Thema der neuesten Paulusforschung" (1967) in *Rekonstruktion und Interpretation* (Munich: Kaiser, 1969), 225-36; Hans Conzelmann, "Die Rechfertigungslehre des Paulus: Theologie oder Anthropologie?" (1968) in *Theologie als Schriftauslegung* (Munich: Kaiser, 1974), 191-206; *An Outline of the Theology of the New Testament* (London: SCM, 1969), 214-20.

[31]Käsemann's debate with Bultmann and Conzelmann was continued in a lengthy footnote to the reprint of his original essay and in the essays "Justification and Salvation History in the Epistle to the Romans" and "On Paul's Anthropology" in *Perspectives on Paul* (London: SCM, 1971). The revisions in the second edition (1971) of Kertelge's "*Rechtfertigung*" reflect the continuing discussion. Peter Stuhlmacher has both

Christian originality exploiting Old Testament resources,[32] partly in its bringing to clearer focus the thematic structure of "righteousness by faith," especially its salvation-historical reference and its dependence on God's own "righteous" fulfillment of his eschatological promises.[33]

amended his own work, *Gerechtigkeit Gottes bei Paulus*, and responded to critics (Klein, Bornkamm, Lohse, Grässer, Schmithals) in later essays, e.g., "Das Ende des Gesetzes" in *Versöhnung, Gesetz und Gerechtigkeit*, 166-91.

[32]"Christian originality" refers to the newly contoured technical status of the term "the righteousness of God" in Pauline texts. How full the Old Testament background to "the righteousness of God" is judged to be depends on the standpoint of the surveyor. The phrase itself occurs very rarely, though cognate phrases (e.g., "thy righteousness") are not uncommon. How to judge the congruence between the theme of world order and that of divine "righteousness" is disputed. (See, for example, the judicious remarks of Joseph A. Fitzmyer in John Reumann, with Joseph A. Fitzmyer and Jerome D. Quinn, *"Righteousness" in the New Testament* [Philadelphia: Fortress; New York: Paulist, 1982], 199-201.) The Old Testament heritage in any case was mediated by intertestmental traditions. Despite the parallels in Qumran (cf. the essays of Otto Betz, "Rechtfertigung in Qumran" in *Rechtfertigung* [Tübingen: Mohr, 1976], 17-36, and "Rechtfertigung und Heiligung," in *Rechtfertigung Realismus Universalismus in biblischer Sicht* [Darmstadt: Wissenschaftliche Buchgesellschaft, 1978], 30-44), there is no Qumran usage giving "the righteousness of God" the kind of preferred thematic status that it has in the epistle to the Romans (cf. E. P. Sanders, *Paul and Palestinian Judaism*, 305-12). Still, the New Testament technical term is "biblical" in horizon and its eschatological force is dependent on pre-Christian apocalyptic traditions.

[33]On the righteousness of God as parallel and akin to his "faithfulness" and as the fulfillment of his promises, see Lyonnet, "Pauline Soteriology," 832-4, 836; Kertelge, *"Rechtfertigung,"* 17-24, 63-109 *passim*; Stuhlmacher, "Die Gerechtigkeitsanschauung des Apostels Paulus," 99-101; Wilckens, "Zu Römer 3, 21-4, 25. Antwort an G. Klein," in *Rechtfertigung als Freiheit*, 50-76; "Lukas und Paulus unter dem Aspekt dialektisch-theologisch beeinflusster Exegese" in *Rechtfertigung als Freiheit*, 196-200; *Der Brief an die Römer I*, 220-22.

The expiatory facet of the Christ event is integral to Pauline thought.[34] It must be purged of foreign accretions[35] and retrieved in biblical terms, specifically in the light of Old Testament tradition.[36] In accord with the correlativity of "problem and solution" in Paul, it specifies as a fundamental element of man's "problem" the lasting effects in him of sin, not only as power and bondage but precisely as willed

[34]Lyonnet, *Sin, Redemption, and Sacrifice*, 120-33; "Pauline Soteriology," 845-51. In Kertelge's view, this theme, dominant in pre-Pauline tradition ("*Rechtfertigung*," 50-9), receives secondary status in Paul's own theology. Paul integrated traditions on expiation (e.g., Rom 3:24-26) into his own schemata ("*Rechtfertigung*," 107-9; 302) without developing them. The sequence by which 2 Cor 5:21 follows 5:18-20 is "somewhat unmotivated," 101. Stuhlmacher, by contrast, in a whole series of studies has made the expiatory death of Christ a condition of the possibility of the Pauline theology of righteousness. Expiation is explicitly brought into relation to this thematic in "Zur neueren Exegese von Röm 3, 24-26" in *Versöhnung, Gesetz und Gerechtigkeit*, 132-5; "Achtzehn Thesen zur paulinischen Kreuzestheologie," 195-7; "Zur paulinischen Christologie," 211f., 215-23; "Die Gerechtigkeitsanschauung des Apostels Paulus," 100-104, 111-14. In Wilckens's studies prior to the commentary on Romans the theme occurs occasionally (e.g., "Über Abfassungszweck und Aufbau des Römerbriefs," in *Rechtfertigung als Freiheit*, 150-2); in the commentary it is given its full importance, *Der Brief an die Romer I*, 201f., 232f., 233-43.

[35]Lyonnet, *Sin, Redemption, and Sacrifice*, 120-84, esp. 122-6; 141-6; 173-84; "Pauline Soteriology," 845-51. The theme of "foreign accretions" appears only by indirect allusion in Stuhlmacher's studies (e.g., "Zur neueren Exegese," 132-5, with notes). Wilckens, *Der Brief an die Römer I*, 201f., 234-9.

[36]In accord with his understanding of Old Testament texts, and in agreement with L. Moraldi, *Espiazone sacrificale e riti espiatori nell' ambiente biblico e nell' Antico Testamento* (Rome: Biblical Institute Press, 1956), Lyonnet rejected interpretations of Christ's suffering and death as "in place of" sinners ("penal substitution"); see *Sin, Redemption, and Sacrifice*, 169; "Pauline Soteriology," 849-51, 856-8; also, and at length, "Conception paulinienne de la rédemption," *Lumière et Vie* 36 (1958): 35-66. Kertelge, on the other hand, accepts the theory of substitution; see "*Rechtfertigung,*" 104f. (2 Cor 5:21), 211 (Gal 3:13), 216f. (Rom 8:3); see also 248, note 123. Stuhlmacher's insistence on the role of Old

transgression with consequent liability to judgment.[37] Salvation-historically, the expiatory death of Christ effected man's return to God — not as an individual returning by his own act of repentance, but as a race alienated from God through its whole history and returning to him in response to God's already accomplished deed of reconciling the world to himself by the death of his Son.[38]

Testament texts for understanding the Pauline conception of expiation is reflected in his wide use of primary and secondary literature (with accent on the work of Hartmut Gese); see, e.g., " 'Er ist unser Friede' (Eph 2, 14)" in *Versöhnung, Gesetz und Gerechtigkeit*, 236f.; "Zur neueren Exegese," 132-5. Wilckens, *Der Brief an die Römer I*, 236-9.

[37]See Lyonnet, *Sin, Redemption, and Sacrifice*, 46-57; "Pauline Soteriology," 826-9; 831-7; 845-51. Kertelge's understanding of the role of universal human transgression in Paul's soteriology emerges from his treatment of Rom 3:21-26 and 2 Cor 5:21; see "*Rechtfertigung*," 53-62, 71-84, 99-107; on the role of the judgment in Paul's thought, 255-7; on why man under the Law is a sinner, see 215 ("not because he constantly transgresses the Law, but because the direction of the Law's way is perverted," since it leads to a righteousness of one's own). Kertelge's view mediated between that of Bultmann (see 221f.) and the opposite extreme expressed by Wilckens, "Was heisst bei Paulus." Kertelge and Wilckens, however, converge on the reality of transgression and expiation in Pauline soteriology, and Wilckens has given these themes their full due in *Der Brief an die Römer I*, 199-202, 233-43.

[38]"The return to God" of Christ and of mankind in Christ was Lyonnet's formulation; see "Pauline Soteriology," 863-5, and "The Return of Christ to God according to St. Paul," in *Word and Mystery*, Baltimore: Newman, 1968. This "return" epitomized God's reconciling the world to himself by the death and resurrection of his Son. It implied the undoing both of transgression ("not counting their transgressions against them" 2 Cor 5:19) and of bondage (the reconcilation is effected exclusively by the initiative of God in Christ, 2 Cor 5:18, 19a). In substance, if not formulation, this concept was affirmed by Kertelge, "*Rechtfertigung*," 106; by Stuhlmacher on "reconciliation" in general; by Wilckens, *Der Brief an die Römer I*, 297-305.

Respecting the "complementarity of Paul's soteriological schemes": the diverse categories of the "solution" — for example, "righteousness by faith"; freedom (mediated by faith/baptism and indivisible from life in the Spirit) from the enslaving power of "sin" and Law; being "in Christ" as signifying "new creation" — are reciprocally defining. Though each, from one or another vantage point, has a characteristic set of advantages,[39] no single one among them is so peculiarly apt to define Pauline soteriology as to constitute its "center" or "guiding concept."[40] The continuing

[39]To exemplify the advantages, diverse in kind and degree, accruing to the themes of justification (cf., e.g., Kasemann), of reconciliation (cf., e.g., Stuhlmacher), and of participation in Christ (cf., e.g., Sanders), see E. Käsemann, "Justification and Salvation History"; P. Stuhlmacher, "The Gospel of Reconciliation in Christ — Basic Features and Issues of a Biblical Theology of the New Testament," *Horizons in Biblical Theology* 1 (1979): 161-90. E. P. Sanders, *Paul and Palestinian Judaism*, 453-511.

[40]The definition of "center" is itself problematic. "Center": (a) point around which all else is organized; (b) most distinctive theme; (c) source or matrix of distinctive themes; (d) most inclusive or comprehensive theme (at least seminally or in principle); (e) structuring principle; (f) controlling thought-form; (g) theological norm. For a recent discussion, see John Reumann, *"Righteousness" in the New Testament*, 105-23; also C. J. A. Hickling, "Centre and Periphery in the Thought of Paul," in *Studia Biblica, 1978. Papers on Paul and Other New Testament Authors*, ed. by E. A. Livingstone (Sheffield: JSOT Press, 1980), 199-214.

Rather than settle on one of Paul's particular soteriological themes, Lyonnet devised a formulation ("the return to God") designed to comprehend all aspects of the redemption. See *Sin, Redemption, and Sacrifice*, 295f. (Lyonnet's composition, despite the book's ambiguity of attribution) and "Pauline Soteriology," 863-5. Kertelge, *"Rechtfertigung,"* 286-304, acknowledged justification as the center of Pauline theology, provided that it be understood not as a closed and absolutized concept (*contra* Paul Althaus) but as a proclamation interpreting the Christ event and an "experiment" open to development. Stuhlmacher's highlighting of "reconciliation" has not prevented him from defining the selfsame center in terms of "the theology of the cross" ("Achtzehn Thesen") or "the gospel of righteousness" ("Die Gerechtigkeitsanschauung des Apostels Pau-

quest of the so-called center prolongs the misbegotten nineteenth-century fixation on essences, e.g., the essence of Christianity itself (*das Wesen des Christentums*).[41] It also lends itself all too easily to theological sloganeering.

lus"). Finally, respecting the views alluded to in the previous note, it should be remarked that the heart of Pauline theology, abstractly articulated, is God's act in favor of man-in-need and the impact of this act on man-acknowledging-and-appropriating it. "Justification," "reconciliation," and "participation in Christ" are specifying particulars that bring this scheme to concrete expression. Debate on the merit of these distinct (but, in Paul's actual writing, inextricably related) themes has not been especially productive. Käsemann has argued ("Justification and Salvation History," 76) that unless justification keeps its status as the be-all and end-all of salvation history, the cross loses its centrality and all theology is distorted; but he has not shown that other soteriological themes in Paul are essentially defective nor that the theme of justification itself is impervious to distortion. Sanders has argued that only the term "participation" adequately signifies the resolution of the plight of man as Paul "really" conceived it (though Paul himself admittedly failed to make this distinction between his "real" conceptions and his other conceptions). But in Sanders' treatment, this entails the downgrading of the central significance of the transgression/expiation thematic in Paul.

[41] See the critique offered by a nineteenth-century thinker, John Henry Newman, *An Essay on the Development of Christian Doctrine* (1878 edition; Garden City: Doubleday, 1960), chapter 1, para. 4: "Sometimes an attempt is made to determine the 'leading idea,' as it has been called, of Christianity, an ambitious essay as employed on a supernatural work, when, even as regards the visible creation and the inventions of man, such a task is beyond us. Thus its one idea has been said by some to be the restoration of our fallen race, by others philanthropy, by others the tidings of immortality, or the spirituality of true religious service or the salvation of the elect, or mental liberty, or the union of the soul with God." Newman, however, adds: "If, indeed, it is only thereby meant to use one or other of these as a central idea for convenience, in order to group others around it, no fault can be found with such a proceeding; and in this sense I should myself call the Incarnation the central aspect of Christianity, out of which the three main aspects of its teaching take their rise, the sacramental, the hierarchical, and the ascetic." Finally, he warns:

Here "the circle of things and words" (*Sache und Sprache*)[42] is pointedly applicable. "The thing" is God's act in favor of man-in-need and the impact of this act on man-acknowledging-and-appropriating it. A first observation is that this "thing" is specified as an unknown-to-be-known by the several Pauline soteriological schemes and comes to expression in and through this variety.[43] A second and decisive observation is that the "thing" in question comes to admittedly still imperfect but nonetheless far more intelligible and far more adequate expression through the aggregate of Paul's soteriological schemes than it does through any one scheme among them. This is attested by Paul's readiness, while developing one scheme, to draw on another as complement and support of the first.[44] It is accordingly clear that Paul has deployed his various conceptual schemes to intend their object as real — hence the semantic analogy and partial convertibility among them.

"But one aspect of Revelation must not be allowed to exclude or obscure another; and Christianity is dogmatical, devotional, practical all at once; it is esoteric and exoteric; it is indulgent and strict; it is light and dark; it is love, and it is fear."

[42]See Emerich Coreth, *Grundfragen der Hermeneutik* (Freiburg: Herder, 1969), 64f., 116f., 123f.

[43] A striking example: the functional correlativity of the themes of the righteousness of God (Rom) and the wisdom of God (1 Cor), observed by Heinrich Schlier, "Kerygma and Sophia" in *Die Zeit ker Kirche* (Frieburg: Herder, 1956), 220f.; Ulrich Wilckens, *Weisheit und Torheit* (Tubingen: Mohr, 1959), 222, Eberhard Jüngel, *Paulus und Jesus* (Tubingen: Mohr,[5] 1979), 30.

[44]Some examples already noted above: Gal 6:15f. (new creation and election-history); 2 Cor 5:16-21 (new creation; reconciliation; justification; expiation; participation in Christ); Rom 3:21-26 (righteousness of God; justification and faith; redemption; expiation; typology of Day of Atonement); Rom 8:1-4 (condemnation/acquittal; participation in Christ; life-giving law of the Spirit; bondage to Law, sin, death; expiation).

Among the numerous classical disputes transcended or resolved on this basis are whether for Paul himself justification was wholly forensic and imputative,[45] and whether man made righteous by faith is judged according to works.[46]

[45]For the subtance of the issue, see Lyonnet, "Gratuite de la justification et gratuité du salut" in *Studiorum Paulinorum Congressus Internationalis Catholicus, 1961*, Vol. I (Rome: Biblical Institute Press, 1963), 95-110, cf. 101f., 105. Kertelge, "*Rechtfertigung*," 113-28 opts strongly for a forensic sense that is "effective," so transcending the terms of confessional debate ("forensic" versus "effective"). Stuhlmacher, "Erwägungen zum ontologischen Charakter," 2, makes essentially the same point. Wilckens, in *Der Brief an die Römer I*, 199-202 and throughout, defines justification in terms of intrinsic change. Cf. Kertelge, "*Dikaioō*," in *Exegetisches Wörterbuch zum Neuen Testament* (Stuttgart: Kohlhammer, 1980), col. 803.

[46]Lyonnet, "Gratuité de la justification," deals directly with the issue. Kertelge, in the context of "soteriological indicative and ethical imperative," treats judgment as a presupposition of the justification thematic. For Stuhlmacher's statement, see "Zur paulinischen Christologie," 222; also "Schriftauslegung in der Confessio Augustana" in *Versöhnung, Gesetz und Gerechtigkeit*, 267-9. Wilckens offers a brief account of his own distinctive view (building on Schlatter but going beyond him) in an excursus on judgment according to works, in *Der Brief an die Römer I*, 142-6.

IX

The Matrix of Pauline Soteriology

The interpretative ideal of working out an understanding of the intended sense of a text, judging how accurate this understanding is, and expressing what one judges to be an accurate understanding of the text, is age-old.[1] In the modern era, however, it has been realized far more effectively than in any earlier era, for the resources at the interpreter's disposal (lexicography, linguistics, literary analysis and history, etc.) have become far more elaborate and exact than ever before. If the question of "the literal (i.e., intended) sense of the text" is age-old, the changes that the emergence of the historical consciousness and the refinement of the historical disciplines have wrought in its current resources are momentous. "Historical-critical" interpretation is the quest of the intended sense of the text pursued with the help of these resources and in the light of a historical context recovered by environmental research and the most elabo-

---

[1] If the interpretative ideal is age-old, still this formulation of it, which is careful to distinguish among understanding, judgment, and presentation, is recent. See Bernard Lonergan, *Method in Theology* (New York: Herder and Herder, 1972), 155-73.

rate social and cultural history.

Historical-critical interpretation nevertheless remains interpretation, not history. The question it seeks to answer is: What is the intended sense of the text? The historical question, on the other hand, is: What actually happened, and why?[2] The account history seeks to give is genetic and explanatory. Over the past two and a half centuries Western man has become ever more thoroughly convinced that human affairs are "explained" only when their origins and development have been traced and described. This kind of explanation is apt to turn texts and their interpretation into mere data relevant to the historical inquirer's own, ulterior, question. Though history thereby goes beyond interpretation, it does not take its place. It simply endues the text and its interpretation with a more intense intelligibility, a historical intelligibility illuminating the text by converting it into an item in a larger story. How might one "explain" in this sense the elements of Pauline soteriology?

When the question is put this way, it is evident that a part, and a crucial part, of the answer is provided by Paul's experience of conversion.[3] It is surely right to urge that "the key to Pauline theology" in this sense is the call of Paul.[4] This is what instigated the revolution in the pattern of Paul's religion.

[2]See, Lonergan, *Method*, 185-96.

[3]In exegetical context (the grasp of Paul's intended meaning) the theme of his call/conversion becomes significant only insofar as it is a topic of Pauline reflection and writing; but it does become such a topic (cf. 1 Cor 9:1; 15:8; Gal 1:15f.; Phil 3:5-9; cf. Rom 1:5; 1 Cor 1:1; 2 Cor 1:1; Gal 1:1, 12). J. C. Beker rightly insists (*Paul the Apostle*, 10) that the call of Paul "is not the entrance to his thought." That is, it is not the starting point nor the center of Paul's expository strategies. But it is indeed a key to the reconstruction of the *genesis* of Paul's thought (as Beker is aware, 236-43) and this inevitably impinges on one's efforts to construe many Pauline texts.

[4]See Joachim Jeremias, "The Key to Pauline Theology," *Expository Times* 76 (1964): 27-30. Ulrich Wilckens, "Die Bekehrung des Paulus als religionsgeschichtliches Problem," in *Rechtfertigung als Freiheit*, 11-32,

Generically, Paul's religion remained his response to the God of Abraham, but now it became the response to a new initiative: this same God's saving act in Christ. The change consisted in a new vision of things and a new allegiance. What follows is a hypothetical account of the coming into being of the vision.

Paul's projection of new horizons followed the logic of revelation, revision, reconstruction. What was revealed? Christ risen from the dead. What was thereby revised? The conventional Jewish view of Jesus and his execution: "Though we once regarded Christ from a human point of view (*kata sarka*), we regard him thus no longer" (2 Cor 5:16). This revelation and revision called for the kind of fundamental and far-reaching reconstruction that could provide *an intelligible total context for salvation through a crucified Messiah.*

It may well be that in pre-Christian Judaism an esoteric tradition of interpretation saw in the Servant of Isa 53 a messianic savior whose way to glory was through humiliation, suffering, and death.[5] Paul, however, gives no hint of this; and if there actually was such an interpretation in pre-Christian Judaism, it remained a single strand of tradition isolated for want of intelligible context. The oracle on the suffering Servant did indeed present itself to the earliest Christian community as the most pertinent hermeneutical resource for conceiving the death and glorification of Jesus in biblical terms (cf., e.g., 1 Cor 15:3-5). But faith-affirmations of this kind met one theological exigence (namely, for biblical testimony to the death and glorifica-

---

cf. 12f. argues for the terminology of "call" and against that of "conversion." If used in a narrow sense for a penitent's return to God or a convert's change of religion, "conversion" would not be a good term to apply to the event; but "conversion" has also the generic sense of a revolution in perspective and purpose (cf. Lonergan, *Method*, 130f.). In this sense the Damascus event was a conversion as well as a call, and "conversion" says something significant about the event, which "call" does not say .

[5]See Joachim Jeremias, *The Servant of God*, 59-79.

tion of Jesus) only to intensify another (namely, for an intelligible total context in which to make sense of the now scripturally attested death and glorification). Paul's distinctive vision of things was his response to this exigence. Essentially, it was the fruit of his effort to make salvation-historical sense of the cross. Whereas the confessional formulas of pre-Pauline Christianity were triumphant affirmations that God had not only undone the death of Jesus but that he had willed it as a saving event, the challenge now was to support the theme of Christ's expiatory death (cf. 1 Cor 15:3; Rom 4:25) by supplying its comprehensive context: a coherent salvation history climaxing in the cross.

That the cross made divine sense was evident from the resurrection of Christ. The challenge that faced Paul was to discover *how* the cross made sense. It was to discover from the scriptures how the cross could have been charged with divine purpose as the climactic feature of the divine plan. Within the religious categories current in Judaism, the question remained unanswerable. The deeper one's involvement in those categories, the less likely was one to see the hand of God in the story of Jesus. Where in the orthodoxy of the Torah was there room for a crucified Christ? Nowhere. Two factors set the death of Jesus outside the horizons of Jewish theology. First, it could not have been expiatory for the world, for the cross signified God's curse (Deut 21:23).[6]

---

[6]Jacques Dupont, "La conversion de Paul et son influence sur sa conception du salut par la foi," in *Foi et salut selon S. Paul* (Rome: Biblical Institute Press, 1970), 67-88, cf. 80f., takes note of the context in which Paul's reference to Deut 21:23 occurs. According to Dupont's exegesis of Gal 3:10b, it is this argument: if the Galatians accept circumcision, they are bound to keep all the prescriptions of the Law, under pain of incurring its curse. This line of thought is foreign to Judaism. Hence Dupont's reluctance to understand Gal 3:13 as inspired by ideas actually held in Judaism, e.g., Paul's own former idea of Jesus (cf. 2 Cor 5:16). Two observations, however, weaken the force of this line of reflection. First, the point of Paul's citation of LXX Deut 27:26 is probably not to support the argument that Dupont formulates (if the Galatians accept circumcision, they are bound to keep all the prescriptions of the Law,

Second, no such expiation could have been necessary, for the economy of the Torah was complete.[7]

The new starting point for Paul, however, had been a decisive experience of revelation. If Torah had no room for Christ crucified, so much the worse for Torah. The presupposition of the words "If righteousness were through the law, then Christ died to no purpose" (Gal 3:21) was not only a divine purpose in Christ's death but a divine purpose defining the role of Christ's death as uniquely and indispensably mediating the salvation of mankind. But why should the salvation of mankind have so hinged on the death of Christ?

Pre-Pauline tradition affirmed Christ's death "for our trespasses" and his resurrection "for our acquittal" (Rom 4:25); but Paul recharged the formulas in two ways. First, he found his way to the missing biblical context for the cross by conceiving it as the solution to a whole human dilemma. (For a theological scheme of this kind the faith-formulas provided no more than a point of departure.) Second, Paul enormously expanded this potentially grandiose scheme on the side of the dilemma by making it comprehend every aspect of sin and death, and on the side of its resolution by making it comprehend every aspect of acquittal and life. Thus, the motif of acquittal was fused with that of participation in pneumatic existence, in accord (as we shall see) with the baptismal liturgy of the *hellenistai*. For Paul, Christ by his resurrection had become "a life-giving spirit" (1 Cor 15:45), the first-born of a new race. Paul's effort to make the

under pain of incurring its curse), but simply to call the scriptures to witness on the tie between the Law (*nomos*) and the curse (*epikataratos*). See E. P. Sanders, *Paul, the Law, and the Jewish People*, 21f. Second, how likely is it that Paul invented the application of Deut 21:23 to Jesus as an extravagant polemical device? In view of the Essenes' use of the Deuteronomic text to refer to crucifixion (see below, note 11), it seems probable to me that Gal 3:13 echoes a non-Christian Jewish view of Jesus.

[7]See E. P. Sanders, *Paul and Palestinian Judaism*, 422f., for a summary exhibiting a certain self-contained completeness in "the common pattern" of Judaic religion.

destiny of Jesus intelligible as "the climactic feature of the divine plan" generated an apocalypticizing interpretation of sin and death as a universal dilemma burdening the whole of history and utterly insoluble apart from the redemptive mission of Christ. From the fact of the cross, then, it followed as the night the day that Torah, which was supposed to have succeeded Chaos as the solution of man's benightedness and aberrancy, had really been futile. If this futility were not to have meant the failure of God's purposes, it must never have been God's intention that Torah should function as a solution.

The conception of history in terms of problem and solution and the identification of Christ as the solution supplied a principle of discernment respecting the legacy of Israel. *"Solution" could only appear in the mode of promise; all else* — the whole legacy of the past — *belonged to "problem."* "There were promises made to Abraham..." (Gal 3:16) that envisaged precisely the solution to the dilemma of man. As for Torah, "it was added for the sake of transgressions" (Gal 3:19), that is, to produce them (Rom 4:15; 5:13, 20; 7:7-13; cf. 6:14) or, in other words, to compound the problem. As Paul's insight into the human dilemma derived immediately from his effort to grasp the rationale of the cross, so his harsh and dark view of the Torah derived immediately from his conception of the human dilemma (not from his desire to bring the gospel to the gentiles).

By the time Paul undertook to spell out a complete defence of himself and his gospel (in a letter to the Christians of Rome), the question of how rightly to conceive the dilemma of man had proved to belong to the center of his debate with Judaism. On the basis of the present analysis it is clear that Paul had already worked out the main lines of his thinking on this theme well before he wrote to the churches of Galatia, for it is presupposed by the treatment of the Torah in that letter. Theologically, Galatians was the tip of an iceberg. The letter left undefined the concrete conceptual suppositions of its remorseless attack on Torah. In Romans, on the other hand, they are spelled out in Adam's introduction of a dynamism of radical disorder into the world. There had never been anything wrong with the Torah. But there was something awesomely wrong with man — he lay under a self-imposed bondage to sin — and because of this the Torah in the flesh-and-blood actuality of history had been sin's lethal tool, a code that killed (cf. 2 Cor 3:6f.). From start to finish Galatians had been charged with this self-same understanding of the situation of man. It is hardly plausible that the rationale provided by Romans is mere afterthought, as if the role of Adam in Romans 5 were no more than a detachable part of an otherwise coherent and interlocking set of judgments on the concrete historical dilemma of man.

What was to blame for this dilemma? "The flesh?" As if the impotence of "the flesh" were not itself in need of explanation! Paul offered his ultimate explanation in the passages of Romans in which he connected bondage with sin and sin with Adam. Romans, written towards the end of his career and under pressure of having to defend himself and his gospel by making both as fully intelligible as possible, provides a rationale of Paul's vision (the Adam-Christ schema) which probably went back to an early moment in his prototypal career as Christian theologian.

The crucial clues to Paul's assembling of a biblically attested total context for the cross were the stock of faith-formulations he derived from Antiochene baptismal liturgy. Baptism was the socially repetitive situation (*Sitz im Leben*) that generated the lapidary, hieratic texts cited by Paul in the letters to Corinth and Rome, e.g.,

> the unrighteous will not inherit the reign of God...
> but you have had yourselves washed,
> you have been consecrated,
> you have been made righteous
> in the name of our Lord Jesus Christ
> and in the Spirit of our God
>   (1 Cor 6:9-11).

The passage is probably traditional in character rather than a totally free Pauline composition. The conception of baptism as a sharing in Christ's death with the hope of sharing in his risen life originated in Antioch or at least was formulated there in terms such as: you have been "baptized into Christ Jesus" and baptized "into his death" (Rom 6:3).[8] According to Judaic tradition death made expiation for sin; this is presupposed by the Judeo-Christian correlation of two facets of baptism, namely, as purificatory of sin and as a participation in the death of Christ. Whereas in Judaic tradition the standard expression was that dying expiates, in Rom 6:7 he who has died stands acquitted (*dedikaiotai*) of sin. This idiom of acquittal belonged to other formulas connected with baptism (e.g., Rom 3:25f.; 4:25).[9]

Of great significance, finally, was the pre- or para-Pauline baptismal motif of conformity to the image of God's Son (Rom 8:29f.). It supposed man's loss in paradise of the "glory" of God (ApocMos 20; Rom 3:23), i.e., of his being in the image and likeness of God. The eschatological recovery of this conformity to the very being of God was only conceptually distinct from the general theme of eschatological sonship, for those called to be God's sons would be sons only by conformity to his Son (Rom 8:29f.). As sonship to God was an already inaugurated reality (Gal 3:26; 4:6f.; Rom 8:14) still to be brought to fullness at the consummation of time (Rom 8:19), so the recovery of man's likeness to God was already inaugurated (2 Cor 3:18; 4:4-6; Phil 3:10; Rom 8:28f.),[10] namely by baptism (Rom 6:3), and would be brought to perfection by the resurrection of the dead (1 Cor 15:49; cf. Phil 3:21).

The generative matrix of Paul's soteriology was therefore a composite of three factors: problem, insight, and resource. The problem, consequent on being won over to the Christian cause, was to retrieve the divine intelligibility of the

[8]See Ferdinand Hahn, "Taufe und Rechtfertigung" in *Rechtfertigung* (Tübingen: Mohr, 1976), 95-124, cf. 109.

[9]See Hahn, "Taufe und Rechtfertigung," 108, 110f.

[10]See Hahn, "Taufe und Rechtfertigung," 115f.

cross. The insight was structural or heuristic: the cross was the solution to a universal dilemma. The resource was a liturgical treasury of soteriological themes or motifs.

Antecedent to conversion to Christ, the problem was Jesus' death on a cross, a stumbling block for Jews (1 Cor 1:23) since the man "hanged" on a tree was "cursed by God" (lit. "a curse of God," *qilĕlat 'ĕlōhîm*, Deut 21:23; Gal 3:13).[11] Such had been Paul's own view in the days when he judged according to the flesh (2 Cor 5:16). Consequent on conversion to Christ, this problem was met in principle by the resurrection, which, as the divine vindication of Jesus, compelled a reconsideration of his death "for us." But this met the problem of Christ's death only in principle; Paul felt the sharp need to find the full context in which the death of Jesus made biblically attested, salvation-historical sense.

The second factor was the strategic insight that confronted this need by conceiving the death on the cross as the comprehensive *solution* to a human *dilemma* manifested by the whole of history. This called for a thoroughgoing revision and re-appropriation of the biblical tradition, no element of which could be allowed to compete with the saving act of God in Christ. "Solution" could appear in history only in the guise of promise, the promise of God's act in Christ. Any other claim to the status of solution would be

[11]That long before Jesus the "hanging" of Deut 21:23 was applied to cases of crucifixion is probable from LXX Jos 8:29; in LXX Est 9:7 *stauroun* renders *tālā*. *Tālā* is correlated with crucifixion in 4QpNah I 7f.; the tie between crucifixion and Deut 21:23 is clear from 11Q Temple 64:7-13. Gerhard Friedrich, *Die Verkündigung des Todes Jesu im Neuen Testament* (Neukirchen-Vluyn: Neukirchener Verlag, 1982), 122-9, has argued that non-Christian Jews would hardly have looked on Jesus as accursed by God on the merely factual basis of his crucifixion; so mechanical a judgment is ruled out by the datum that among those executed by crucifixion before and during Roman rule in Palestine were numerous heroes of Judaism. This is true but not decisive. The probability remains that Deut 21:23 was applied to the crucified Jesus in the light of his condemnation — considered (as indeed it is implicitly considered in Gal 3:13) to be in accord with the Torah — for the ostensibly false and blasphemous claim to be in the (messianic) Son of God (Mark 15:61-63; par. Matt 26:63-65; John 19:7; cf. Luke 22:70f.

exposed as deceptive, and the claimant's real role in salvation history would be redefined. The controlling supposition of the whole project was that the story of God and Israel reflected a deliberate plan, the clue to the dimensions and features of which was the status of Christ's death and resurrection as the plan's climactic goal within history.

The third factor was an extraordinarily rich resource of pointers to the accomplishment of this theological project. This resource was the baptismal liturgy of the *hellēnistai*, with its motifs of acquittal, participation in the paschal mysteries of Christ, and recovery of sonship and glory by solidarity with the glorified Son. This liturgy sowed seeds of vision, a vision of the risen Christ as "life-giving spirit" and of those baptized "into him" as a new mankind.

This hypothesis relates the genesis of Pauline soteriology to the world mission in an indirect, densely mediated way. It thus stands in contrast to proposals that make Paul's appointment as Apostle of the gentiles the commanding principle of the development of his thought. Such proposals attribute to Pauline theology an adventitious quality that it seems not to have, as if the young Paul (like the young Lenin) were a man with a mission in search of a theory to sustain it. The genetic account offered here has the advantage of positing no dramatic chasm between itself and the expository strategies and themes to which we have direct access. Paul's early theological work was done in the Antiochene context of soteriological universalism, which reached an explosive point, at which Antioch launched its mission. But the commanding obsession of Paul's thought was to find the wisdom concealed in the folly of the cross.

Conclusion

Paul's soteriological reflection stood in the line of Antiochene tradition: Christianity was more than the restoration of Israel, more even than a mere restoration of mankind. Baptism, to be sure, restored man to the image and likeness of God (Gen 1:26f.), but by a new creation: assimilation to the risen Christ (cf. 2 Cor 3:18; Rom 3:23; 8:28-30). Paul, moreover, went beyond Antiochene tradition, filling out its vision of things and forging a missionary policy fully coherent with that vision. He redefined Christianity as the reversal of a disaster afflicting all mankind through the whole of history. Attested in advance by the scriptures, this reversal brought into being a new, climactic, definitive economy of salvation. Its hallmark was openness to all human beings without distinction.

From the start the *hebraioi* led by Cephas had been aware of their unique ecclesial status: they embodied the restoration of Israel. On the one hand, they were Israel *par excellence*, calling on the nation to enter into its rightful heritage. On the other, there was no entry into this heritage except by the positive acts of being baptized and confessing the risen Messiah. This and only this would secure Israel's election-historical identity as God's people. Thus, every Christian group of which we have knowledge was explicitly aware, whatever its allegiances to empirical Israel, that it shared in an ecclesial identity that was new and distinctive and normative.

Paul's great forward step consisted in his laying of foundations at once biblical and kerygmatic for the Torah-free self-definition of gentile Christianity. The two facets of his historic achievement — his comprehensive soteriology and his successful missionary labor — were inseparable and reciprocally defining. His message made the common Christian kerygma and the missionary drive of the *hellēnistai* intelligible and feasible in the Mediterranean world.

But in the end — and this will be a topic in our next and final chapter — Paul's forward step should be described less as a grounding of the self-definition of Torah-free Christianity than as a relativizing of all self-definitions in favor of the unity of the church.[12] Neither circumcision nor uncir-

[12]Holmberg, *Paul and Power*, 25, cites with seeming approval a view of Traugott Holtz to the following effect: the Antioch incident "shows that

cumcision counts (Gal 6:15; cf. 1 Cor 7:19). Paul deployed his soteriological themes, his practical parenesis, and his missionary labor in the cause of an ecclesial identity that transcended without abolishing diverse communitarian policies respecting the Law. He promoted a soteriology valid for all alike, regardless of any and all such differences.

His greatness, in fact, came to light precisely in the situation of conflicting Christian self-definitions. Here he was unique and alone, as in the confrontation with Cephas at Antioch. His principle was authentic church unity. For this, as Paul would later argue, the authentic offspring of Abraham and heirs of the promise must be "heirs in token of faith, in order to be heirs by God's pure favor, so that the promise should be guaranteed to all his offspring" (Rom 4:16). Here was a value that time showed to outweigh by far the well-intentioned but futile pragmatism of James, to which Cephas and "even Barnabas" deferred (Gal 2:11-13). In this as in comparable conflicts (e.g., between "the strong" and "the weak" in Corinth and Rome) Paul went beyond the rationale, however well- or ill-justified, of any given self-definition to a superior court of appeal: one God and one Lord requiring a church truly one (1 Cor 8) and one way, "the way of love" (Rom 14:15), as its emblem.

It was the resolution of missionary conflicts that accounted for the distance between Antioch's sublime

the unity of the Church is not of supreme value for Paul (the supreme value is the truth of the Gospel)." The view I am urging here is that a hallmark of Paul's theology before, during and after the Antioch incident, is precisely his refusal to entertain as possible the disjunction between the truth of the gospel and the divinely willed unity of the church. For Paul the supreme value was indissolubly this unity and this truth. Hence, his protests against the subversion of unity in Antioch and Galatia (Gal 1-2), in Corinth (1 Cor 8:7-13) and Rome (Rom 14:1-15:13), appeal — to what? Precisely to the truth of the gospel (Gal 2:4-14; cf. Rom 14:17-21). J. C. Beker, *Paul the Apostle*, 130, puts the matter as follows: "...the unity of the church and the truth of the gospel constitute the permanent, uneasy dialectical components of Paul's apostolate and thought."

liturgy and Paul's hard realism. With the Antiochene baptismal libretto Paul affirmed that to be "in Christ" was "new creation" (2 Cor 5:17), but the harsh experience of conflicting self-definitions, of mission and counter-mission, made him translate this into: neither circumcision nor uncircumcision counts at all (Gal 6:15). The net result, as the writer of Ephesians saw, was to show that Christ's death had broken down the dividing wall between Jew and Greek (Eph 2:14).

X

Identity and Development

We have found a paradigm of swiftly changing self-definition in the story of the Christian commitment to the world mission. Concentrating on main lines of development, we have given most of our attention to massive phenomena: the original self-definition of the Jerusalem *hebraioi*, the divergent self-definition of the *hellēnistai*, the Antiochene initiative of a mission to the northeastern Mediterranean world, the successful defence of the Torah-free mission by Paul and Barnabas, Paul's striking soteriological development of the faith-affirmations of Jerusalemite and Antiochene Christianity.

We have paid less attention to significant but secondary phenomena such as the effort of James to impose on gentile Christians the Torah prescriptions proper to all men (Gen 9:4 together with the laws on the "alien" [*ger*] dwelling in Israel, Lev 17-18). If the decree of James was the issue behind the conflict between Paul and Cephas in Antioch (Gal 2:11-21),[1] this might well explain why Acts offers an account of the world mission so different in detail from that suggested by the data of the Pauline letters: Luke, following

---

[1]See David R. Catchpole, "Paul, James and the Apostolic Decree," *New Testament Studies* 23 (1977): 428-44; P. Stuhlmacher, "Die Gerechtigkeitsanschauung des Apostels Paulus," 96f.

Antiochene tradition, accepted the Jacobite decree; Paul did not. In the light of this division, Jacob Jervell has argued that the last quarter of the first Christian century was a time of vital influence and leadership by "the mighty minority" of Jewish Christian churchmen.[2] If this was indeed the case, the reason for scholarship's having misconstrued the fortunes of Jewish Christianity immediately after 70 A.D.[3] is that Paul's entirely Torah-free policy did win out in the long run. The beginnings of this victory are already evident in the status attributed to Paul by the Pauline pseudepigrapha (especially Colossians and Ephesians) and in the beginnings of the process of canonizing the Pauline and Deutero-Pauline letters. To this theme we shall return at the conclusion of this chapter.

Meantime, our purpose is to reflect on and try to digest the historical process we have reviewed. We should like to expose and commend a view of "Christianity and change" that significantly differs from the evolutionary account offered by the history-of-religions school and its many and varied heirs. The thesis proposed here is that in "the Easter experience" the first Christians appropriated a consciously ecclesial and election-historical identity; that this identity, articulated and secured by kerygma and confession, allowed scope for various concrete self-definitions, simultaneous and successive; that the main appropriate category for understanding early Christian change is "development"; and that early Christian development took place primarily by transpositions of meaning.

Earlier we asked what we should make of the conflict between the ancients' suppositions or express convictions of Christian unity and continuity and rootage in a common origin (cf., e.g., the Acts of the Apostles) and the moderns'

---

[2]Jacob Jervell, "The Mighty Minority," *Studia Theologica* 34 (1980): 13-38.

[3]To be sure, this common misjudgment usually omits consideration of Greek-speaking centers such as Antioch.

discrimination among the many points of vantage and fields of vision simultaneously or successively characterizing the Christians of antiquity. Our present purpose is to indicate how this conflict might be resolved. Both are right in their affirmations but unsatisfactory in their omissions. The ancients in question celebrated their common ecclesial identity, but they did not acknowledge what they lacked the conceptual tools to explain (discovery and development, their novelty and unpredictability, the fact of change in ecclesial self-definition and policy). Instead, they took the tack of retrojecting the gains of historic experience to the original saving act of God (thus the world mission was made to derive from the explicit mandate of Christ). Our interest, however, centers on complementing and modifying not so much the views of the ancients as those of the moderns, who readily acknowledge variety, change, and discontinuity, but are unable to find the unity claimed and cherished by the ancient church. The theme of these reflections is accordingly identity and development, and we begin with identity.

Experiential Roots of Identity

We have used the term "identity" to specify an issue distinct from that of self-definition and have entertained the possibility that the ecclesial identity of Christians might have been, not jeopardized and lost, but actually maintained owing precisely to changes in Christian self-definition. If the gentile Church of the second and third centuries looked on contemporary Jewish-Christian sects as having forfeited their identity as Christians, the modern who ponders this historically might well agree on the issue of lost identity and attribute this situation to a glacially conservative self-definition, which, in the wake of repeated disasters and growing isolation, gradually retreated from its own commitments and decayed.

"Identity" is what the core of one's allegiance makes one to be; "self-definition" is identity culturally and historically incarnated. To be more concrete, let the New Testament faith-formulas serve as point of departure. The formulas themselves, taken rigorously by a strict constructionist, are indices to identity; placed in the larger context of the historically and culturally conditioned horizons, self-understanding, and self-shaping of concrete groups and individuals, the same formulas contribute to a retrieval of social self-definition. Since Torah piety belonged to their horizons, the *hebraioi* of Jerusalem assimilated the experience of salvation in a way that left allegiance to the Torah intact. Nevertheless, as we have seen, Paul could mount an appeal to the *hebraioi* — "we...who have come to know [by our encounter with the risen Christ] that man is made righteous not by works of the law but through faith in Christ..." (Gal 2:15f.) — that differentiated between Torah piety and the heart of the Christian experience (namely, the Easter experience). The Easter experience by-passed the Torah, neither comprehending nor entailing it. The same was true of the Galatians' charismatic experience of the Spirit (Gal 3:2-5). How had the Torah figured in this experience? Not at all! This same principle of discrimination, according to Acts, was the linchpin in Peter's apologia for having baptized Cornelius and his household without requiring circumcision (Acts 11:15-17). In a word, an index to Christian identity was the Christian experience of salvation, which found spare, precise expression in the confessional acclamations, hymns, confessions, and proto-credal texts preserved in the New Testament.

In the three examples just alluded to (Paul's appeal to the Galatians' charismatic experience of the Spirit, Gal 3:2-5; Acts' presentation of Peter's appeal to the mini-Pentecost that came upon Cornelius and his household, Acts 11:15-17; Paul's appeal, probably to the Easter experience itself, and in any case to the experience of reconciliation to God of Jews such as Cephas and himself without reference to the Torah, Gal 2:15f.), *the argument makes the experience of God's saving act a principle of discernment.* This experience is not yet man's response to God's act; it grounds and calls for his response. Moreover, it provides a measure of what that response should be, a specification of *appropriate* response. The Galatians had had no contact with the Torah and Cornelius and his household had not been circumcised; still, God did not stint in pouring out the climactic gifts of the Spirit. Conclusion: for the Galatians and Cornelius circumcision and the Torah did not condition salvation.

No argument holds except within the horizon that makes it intelligible. Elements of the horizon supposed by the arguments sketched above include at least two convictions: first, that the object of these experiences was the act and gift of God as savior; second, that God's act and gift belonged unambiguously, integrally, coherently to an economy of salvation realized and revealed in this privileged experience.

"The experience of salvation" as principle of discernment was by no means a new idea. It was a biblical commonplace, as the creeds and other covenantal texts of ancient Israel attest by their grateful recollection of the experience of salvation. In contradistinction to the New Testament texts, we have been considering, this age-old tradition made sure of including the Torah. The experience of salvation called for a proper response and it was precisely the Torah that specified that proper response. In the text that follows, the theme of the experience of salvation is immediately complemented by the theme of the conditional blessings of the covenant:

> You have seen what I did to Egypt
>   and how I bore you on eagles' wings
>   and brought you to myself.
> Now, therefore, if you obey my voice
>   and keep my covenant,
> you shall be my own possession among
>   all peoples, for all the earth is mine.
> And you shall be to me a royalty of
>   priests and a holy people (Ex 19:4-6).[4]

---

[4]For the data commending this translation of *mamleket kohănîm* in the last line, see W. L. Moran, "'A Kingdom of Priests,'" in *The Bible in Current Catholic Thought* (New York: Herder and Herder, 1962), 7-20, cf. 11-17.

In a particularly reflective and precise appeal to the experience of salvation as normative respecting the right response to salvation, the late Exilic or post-Exilic author of Deuteronomy 4 made the people's experience at Horeb the decisive measure of the primary stipulation of the covenant (which he took to be the prohibition of images, i.e., idolatry). The text first represents the experience at Horeb. Moses speaks:

> Yahweh said to me,
> Assemble the people for me; I will have them hear my words, that they may learn to fear me all the days that they live on the earth, and may so teach their children. And you came near and stood at the foot of the mountain, while the mountain, burning with fire to the heart of heaven, was wrapped in darkness, cloud, and thick murk. Then Yahweh spoke to you from the midst of the fire, and you heard the sound of words but saw no form; there was only a voice. And he declared to you his covenant, which he commanded you to perform, namely, the ten commandments; and he wrote them on two tablets of stone (Deut 4:10-13).

Next, the text draws the lesson from the Horeb experience. It is deftly summed up in the words: "no form seen, therefore no images; the heavens shrouded in deepest darkness, therefore no cult of heavenly bodies."[5]

> Since you saw no form at all on the day that Yahweh spoke to you at Horeb from the midst of the fire, beware lest, acting corruptly, you make for yourselves the image of any figure, a (human) image, the likeness of male or female, the likeness of any beast on the earth, of any winged bird that flies in the air, of anything that creeps on the ground, of any fish in the water under the earth (Deut 4:15-18).

[5]W. L. Moran, "Deuteronomy" in *A New Catholic Commentary on Holy Scripture* (London: Nelson, 1969), 263.

Having ruled out cult images by reference to the lack of images in the Horeb experience, the writer next rules out, implicitly on the same basis, the cult of heavenly bodies:

> And beware lest, raising your eyes to heaven and seeing the sun and moon and stars, all the host of heaven, you be seduced and worship them and serve them, things that Yahweh your God has allotted to the mass of peoples under the whole heaven (Deut 4:19).

Here we have a late Deuteronomistic redactor, at home in the priestly tradition, intent on concentrating the saving act of God in the moment of Horeb, on reconstructing Horeb as a purely auditory, non-visual experience, and on appealing to that experience as the norm of the supreme commandment (cf. Deut 5:6-10). True, the experience of Horeb as presented here is a reflective stylization composed many centuries after the event, whereas Paul's appeals to experience are immediate and the experiences themselves are recent. Still, the Deuteronomic text brilliantly illustrates the appeal to the experience of salvation as ultimate norm for the life of Israel. Like Paul's argument from the experience of salvation, whether of Cephas and himself or of the Galatians, the writer supposes that this experience is an integral revelation of the economy of salvation. Thus, he excludes from religious practice what the experience of salvation itself excluded by the "darkness, cloud, and thick murk" hiding Horeb up "to the heart of heaven."

In the earliest Christian consciousness the definitive saving act of God was without any doubt the sequence of Jesus' death and resurrection. But it was only through the evidence of resurrection that Jesus' death could take conscious shape as saving event. The cardinal experience of salvation was accordingly "the Easter experience of the disciples." It was cardinal in the sense that on it hinged the very proclamation of the gospel (2 Cor 5:19; cf. 1 Cor 2:10-16; 9:1f.; 15:1-11). This revelation of the risen Jesus to the disciples evidently belonged, in early Christian conviction, to the economy of eschatological salvation. It revealed God's way; hence its normative character. It was a charged experience: not only a revelation but a reconciliation, the reconciliation to God, through the communion offered by his risen and glorified Son, of men who had earlier rejected this same Son (James), or abandoned him (the disciples in general), or "denied" him (Peter), or "persecuted" him (Paul). Neither the prescriptions of the Torah nor its remedies for transgression had had any role in this drama. It had not named and condemned the transgressions nor, much less, expunged them. The Easter experience alone had been — integrally and self-containedly — revelation and reconciliation and mandate. The economy of salvation thus brought to light, as some saw with particular clarity, was a radically "new thing" (Isa 43:19).

It was the Easter experience, in short, that gave the disciples dramatic access to what God's good pleasure as savior finally was. This experience showed that Christ had been

> delivered up for our transgressions
> and raised for our acquittal (Rom 4:25).

What, then, of the new "we" established by initiation into this economy of salvation? The question was: Who and what are we? The answer was: the witnesses and beneficiaries and confessors of God's saving act. We are those for whose transgressions he was delivered up, for whose acquittal he was raised. Christian identity, a precipitate of the experience of salvation, was expressed, mediated, secured by confessional formulas.

The theorem rooting Christian identity in the experience of God's saving act is by no means calculated, however, to foreclose the possibility of development. The historic process of discerning and appropriating Christian identity is well attested in early Christian literature.

In pre- or para-Pauline tradition the event of salvation was conceived as a three-act drama: the entry into history of the pre-existent one who was on a par with God; his obedience unto death; his glorification as *kyrios* (Phil 2:6-11). If such were the dimensions of the divine act of salvation, how

might the *experience* of salvation be conceived? The possibilities were great. It might be described simply as "being
with him" (namely, in his public career, cf. Mark 3:14). This
surely went hand in hand with the transmission of the Jesus
tradition. It accorded perfectly with the Lukan definition of
"Apostle." The "Apostle" had to have been chosen from
among those who, in Peter's words, had "accompanied us
during the whole time that the Lord Jesus went in and out
among us" (Acts 1:21f.). And if such was the experience of
salvation, its proclamation had to include the earthly career
of "the Christ of God" (Luke 9:20).

The experience of Christ, with retrospective accent on the
earthly Christ, was highlighted in the overcharged opening
of 1 John:

> That which was from the beginning, which we have
> heard, which we have seen with our eyes, which we have
> looked upon and touched with our hands, concerning the
> word of life — and life appeared and we saw it and testify
> to it and proclaim to you the eternal life, which was with
> the Father, and appeared to us... (1 John 1:1f.).

Like other New Testament texts on the experience of salvation, this makes experience itself thematic, appeals to experience, and makes at least implicit claims by that appeal;
and, like other New Testament texts on the experience of
salvation, though perhaps more dramatically than any
other, this text terminates in the object of that experience.
Indeed, a major reason for recalling such texts is that they
regularly include just what historical reconstructions of the
Christian experience of salvation regularly exclude: the
object of the experience (here, the earthly Christ grasped in
the light of the Easter experience). Unlike major currents of
theology today, for which the object of the early Christian
experience of salvation is historically unknowable, i.e.,
bracketed, removed in principle from historical inquiry, this
text in its main intention resolutely fixes, not on a christology, but on Christ himself, "the gift God has made of

himself to us in his Son."[6] Such texts, then, interfere with the habit of mind that tendentiously posits a christologically meager starting-point for the Christian experience of salvation. On the testimony of the New Testament, the actual point of departure for Christian development of whatever kind was an experience whose extraordinary character derived not from the horizons of its subjects but from the transcendent reality of its object.

Though a greater variety of such texts might be considered, let it suffice to have indicated a few of the ways in which early Christianity could conceive and express the experience of salvation. One last observation on this experience is appropriate. It bears on the distinction between once-for-all experiences and ever renewed experiences. The primary supposition of the category of once-for-all experiences is that the revelation of the risen Christ had a fixed terminus (cf. the Pauline "last of all. . ." in 1 Cor 15:8; also, the Lukan "forty days" of Acts 1:3). Again, the concrete human experience of "accompanying the Lord Jesus" through his earthly career was historically unrepeatable. The combined eye-witness and faith-witness of the Apostles was accordingly endowed with a once-for-all character. Primitive Christianity nevertheless attests an experience of salvation that is ever renewed — instanced, for example, in the pneumatic experience of the Galatians (Gal 3:2-5). Hence the solidity of the thesis that the true heritage of the church is not a christology but Christ himself, that the true tradition of the church is not a doctrine but "the Holy Spirit of God, the very reality, then, of what the Apostles experienced in Christ."[7]

[6]Henri de Lubac, "Le problème du développement du dogme," *Recherches de science religieuse* 35 (1948): 130-60, cf. 156.

[7]Karl Rahner, "The Development of Dogma," in *Theological Investigations*, vol. I (Baltimore: Helicon, 1961, 39-77), cf. 68. Josef Blank, *Paulus und Jesus* (Munich: Kösel, 1968), 143-70, rightly accents a richness in the experience of salvation that is not, cannot be, carried over intact into the kerygma (apropos of the content of 1 Cor 15:3-5).

Identity: Ecclesial, Correlative to "Gospel," Open to Diversity

The Christian experience of salvation was embedded in an eschatological context, climactic respecting the whole past of ancient Israel. From the outset, then, Christian self-understanding was covenantal, qualified in its earliest moment by the ecclesial and election-historical conception of "the remnant of Israel."[8]

As Christianity expanded into the gentile world and began to grow rapidly, the consciousness of being a "people" grew as well. Old (their story was told by the whole Bible) and new (they were born of the last Adam, lately raised from the dead), Christians were distinct equally from Jews and Greeks. Paul had urged the Corinthians to "give no occasion of sin to Jews or to Greeks or to the assembly of God's people" (*tę ekklēsią tou theou*, 1 Cor 10:32). In the last-named third entity, the church of God, the ruling distinction between Jew and Greek (Gal 3:28; 5:6; 6:15) as between slave and free man (Gal 3:28; 1 Cor 12:13) had been sublated in a higher unity. After Paul's day this self-understanding held (Col 3:11; Eph 2:11f.); it grew through the following century into a Christian self-understanding, and an understanding of Christians by the surrounding Greco-Roman world, summed up in the term "third race" (*triton genos, tertium genus*).[9] This was a race set off from Jew and Greek in its own view by the history of election, and in the view of its surrounding world by a distinctive — hence, offensive — way of life.

---

[8]B. F. Meyer, *The Aims of Jesus*, 239f.

[9]Harnack, *Mission and Expansion*, ch. VII, "The Tidings of the New People and of the Third Race," 24-65, followed by an Excursus, "Christians as a Third Race, in the Judgment of their Opponents," 266-78, took into account the migration of Christianity to the gentile world, the fall of

The issues that the history of election raised for Christianity can be discerned in very early data supplied by Paul. Ecclesial continuity and discontinuity with the past might seem to the modern mind a matter of minor importance, but it was not so for Paul and his contemporaries. *Most, and perhaps all, of Paul's battles were rooted in divergent views of what was requisite to the authentic ecclesial identity of Christians.* They were an election-historical people, old and new. How much of the old was indispensable? What demands of the new were peremptory? Once the gentile mission took hold, this became the burning issue.

"Identity," then, was not a marginal epiphenomenon. It was the answer to bedrock questions: Who are we? What are we? What ought we to be? The generic answers were: we are the people of God, a people of his own possession, bought at a price, rescued and reconciled by the blood of the Lord, a new creation in Christ, the Israel of God, the new sanctuary not built with hands... But all this was conditional. It hinged on *a proper response* to the God who summoned into being this new people. The divergent views held respectively by Christian *hebraioi* and *hellēnistai* in Jerusalem led to later battles over circumcision, to the decree of James (ignored in the Pauline churches), and to the tensions between gentile and Jewish Christianity, which, though variously sorted out by Paul, were still formidable in the aggregate.

For Paul the differences between his own missionary churches and those of Judea were a massive cultural fact; to bridge them (for example, by the symbolic and practical

Jerusalem, persecution in the Empire, the work of the Apologists and the Alexandrian Fathers, and the reactions of Greek and Roman opponents of Christianity up to and through the third century. For an update on the second century, see Robert L. Wilken, "The Christians as the Romans (and Greeks) Saw Them," in *Jewish and Christian Self-Definition*, vol. I (Philadelphia: Fortress, 1980), 100-25. See also Dix, *Jew and Greek*, 87.

gesture of the collection)[10] was among his prime purposes. Why this concern? It was a question of unity and identity. The new creation, the Israel of God, the body of Christ, could not be, must not be allowed to be, split. ("Is Christ divided?" 1 Cor 1:13.) How then did Paul understand the differences between the churches of Judea and those of Achaia? As in themselves constituting a breach of unity? Evidently not. It follows that he drew a decisive distinction between unity and uniformity. Paul cherished the unity of the church in the full consciousness that uniformity for Jewish and gentile spheres was out of the question. He himself could move in both worlds, accommodating to each "for the sake of the gospel" (1 Cor 9:23):

> Free from all, I made myself a slave to
>   all to win over as many as I could;
> to the Jews I became like a Jew to win
>   over Jews,
> to those under the law like one under
>   the law (though I am not myself under the law)
>   to win over those under the law,
> to those free of law, like one free of
>   law (though I am not free of God's
>   law, but am bound to Christ's law)
>   to win over those free of law
>   (1 Cor 9:19-21).

Christian identity — obviously more fundamental in Paul's view than the diverse self-understandings that qualified it — was correlative to "the gospel" in whose name Paul accommodated himself to all.

---

[10]For the symbolic aspect of the collection, see Roger D. Aus, "Paul's Travel Plans..." (An alternative, or perhaps supplementary, interpretation of the meaning of the collection — namely, that it was an offering owed to the sacral central community of Jerusalem, comparable to the Jewish temple tax [Karl Holl] — is reviewed and defended by Peter Stuhlmacher, *Das paulinische Evangelium*, 100-5. See also Martin Hengel, *Acts and the History of Earliest Christianity*, 118.)

Admittedly, this could not be, if for Paul there were more than one gospel. But it seems hardly possible that he considered the church of Jerusalem, which operated as he himself did "for the sake of the gospel," was committed to a *different* gospel and one that, in the words of J. D. G. Dunn, "involved a greater subjection to the Law than he himself thought right."[11] But did Paul find fault with Jerusalem on these grounds? Did he not appeal to the conviction, common to Cephas and himself, Jews by birth but no less sure on that account of having attained to righteousness in Christ in no wise through "works of the law" but exclusively by entry into Easter faith (Gal 2:15-17)? Did Paul ever allude to a Jerusalem "gospel" that included any stipulation whatever of subjection to the Law? Did Paul in fact understand there to be several gospels?

According to Dunn, Paul in Galatians speaks of "no less than three gospels."[12] Does he? In Gal 2:7 Paul does make reference to "the gospel of the uncircumcised" (lit., "of the foreskin," i.e., of the gentiles) and to "the gospel of the circumcised" (lit., "of the circumcision," i.e., of the Jews). But does this refer to two gospels or to two mission fields? The next verse specifies the sense by substituting the word "mission" (*apostolē*) for "gospel": "for he who worked through Peter for the mission to the circumcised worked through me, too, for the gentiles" (Gal 2:8). Now, the phrases distinguishing these two missions are not coinages taken up out of common Christian tradition; they are Paul's own.[13] What view of Paul's do they imply ? Can there have been for him more than one "power of God for the salvation of all who believe" (Rom 1:16; cf. 1 Cor 1:18)? If not, then there cannot have been for him more than one gospel. this seems to be the point of Galatians. As for what Dunn counts as the third gospel in Galatians, it is what Paul refers to as "a

[11]J. D. G. Dunn, *Unity and Diversity in the New Testament* (Philadelphia: Westminster, 1977), 23.

[12]*Unity and Diversity*, 23.

[13]See Peter Stuhlmacher, *Das paulinische Evangelium*, 95-7.

different gospel" (Gal 1:6); but he immediately adds: "not that there is any other gospel, but there are some who disturb you and wish to pervert the gospel of Christ" (Gal 1:7). The final words summed up Paul's view: there could be, and was, only one gospel.

It further follows that Christian identity, the subjective correlative of the gospel, lay open to diversity of self-definition (i.e., diverse horizons, self-understanding, and self-shaping). Even apart from the wholly legitimate diversity between the life of Jewish Christianity in Palestine and that of gentile Christianity in the diaspora, Paul affirmed the superior claims of the gospel over the otherwise unimpeachable self-definition of "the strong." In Rom 14-15 the great champion of freedom became the defender of "the weak." When brought into tension with "gospel" (cf. 1 Cor 9:23) or "reign of God" (Rom 14:17), neither circumcision nor uncircumcision counted for anything at all (cf. Gal 6:15). Such was the Christian self-discovery born of the world mission.

Syncretism vs. Development;
Development and Orthodoxy

We can approach the theme of development concretely by tracing its fortunes in two critical discussions: on Christian syncretism and on orthodoxy and heresy.

The discussion of Christian syncretism and of historical data bearing on it goes back to the English deists and the Enlightenment; it became more fully informed and sophisticated during the *floruit* of the history-of-religions school (1890-World War I). In 1903 Hermann Gunkel's slim, 96-page essay on the history-of-religions understanding of the New Testament[14] first of all offered a packed survey of data pertinent to syncretism in pre-Exilic Israel; in the light of

---

[14]Hermann Gunkel, *Zum religionsgeschichtlichen Verständnis des Neuen Testaments* (Göttingen: Vandenhoeck & Ruprecht, 1903).

more extensive discussion it argued that post-Exilic Judaism was a new, syncretistic religion; finally, it detailed evidence relevant to the syncretistic character of early Christianity. Gunkel's representative statement ("Christianity is a syncretistic religion")[15] has been widely taken, at least in Germany and to a lesser extent in America, to be among "the inalienable results of history-of-religions research into primitive Christianity."[16]

Popularized as such in the period following World War II, this view found conveniently compendious exposition in Bultmann's *Primitive Christianity in its Contemporary Setting*.[17] Here the writings of Paul, John, and the Epistle to the Hebrews were invoked to attest the syncretism of hellenistic Christianity. As "Lord" (namely, of Christian cult), Jesus was assimilated to the mystery deities.[18] By baptism and the eucharist the initiates participated in his death and resurrection.[19] At the same time, the sacraments were gnostic symbols and Christian sacramental theology was indistinguishable from that of gnosticism.[20] Again, as "redeemer," Jesus was conceptualized on the model of the myths of pre-Christian gnosis.[21] Gnostic categories were equally at the root of his having lost his identity as "an individual human person" and become a cosmic figure, to whom (or to whose "body") all who had been joined to him by faith and baptism belonged.[22]

It should be emphasized that, having thus described Christianity in syncretistic terms, Bultmann posed an ulte-

[15]*Zum religionsgeschichtliches Verständnis*, 95.

[16]Günter Klein, "Der Synkretismus als theologisches Problem in der ältesten christlichen Apologetik," in *Rekonstruktion und Interpretation* (Munich: Kaiser, 1969), 262-301, cf. 262.

[17]See 175-9.

[18]*Primitive Christianity*, 177.

[19]*Primitive Christianity*, 177.

[20]*Primitive Christianity*, 201.

[21]*Primitive Christianity*, 197f.

[22]*Primitive Christianity*, 178, 202f.

rior question:

> Is Christianity then really a syncretistic religion? Or is
> there a fundamental unity behind all this diversity? . . .
> Does Christianity contain a single, new and unique doc-
> trine of human existence?[23]

The implication, since in fact Bultmann met this test-
question with a triumphant yes, was that, despite a fundamental and far-reaching syncretism at the level of historical
phenomenon, primitive Christianity as self-understanding —
in accord with a "single, new and unique doctrine of human
existence" — relativized and transcended its own syncretistic make-up.

Two issues, distinct but related, have consequently commanded recent discussion of early Christian syncretism.
They are respectively the historical and the analytic issue.

The historical issue is vast and the debate on it volumi-
nous, for "syncretism" is an issue of importance for biblical
religion throughout its whole history. But there is syncretism and syncretism. Syncretism in the strong sense qualifies
the kind of religion that has little identity of its own, but is
the sum of elements assembled from outside itself. Syncretism in the weak sense qualifies the kind of religion that,
having a distinct identity of its own, borrows, transforms
what is borrowed, and enhances its native identity by this
borrowing and transforming. The era of positivism could
not draw any such distinction, for it conceived of identity in
terms of isolation (in Collingwood's phrase, "cut off from
everything else," like a stone).

The two religions attested and celebrated by the Christian
Bible — the religion of Israel in the Old Testament and the
religion of the new Israel in the New — both have had strong
identities, which on the whole were enhanced, not adulter-
ated nor perverted, by openness to the surrounding world
(weak-sense syncretism). To the extent that Yahwism, for

[23]*Primitive Christianity*, 179.

example, found itself actually threatened by syncretism, its champions could not simply accommodate to this by having Baal share the honors with Yahweh, but went on the warpath against Baal. When, during and after the Babylonian Exile, Yahweh was wholly without competitor, Yahwism was still able to absorb foreign influences — again, selectively and constructively. Whereas it was a condition of hellenistic syncretism that gods and goddesses be phenomenal, standing for a reality more basic and real than themselves, Yahweh was absolute, non-interchangeable with other gods, nonsymbolic, irreducible to a figure embodying and revealing a reality more ultimate than himself. The same held true in Christianity, which registered and selectively integrated into itself the influences not only of Judaic apocalyptic, but of the mysteries, of gnosis, and, eventully, of the philosophers from Plato to Proclus. In Gunkel's view classical Yahwism, post-Exilic Judaism, and primitive Christianity were all syncretistic religions; but this is true only if syncretism is understood in the weak sense defined above.[24]

Meantime, research in gnosticism and in the mysteries has been fine-tuned by a more exact definition of terms, a more complete survey of data, and a more rigorous interpretation of data. But the most determinant factor in history-of-religions research is the embodiment of heuristic anticipations in research models or paradigms. It is evident in retrospect that the history-of-religions school, by converting an evolutionary taxonomy and the supposition of important syncretistic borrowing into the main heuristic tool of research, settled in advance the question of whether early Christianity was significantly syncretistic.

Many of those unsympathetic to the undiscriminating

[24]See Ulrich Wilckens, *Der Brief an die Römer, II*, 42-62, on the test-case of baptism as understood in Rom 6. On gnosticism, see R. McL. Wilson, "Nag Hammadi and the New Testament," *New Testament Studies* 28 (1982): 289-302; George W. MacRae, "Nag Hammadi and the New Testament in *Gnosis* (Gottingen: Vandenhoeck & Ruprecht, 1978), 144-57.

theses of Christian syncretism have attempted to counteract or refute it by adopting an alternative analytic model: that of organic process.[25] The analogy with organic process is not useless. It has provided suggestive pointers for the distinction between straightforward syncretism and the power to retain identity while assimilating resources from the surrounding environment.[26] But, as a model designed to interpret change, it is fatally defective. Religions are not living organisms, and little is gained by devising heuristic tools in accord with the broad and downhill path of analogy. The question, then, is whether there is a third model, distinct equally from that of evolution-by-borrowing and from the analogy of organic process.

There is, in fact, a third model, developmental rather than evolutionary. It is transposition, or translation.[27] It supposes that every act of meaning is embedded in a context and that the maintenance of meaning is conditioned by the more or less creative act of transposing meaning from one context to another. In contradistinction to the model of evolutionary syncretism, it affirms, as the starting point of early Christian development, not a low christology, low ecclesiology, etc., but an experience of salvation — "the Easter experience of the disciples," the object of which was

[25]Henri de Lubac, "Le problème du développement du dogme," *Recherches de science religieuse* 25 (1948): 130-60, long ago attacked the "vitalist fallacy" as a model for understanding development. C. F. D. Moule paid close attention to the defects of evolutionary models but little attention to the shortcomings of the "organic development" model, which he argued for in *The Origin of Christology* (Cambridge: Cambridge University Press, 1977), 1-10, 135-41.

[26]See Raimundo Panikkar, "Some Notes on Syncretism and Eclecticism Related to the Growth of Human Consciousness" in *Religious Syncretism in Antiquity* (Missoula: Scholars Press, 1975), 47-62.

[27]It was a joy to me to discover that Newman agreed. He penned a note in a copy of his *Essay on Development*, which reads: "Development equals translation into a new language." See John Coulson, "Front-Line Theology — A Marginal Comment on Newman and Lonergan," in *Looking at Lonergan's Method* (Dublin: Talbot, 1975), 187-93, cf. 188.

the risen Christ — with intrinsic implications of high christology, high ecclesiology, etc. What Dix called Christianity's "leap for life" from the Jewish to the Greek world[28]
imposed the task of signifying in new conceptual as well as
new linguistic terms the realities first encountered and thematized by the first Christians of Jerusalem. In this as in all
comparable cases something of the old was (both deliberately and indeliberately) lost in the translation and significant new elements were gained.

"Development" in this sense was not envisaged in the
work of the history-of-religions school and its heirs. On the
contrary, it was systematically excluded in advance. This
can be verified in some detail respecting, for example, the
history-of-religions account of how Paul (and, we could
now add, the Christian community of Antioch) arrived at
the understanding of Christian baptism found in Romans 6
and allied passages.[29] "Development by transposition"
methodically takes into account (as "evolution by borrowing" methodically leaves out of account) the continuity
between baptism adopted in post-Easter Jerusalem and
baptism as Paul conceived it.[30]

---

[28]Dix, *Jew and Greek*, 55. The phrase is well chosen. As Harnack
observed in *Mission and Expansion* I, 48, the end of relative toleration
for the Christian sect within Judaism coincided with the launching of the
mission to the gentiles.

[29]See Günter Wagner, *Pauline Baptism and the Pagan Mysteries*
(Edinburgh: Oliver & Boyd, 1967); Dix, *Jew and Greek*, 95-9; Wilckens,
Der Brief an die Römer, II, 42-62.

[30]Dix, *Jew and Greek*, worked from start to finish (though without
theoretical elaboration) with a model of "development by transpositions
of meaning" (cf. "translation," 80f.). This may be the secret of the book's
extraordinary sensitivity to the nuances of historical change. Dix's two
cardinal insights were, first, that from the outset Christianity had an
identity of its own (see the treatment of "de-Judaisation" and of the
gospel as a factor distinct from both Judaism and Hellenism, 109-111);
second, that it maintained this identity by bold transpositions of meaning
during and after the swift leap of the gospel from the Jewish to the gentile
world. On baptism, see the previous note.

Finally, a comment on "the analytic issue" in the discussion of Christian syncretism, with a view to signaling its importance in the long run for the theme of Christian development — the nascent development of dogma in the New Testament itself and the immense dogmatic developments in Christianity ever since. It was Hans Jonas's interpretation, not of Christianity but of gnosticism, as a religious philosophy expressing in a maze of myth, symbol, and image a coherent self-understanding and understanding of the world and of the beyond, that helped crystallize Bultmann's grasp of Christianity, too, as a coherent self-understanding and understanding of the world and of God.[31] *E pluribus unum*: regardless of the diverse provenance of myths, symbols, conceptual schemes, and practices, Christianity, like gnosticism, could be recovered as a unified self-understanding. Adopted by kerygma theology as its solution to the problem of Christian syncretism and as a criterion crucial to its program of demythologizing the New Testament, this of itself brilliant interpretative advance was burdened by Jonas with a thesis (on the objectifying function in human cognition)[32] calculated to generate radical misjudgments of Christian development. Thus, the positive functions of the watchword "self-understanding" were frozen into a rigorously limited existentialistic theology unable to make positive sense of the Christian thematization of "truth" in antiquity.[33] This predetermined that theology's

[31]See James M. Robinson, "The Pre-history of Demythologization," *Interpretation* 20 (1966): 65-77, a translation of Robinson's introduction to the second edition (1965) of Hans Jonas's book on Augustine and the Pauline problem of freedom.

[32]Robinson, "Pre-history," provides an account of the context in which Jonas's 1965 Appendix on "The Hermeneutical Structure of Dogma" in his book on Augustine has been significant and influential. The kind of cognitional theory Jonas offered here has come under incisive review and critique by Frederick Lawrence, "Method and Theology as Hermeneutical," in *Creativity and Method* (Milwaukee: Marquette University Press, 1981), 79-104, cf. 83-9, 94-104.

[33]See Bernard Lonergan, *The Way to Nicea* (Philadelphia: Westminster, 1976), 1-19, for a dialectical analysis of development attesting the

view of the debate on early Christian orthodoxy and heresy.

The contemporary conversation on this topic took its point of departure from Walter Bauer's 1934 monograph on second-century Christianity.[34] Bauer's positive achievement was, first, to test the classic Eusebian schematization of the history of orthodoxy and heresy and to lay bare its systematic character, so distinguishing it from history in the modern sense; second, to establish in some detail the fact of variety in second-century Christianity.[35] For the rest, his leading theses, whether on the chronological priority of heresy to orthodoxy in a whole series of Mediterranean centers or on the all but exclusive role of the church of Rome in the late second-century triumph of orthodoxy, have fallen victim in varying degrees to sober and telling critique.[36]

Bauer did not deal with the period that concerns us. The discussion of "diversity" in this period, however, has taken its inspiration from Bauer and extended into this new field of labor the oversights, unserviceable definitions, and strained interpretations to be found at critical points in

remarkable thematization of truth in early Christianity. On the historically unparalleled heightening of this issue in early Christianity, see also the treatment of non-Christian parallels in the forthcoming article of Norbert Brox, "Häresie," in *Reallexikon für Antike und Christentum.*

[34]Walter Bauer, *Orthodoxy and Heresy in Earliest Christianity* (Philadelphia: Fortress, 1971).

[35]See the conclusion of Daniel J. Harrington's review of literature from 1970-1980: "The Reception of Walter Bauer's *Orthodoxy and Heresy in Earliest Christianity* during the Last Decade," *Harvard Theological Review* 75 (1980): 289-98, cf. 297f.

[36]F. W. Norris, "Ignatius, Polycarp, and I Clement: Walter Bauer Reconsidered," *Vigiliae Christianae* 30 (1976): 23-44, offers a trenchant critique not only of Bauer's treatment of Antioch, Asia Minor, and Rome, but of his two leading theses (the priority of heresy to orthodoxy in many centers and the dominant role of Rome in the victory of orthodoxy) and of the methods that Bauer used to substantiate them. The "pre-history" of the McMaster Project (see the preface to the present book) included several dissertations critical of Bauer and variously

Bauer's book.[37] Let Dunn's study of "unity and diversity"[38] illustrate. Among its main purposes was that of extending Bauer's inquiry back into the apostolic era. In the "introduction," where, according to Dunn, the theological and historical issues "are clarified and sharpened," we find gathered in a few pages every prejudicial cliche that has figured in the discussion. Orthodoxy, it seems, has some cumbersome traits. It is "absolute truth," "single" and "clearly defined," any deviation from which is heresy; it is a "final expression" reducing truth to a "formula," which, moreover, is "eternal and unchangeable"; it does not balk at converting Jesus of Nazareth into "a statement." Orthodoxy, in short, is absolute, clearly defined, single, final, eternal, unchangeable propositional reductionism.[39]

What this rhetoric betrays is how out of touch many New Testament scholars are with the now generations-long theo-

reflected in published literature. Harrington (see the previous note) took notice of the articles of Brice L. Martin, "Some Reflections on the Unity of the New Testament," *Studies in Religion* 8 (1979): 143-52 and of David J. Hawkin, "A Reflective Look at the Recent Debate on Orthodoxy and Heresy in Earliest Christianity," *Église et Theologie* 7 (1976): 367-78: not included in Harrington's survey, however, is John C. Meagher, *The Way of the Word* (New York: Seabury, 1975), which took the positive tack of locating in the work of the New Testament writers themselves the norms grounding and regulating their witness.

[37]Bauer's principal oversight: the existence of a native Christian identity correlative to the gospel, and of Christian reflection on it, going back to the earliest Christian literature (the letters of Paul). Unserviceable definitions: those that Bauer gave to "orthodoxy" and "heresy" (see Hawkin, "A Reflective Look" and Norris, "Ignatius, Polycarp, and I Clement," 35f.). Strained interpretations: see Norris not only on how Bauer construed silences but on how he read texts. Norris, 42, rightly protests against the sometimes facile way in which scholars acknowledge the defects of Bauer's argumentation but repeat his conclusions as if they were somehow independent and still intact.

[38]J. D. G. Dunn, *Unity and Diversity in the New Testament* (Philadelphia: Westminster, 1977).

[39]Dunn, *Unity and Diversity*, 1-7.

logical discussion of "development."[40] If primitive Christianity was a living, moving process, developing all the time, so was orthodoxy. How often Paul had to differentiate between successful and failed effort to articulate the gospel, or to draw conclusions from it, or to translate it into life. To be sure, the term "orthodoxy" was absent, but the distinction between successful efforts and failed efforts was no less real on that account.[41]

There seems to be no good reason for agreeing to the strict separation that Dunn has posited between orthodoxy and the historical process, as if orthodoxy itself must share the fate of its Eusebian schematization. Indeed, no good reason appears for conceiving orthodoxy as "absolute," nor as "single," nor as "final," nor as "eternal and unchangeable."[42] "Orthodox" especially qualifies "truth," and the

[40]On the "pre-history" of the theme of development, see Owen Chadwick, *From Bossuet to Newman: The Idea of Doctrinal Development* (Cambridge: Cambridge University Press, 1957), 1-95. On Newman, see Nicholas Lash, *Newman on Development. The Search for an Explanation in History* (Shepherdstown: Patmos, 1975). Lash also offers a select bibliography of literature (up to 1975) on development, 213-45.

[41]C. K. Barrett, "What is New Testament Theology? Some Reflections," *Horizons in Biblical Theology* 3 (1981): 1-22, cf. 12f.: "Truth is best defined over against error; creeds may need the sting of anathemas in their tail. This observation is needed as a supplement to W. Bauer's study of orthodoxy and heresy in the early church. If it is true that Paul conducted no heresy-hunts, it is equally true. . . that he was constantly at work establishing truth over against what he took to be error."

[42]On the inevitable limits of all doctrinal formulation, see Bernard Lonergan, "Philosophy and Theology," in *A Second Collection*, 193f., 197-9, 207f.; see also *Method in Theology*, 323-6. ("Immutability" is a less apt term to apply to dogma than "permanence." Moreover, "dogma" comprehends both a formula and its meaning; "permanence" attaches only to the meaning.) Finally, Nicholas Lash, *Change in Focus* (London: Sheed & Ward, 1973), 36, observes that today "dogmatic" is applied "to something stated in such a manner as to inhibit rational discussion." In contrast to this common usage and connotation, I use "dogmatic argument" in the present chapter to signify an argument having a premiss the truth and certainty of which is appropriated by faith.

truths that come to light whether in Christianity or elsewhere are relative to contexts; these contexts change; development is attendant on the transposition of truth from one
context to another; history includes the study of such transpositions; it thus helps one both to distinguish between
successful and failed transpositions in the past and to effect
successful transpositions in the present.

Behind the flawed discussions just depicted lay a massive
cultural phenomenon: the recoil of the West from its religious heritage, or at least from the classical form of its
religious heritage. This entailed recoil from the thematization of truth-claims and, above all, from any form of dogmatic argument. But such argument has been a part of
Christian history from the start. Without attention to it and
without a serious effort to understand it, the course of
Christian development ceases to be intelligible.

Kerygma and Dogma

When some in Corinth urged the proposition "there is no
raising of dead men" (1 Cor 15:12f.; cf. 15:15f., 29, 32), Paul,
observes Dunn, does not denounce them, he "merely argues
against [their opinion]."[43] He is equally broad-minded on
baptism, not insisting on the sole legitimacy of any particular view.[44] If to the Jews he became like a Jew and to those
outside the Law like one outside the Law, this "clearly
implies" that Paul "varied his proclamation of the gospel
according to circumstances."[45] Undogmatic flexibility was
likewise the key to Paul's "development," illustrated by his
fluctuating eschatological expectations.[46] Basic to the line
of reflection we are following in this chapter is the opposite
view, namely, that primitive Christianity, unabashedly dog-

---

[43]Dunn, *Unity and Diversity*, 24.
[44]Dunn, *Unity and Diversity*, 24.
[45]Dunn, *Unity and Diversity*, 25.
[46]Dunn, *Unity and Diversity*, 25.

matic, was one church committed to one gospel. If Dunn's is a generally accurate account of Paul, it is hard to see how Paul in his own day could have failed to please all parties. If, on the other hand, Paul made himself objectionable to Jews, gentiles, and a great many fellow-Christians, it may be that the portrait of him as free-spiritedly tolerant and self-restrainedly undogmatic is an anachronistic howler. There was plenty of diversity in early Christianity, but neither Paul nor the early Christians in general cultivated an ideal of undogmatic allegiance and opinion.

The kerygmatic and confessional faith formulas that Paul cited in the letters to Rome and Corinth were inherently open to dogmatic use and he sometimes used them dogmatically. Perhaps the best illustration of this is his refutation of those who argued that "there is no raising of dead men" (1 Cor 15:12f.). The faith formula of 1 Cor 15:3-8 is cited as authoritative common ground. The "gospel" that Paul proclaimed was common to all the Apostles: "So, be it I or they, it is in these terms that we proclaim the gospel and it was in these terms that you accepted it in faith" (15:11). This gospel now became the premise for an argument (15:12-34) over whether there was such a thing as the raising of dead men (*anastasis nekron*). The first step was to establish the incompatibility of an answer in the negative with the proclamation of the gospel of Christ's own death and resurrection.[47] This was designed to expose the full destructiveness of "there is no raising of dead men" (vv. 12f.) or "dead men are not raised" (vv. 15f., 29, 32). If it was true that "dead men are not raised," then Christ was not raised (15:13, 16); but if Christ was not raised, the "proclamation" and the "faith" that responded to it were equally empty (15:14), the proclaimers

[47]See Michael Bachmann, "Zur Gedankenführung in I. Kor. 15, 12ff.," *Theologische Zeitschrift* 34 (1978): 265-76. To specialists it will be evident from the following pages that I have rejected exegeses that so construe the argument of 1 Cor 15:1-28 as to put in question Paul's acknowledgement of the independent validity of the kerygma (vv. 1-11). An example: Klaus Wengst, "Der Apostel und die Tradition," *Zeitschrift für Theologie und Kirche* 69 (1972):145-62.

were false witnesses (15:15), the accepters of the proclamation were still in their sins (15:17), dead Christians were lost (15:18), and living Christians were "the most pitiable people of all" (15:19).

Thus far, Paul had simply exploited the logic of "dead men are not raised." But truth mediates reality. If "dead men are not raised" was true, there followed as the real state of affairs the dismal consequences spelled out by Paul. We have to do here not with a shuffling of abstractions but with crucial consequences of incompatible claims to truth. At this point, and for the first time since opening the argument in v. 12, Paul affirmed what he took to be true:

> Now, the truth is that God has raised Christ from the dead, the first-fruits of those who have fallen asleep (1 Cor 15:20).

The next step in the argument was to reaffirm the gospel of 15:3-8 as the premise of a *qal wāḥômer* argument:

> for, just as through a man there came
>   death
> so all the more surely through a man
>   there shall come the resurrection of
>   the dead;
> just as by solidarity with Adam all men
>   die,
> so all the more surely by solidarity
>   with Christ shall all be made to live
>   (15:21f.).

Thereupon Paul presented an apocalyptic preview of the end (15:23-28) and a return to the counter-thesis or antithesis ("dead men are not raised") in order to underscore its incompatibility, first, with baptism "for the sake of [reunion with] the dead [in Christ]" (15:29),[48] then with Paul's own

---

[48]See Maria Raeder, "Vikariatstaufe in 1 Cor 15:29?," *Zeitschrift für die neutestmentliche Wissenschaft* 46 (1955): 258-60.

death-defying mission to the world (15:30-32). The logic of "dead men are not raised" called for a conclusion such as "let us eat and drink, for tomorrow we die" (15:32b).

Dunn represents the Paul of 1 Cor 15 as follows:

> The basic outline of Paul's kerygma in 1 Cor 15.3ff. is limited to the statement about Jesus' death and the assertion of his resurrection. He insists that the Corinthians adhere to that. But when it comes to diversity of belief about whether or not there is a general resurrection to come (15:12 — a question central to the kind of salvation offered in the kerygma), Paul does not denounce those who hold the contrary view to his own as apostates and renegades; he merely argues against it.[49]

These sentences are not false, but they amount to a *suggestio falsi*: as though Paul's non-denunciation of persons set a brake or check on, or otherwise moderated, his denunciation of their propositions. Paul not only "insists that the Corinthians adhere to that," i.e., to the kerygma, he also insists that they abandon what is flatly incompatible with it. The proposition he challenges ("there is no raising of dead men" or "dead men are not raised") so strikes at the truth of the kerygma that, if it is true,

> your faith is futile
> you are still in your sins (15:17).

With v. 20 ("Now, the truth is that God has raised Christ from the dead"), the view that "dead men are not raised" is apodictically rejected. It would reductively invalidate the kerygma (vv. 13-19). Inasmuch as the kerygma is valid (v. 20), the opinion that would invalidate it falls to the ground, false and untenable.

This much seems inescapable. But Paul's dogmatic argument hinged on the *truth* of the kerygma and in 1 Cor 15 he

[49]Dunn, *Unity and Diversity*, 24.

merely presented the content of the kerygma (vv. 3-5) and the authoritative witnesses to the reality of the resurrection (vv. 5-8). Otherwise he appealed to the truth of the kerygma but did not detail its unique status. Earlier, however, namely in 1 Cor 1-4, Paul dealt explicitly with the nature of kerygmatic truth, playing off the kerygma against the wisdom of the world. The historical context was apparently set by the Corinthians' readiness to interpret the message of each teacher as his *logos*, or expression of wisdom, and to choose among them.

Whatever "wisdom" meant to the Corinthians, Paul understood it as a worldly enterprise put out of commission by the wisdom incarnate in Christ crucified. What had wisdom "in this age" (1 Cor 3:18) arrived at? At recovery of the acknowledgement of God, the source of being? No (1 (Cor 1:21). Rather, at an unknowing of God (1 Cor 2:14), a mistaken boasting (1 Cor 1:29-31; cf. 3:21; 4:6-8), and an endless round of debate (1 Cor 1:20; 4:20). The cross disqualified as "futile" the deep thoughts and exchanges of the wise (1 Cor 3:20; cf. Rom 1:21).

But was the truth that had made nonsense of this wisdom itself grounded? Paul's answer pointed to the ineffable. "No one comprehends the things of God (*ta tou theou*) except the Spirit of God" (1 Cor 2:11). The wise man in this age is still Adamic man (*psychikos anthropos*), to whom the gifts of the Spirit are folly (1 Cor 2:14). To Paul the wisdom of God disposing all things neither had nor could have a "ground" more final than itself. Entirely self-authenticating, it could not be measured, plumbed, pronounced upon, for God's "judgments" were unsearchable and his "ways" inscrutable (Rom 11:33). They were not themselves "grounded"; they grounded everything. As realized in the destiny of his Son and formulated in the kerygma, the judgment and the way of God definitively settled issues that left the wise of the world installed in their folly or, at best, unclear and unsure. For the judgments and ways of God determined what was finally wise and finally foolish. They came to the notice of man only by God's gracious gift.

The supposedly startling difference between Gal 1:12 and

1 Cor 15:2[50] on how Paul came into possession of his "gospel" was actually a difference of perspective, no more. The question Paul met in Galatians was whether his participation in this ministry was derived, dependent on those who were Apostles before him. He denied it. Like the other Apostles he had been immediately commissioned by the risen Christ (a point also explicitly made in 1 Cor 15:8). For Paul there was always one and only one gospel communicated by revelation and by tradition, for the point of tradition was to hand on a revelation. This gospel was the disclosure, variously honed to formulaic expression, of Christ as *kyrios*, of salvation in Christ as *kyrios*, and of the events — his death "for us" and resurrection from the dead — that showed him to be the *kyrios* of all.[51] The content of the gospel was both an immediate revelation to Paul (Gal 1:12; cf. 1 Cor 15:8) and a tradition that he himself received (1 Cor 15:2). It could not have been otherwise if, as Paul insisted, the gospel was the power of salvation for all who accepted it in faith.

In one sense then, namely, as incarnating the wisdom of God, the gospel was not "grounded" at all; there was nothing more fundamental than itself to ground it. But as coming to the notice of man, it was grounded in a revelation event. God himself, by the revelation of his Son, "gave us the ministry of reconciliation" (2 Cor 5:18: cf. vv. 19f.). In between God's shaping an economy of salvation and his enacting it in the world through that ministry, was this moment of "revelation" (Gal 1:12, 16: cf. *idein/ōphthēnai*: 1 Cor 9:1; 15:5-8) to chosen witnesses and envoys. In the order of man's coming to know, it was this revelation that

---

[50]See, e.g., Leonhard Goppelt, *Theology of the New Testament*, II, Grand Rapids: Eerdmans, 1982, 40f., on the tension (which, however, Goppelt takes to be resolvable) between the two texts.

[51]This is a paraphrase of Schlier's definition of the kerygma in "Kerygma und Sophia," 214. For a summary of Schlier's treatment of dogmatic thought and practice in the New Testament, see Werner Löser, "Dimensionen der Auslegung des Neuen Testaments," *Theologie und Philosophie* 57 (1982): 481-97, cf. 492-6.

grounded the gospel, grounded man's discovery of the status of the cross as wisdom and its reduction of this-worldly wisdom to nonsense. Here was new creation in the sphere of truth (cf. "the truth of the gospel" in Gal 2:5, 14); and, inasmuch as reality becomes known by one's knowing what is true (*ens per verum innotescit*), here was — illuminating, mysterious, enhancing mystery by illuminating it — an unconcealing (*a-lethēia*) to faith of a new order of reality.

Primitive Christianity, through its spokesman Paul, understood the reception of the gospel as submission to God's power (1 Cor 1:18, 24; Rom 1:16), wisdom (1 Cor 1:24) and righteousness (Rom 1:17; 10:3). True in itself, the gospel mediated to whoever accepted it in faith the fulfillment of the promises. Foundational to the quest of further truth, it was a premise of apodictic argument. This gospel was "grounded" only in the sense that the promise to the patriarchs and the prophets came to the light of fulfillment in the Easter revelation to the Apostles, from Cephas to Paul (1 Cor 15:5-8). The content of kerygmatic truth was the resurrection of Christ, with an open "as-structure": as revelation (Gal 1:16), as fact (1 Cor 15:3-5; cf. 1 Thess 4:14), as reversal (Acts 2:23f.; 3:15; 4:10f.; 5:30; 10:39f.), as vindication (Acts 2:22-24; 3:13-15), as reward (Phil 2:9), as fulfillment (Rom 8:34), as sign and promise (1 Cor 15:20; Rom 8:29; Acts 26:23), as new creation (1 Cor 15:45), as enthronement (Rom 1:4; 8:34), as blessing (Rom 4:25), as pattern (Rom 6:5), and, finally, in "the Easter experience of the disciples," as the justification of the ungodly.

"One New Man"

The New Testament writers were all churchmen. Paul and the Paulinists, Mark and Matthew, Luke and John and the rest all seem to have been aware of ecclesial diversity and of its potential challenge to unity. They recoiled from division. They were intent on Christian unity as a goal of Christian existence. The givenness of unity through baptism and the eucharist and the cultivation of this given unity were particularly insistent New Testament themes.

If diversity be confounded with division, the canon of the New Testament would indeed ground the divisions of the church.[52] But does diversity amount to division? We have adopted three terms — identity, self-definition, and development — meant to mediate an insight into the possibility and reality of unity in diversity. Christian identity, rooted in the experience of salvation, correlative to the gospel, susceptible of diverse self-definitions, open to progress as to regress and collapse, grounded the possibility of the unity passionately sought by Paul and celebrated as his achievement by the post-Pauline church. Carried by refugees to Syria and by missionaries to the Mediterranean world, this "identity" was as much a part of early Christian history as the solid antiquities that engage a coin-collector. (If antiquarians and their positivist brethren among the historians are hard put to acknowledge this, it simply shows that the history of early Christianity is too important to be left to them.) Our concluding observations on identity, self-definition, and development touch the impact of the world mission on the church that launched it and illustrate this impact by the deutero-Pauline letters to the Colossians and Ephesians.

The mission was a transforming experience. It changed the world of the mission field, for it proved to have unique relevance to Mediterranean man and a uniquely deep impact on him — hence the steady and finally irresistible success of the mission. It changed the men who carried out the mission, converting their lives into a dangerous venture (1 Cor 15:30-32; 2 Cor 11:23-29), shaping their thought in explicitly universalist terms (Pauline letters), turning the eschatological scenario (Rom 9-11) into a cosmic and sacramental vision of things (Col and Eph). It changed the fortunes of Christianity, effecting its transition from a Jewish

---

[52]See Ernst Käsemann, "The Canon of the New Testament and the Unity of the Church," in *Essays on New Testament Themes* (London: SCM, 1964), 95-107.

sect with a self-understanding as "Israel restored" to a world-wide movement with a self-understanding as "one new man" (Eph 2:15).

Colossians, a letter addressed in the last analysis to the whole circle of the baptized in Asia Minor, was meant to commend Christian fidelity in the face of the incursions of a syncretistic (gnostic) "philosophy" (Col 2:8). It exhibited a post-Pauline christology, ecclesiology, sacramentology, and eschatology. Since in some instances the point of departure was definably Pauline, at least some of the letter's transpositions of meaning can be more or less exactly traced and others made the object of reasonably probable conjecture. Behind the christology of the Christ hymn in Col 1:15-20 stood, not a gnostic hymn,[53] but a Jewish-Christian transposition of wisdom motifs into christology. Behind the body-of-Christ ecclesiology of Colossians stood Paul's view of the baptized as simultaneously the Israel of God, a new creation sublating all human divisions "in Christ," and the body of Christ realized in each ecclesial community. In deutero-Pauline theology this became the theme of "one new man" composed of body (Jews and gentiles baptized into Christ), which had yet to grow to full stature, and head (Christ), which gave articulation and vitality to the whole. Behind Colossians' theology of baptism stood that of Antioch and of Paul. Finally, the Pauline eschatological scenario — the world mission, understood as the winning over of "the full number of the gentiles" (Rom 11:25) and as the foreordained condition of the parousia; the age-old theme of the pilgrimage of the nations converted into Paul's "offer-

---

[53]Käsemann argues for a gnostic hymn, "A Primitive Christian Baptismal Liturgy," in *Essays on New Testament Themes*, 154-9; but see the critiques of Reinhard Deichgräber, *Gotteshymnus und Christushymnus in der fruhen Christenheit* (Göttingen: Vandenhoeck & Ruprecht, 1967), 153f.; J. T. Sanders, *The New Testament Christological Hymns* (Cambridge: Cambridge University Press, 1977), 79-87; Klaus Wengst, *Christologische Formeln und Lieder des Urchristentums* (Gütersloh: Mohn, ²1973), 171-80; and Eduard Lohse, *Colossians and Philemon* (Philadelphia: Fortress, 1971), 45f.

ing of the gentiles" (Rom 15:16); and, last, the parousia to be accompanied by the salvation of "all Israel" (Rom 11:26) — yielded to a vision of the baptismal transfer of Jew and gentile alike "from the dominion of darkness" to "the kingdom of his beloved Son" (Col 1:13). What remained of the eschatological scenario was the expectation of finally "appearing" together with Christ when he "appeared" (Col 3:3). The content of history had now become simply the coming to term of "the secret," namely "Christ in you" (i.e., in the gentiles).

Unlike Colossians, Ephesians did not target a concrete danger. Still, both compositions belonged to the same spiritual world: a Christian counter-gnosis, rooted, like Pauline theology itself, in the biblical heritage and, like Pauline theology, pervasively conditioned by the soteriology of the world mission. Its contrasts were as remarkable as its positive ties with the theology of the certainly authentic Pauline letters. Much of the sting had been taken out of the Pauline dialectic in the present of pain, anxiety, humiliation, privation, and failure with the joy and peace of the Spirit (but cf. Col 1:24). Baptism was now conceived (in closer accord with the liturgical tradition on which Paul drew than with Paul's own view of baptism) as already realized resurrection — a conclusion Paul had been careful to avoid. Above all, the eschatology of the parousia, which had been a constant in Pauline thought from the first to the last of his letters, now suffered a sharp loss of meaning to the advantage of sacramental soteriology.

The role of the parousia was reduced to the public revelation of what had already been settled (Col 3:3f.). But it remains unclear whether the spiritual world of Colossians and Ephesians had its genetic explanation in a collapse of the expectation of an imminent parousia. Without hazarding this common but dicey conjecture, let it suffice to define the main thematic focus on "the secret that is Christ" (Col 4:3; Eph 3:4; cf. Col 1:26f.; 2:2; Eph 1:9; 3:3, 9): the vision of Greek with Jew in the inheritance of eschatological promise. This — the outcome of the world mission — had been "the secret hidden for ages and generations" (Col 1:26), reserved for "the fullness of time" (Eph 1:10). In the eschatologically "new man" (Eph 2:15) destined to come to maturity as "perfect man" (Eph 4:13) post-Pauline theology projected its interpretation of the glorified Christ, who, having shed his blood (Col 1:20, 2:14; Eph 2:13) in the cause of the reconciliation (Col 1:20, 22; Eph 2:16) of man with man and of all with God, encompassed in himself the transcendent unity of Jew and gentile.

In this redemptive context "church" was no mere social phenomenon. It was mankind made new in the new Adam. The fruit of the world mission, it was the resolution in principle of the human dilemma, the human drama of division and conflict.

This universal church stood in conscious continuity with the confessional traditions of Jerusalem and Antioch. It made explicit what we had to postulate as a faith conviction of the *hellēnistai*, namely, that the world church — and, both explicitly (Eph 2:13-18) and by implication, the world mission — hinged on the already realized universal Lordship of Christ (Col 1:15-20; 2:9f.; 3:1, 11; Eph 1:9f., 20-23; 2:6f., 13-18; 4:4-10). The inclusion of the gentiles in God's saving act had been integral to the faith convictions of both Jesus and the *hebraioi* of Jerusalem. The innovation of the *hellēnistai* lay, not in pioneering the idea of this inclusion, but in rescheduling its fulfillment from "the end" to the present. The affirmation of the already realized universal Lordship of Christ found robust expression in Paul and grandiose expression in the Pauline school.

Though biblically grounded, Jesus' inclusion of the gentiles in salvation was a basic and distinctive intention (see especially the eucharistic words) far from common among his contemporaries. The universalist aspect of their realized eschatology made the Christian *hellēnistai* of Jerusalem pariahs in Judaism. Though the final and climactic form of the expression of Christ's universal Lordship had to await the deutero-Pauline letters, it is clear in retrospect that Christianity had never been more itself, more consistent with Jesus and more evidently en route to its own future, than in the launching of the world mission. If the words of

Jesus on the pilgrimage of the nations (Matt 8:11f.; par. Luke 13:28f.) breathe an atmosphere entirely different from the learned theology of Colossians and Ephesians, it was nevertheless not without historic transpositions of meaning from one such context to the other that the apostles from Cephas and John to Paul and his followers made the world mission a reality.

The mission became a reality in continuous dependence on what Christ himself was. And he was, first of all, what Israel had understood her scriptures to say she herself would become: one like a (son of) man, whose reign would be everlasting (Dan 7:13f.),[54] appointed Servant (Isa 44:1f.; 49:6; cf. Mark 1:11; parr. Matt 3:17; Luke 3:22; Mark 9:7; parr. Matt 17:5; Luke 9:35; Luke 2:32; Acts 13:47), and Son of God (Hos 11:1; Ex 4:22; Matt 2:15; cf. 4:3f.; par. Luke 4:3f.). In accord with Israel's messianic dream, he had been the Messiah of promise, who would build God's house: a sanctuary secure against death (2 Sam 7:13; cf. Hag 1:1f.; 2:20-23; Zech 6:12f.; Matt 16:18; Mark 14:58; parr. Matt 26:61; John 2:19). Far beyond the messianic dream, he became by his resurrection from the dead the last Adam and life-giving spirit (1 Cor 15:45). He offered, free, what the world at large had not dared to hope for: a share in eternal life, resurrection from the dead, the final triumph of good. In time this offer would penetrate and newly integrate all classes of society in the Empire and inspire a thorough revision of all their categories of meaning. The Lord of the mission remade both man and his world.

[54]See C. F. D. Moule, *The Origin of Christology* 151f.

Bibliography

Arens, Eduard. *The ELTHON-Sayings in the Synoptic Tradition. A Historico-Critical Investigation.* Freiburg: Universitätsverlag; Göttingen: Vandenhoeck & Ruprecht, 1976.

Aus, Roger D. "Paul's Travel Plans to Spain and the 'Full Number of the Gentiles' of Rom. XI 25." *Novum Testamentum* 21 (1979): 232-62.

Bachmann, Michael. "Zur Gedankenführung in I. Kor. 15, 12ff." *Theologische Zeitschrift* 34 (1978): 265-76.

Barrett, C. K. "Paul and the 'Pillar' Apostles." in *Studia Paulina in honorem Johannes de Zwaan, septuagenarii.* Haarlem: Bohm, 1953. Pp. 1-19.

——————. *From First Adam to Last. A Study in Pauline Theology.* London: Black, 1962.

——————. "The House of Prayer and the Den of Thieves." In *Jesus und Paulus.* [W. G. Kümmel Festschrift.] Edited by E. Earle Ellis and Erich Grässer. Göttingen: Vandenhoeck & Ruprecht, 1975. Pp. 13-20.

_____. "What is New Testament Theology? Some Reflections." *Horizons in Biblical Theology* 3 (1981): 1-22.

Bauer, Walter. *Orthodoxy and Heresy in Earliest Christianity.* 2nd ed. Edited by Georg Strecker. Translated by R. A. Kraft and others. English Translation edited by R. A. Kraft and Gerhard Krodel. Philadelphia: Fortress, 1971.

Beker, J. Christian. *Paul the Apostle. The Triumph of God in Life and Thought.* Philadelphia: Fortress, 1980.

Betz, Otto. "Rechfertigung in Qumran." In *Rechtfertigung.* [Ernst Käsemann Festschrift.] Edited by Johannes Friedrich, Wolfgang Pohlmann, and Peter Stuhlmacher. Tübingen: Mohr; Göttingen: Vandenhoeck & Ruprecht, 1976. Pp. 17-36.

_____. "Rechtfertigung und Heiligung." In *Rechtfertigung Realismus Universalismus in biblischer Sicht.* [Adolf Köberle Festschrift.] Edited by Gotthold Müller. Darmstadt: Wissenschaftliche Buchgesellschaft, 1978. Pp. 30-44.

Blank, Josef. *Paulus und Jesus. Eine theologische Grundlegung.* Studien zum Alten und Neuen Testament 18. Munich: Kösel, 1968.

Brown, Raymond E. and John P. Meier, *Antioch and Rome. New Testament Cradles of Catholic Christianity.* New York-Ramsey: Paulist, 1983.

Brox, Norbert. "Häresie." *Reallexikon für Antike und Christentum* (forthcoming).

Bruce, F. F.   "Further Thoughts on Paul's Autobiography (Galatians 1:11-2:14)." In *Jesus und Paulus.* [W. G. Kümmel Festschrift.] edited by E. Earle Ellis and Erich Grässer. Göttingen: Vandenhoeck & Ruprecht, 1975. Pp. 21-9.

Bühner, Jan-Adolf.   *Der Gesandte und sein Weg im 4. Evangelium. Die kultur- und religionsgeschichlichen Grundlagen der johanneischen Sendungschristologie sowie ihre traditionsgeschichtliche Entwicklung.* Wissenschaftliche Untersuchungen zum Neuen Testament, 2. Reihe, 2. Tübingen: Mohr, 1977.

Bultmann, Rudolf .   *Theology of the New Testament.* Translated by Kendrick Grobel. New York: Scribners, 1951-55.

_____.   *Primitive Christianity in its Contemporary Setting.* Translated by R. H. Fuller. New York: World, Meridian, 1956.

_____.   "DIKAIOSYNE THEOU." *Journal of Biblical Literature* 83 (1964): 12-16.

_____.   "The Significance of the Old Testament for the Christian Faith." In *The Old Testament and Christian Faith.* Edited by B. W. Anderson. New York: Harper & Row, 1963. Pp. 8-35.

_____.   "Prophecy and Fulfillment." In *Essays on Old Testament Hermeneutics.* Edited by Claus Westermann and James L. Mays. Richmond: Knox, 1960. Pp. 50-75.

Burkitt, F. C.   *Christian Beginnings.* London: University of London Press, 1924.

Butterworth, E. A. S.   *The Tree at the Navel of the Earth.*
Berlin: de Gruyter, 1970.

Catchpole, David R.   "Paul, James and the Apostolic
Decree." *New Testament Studies* 23 (1977): 428-44.

Causse, Antonin.   "Le pèlerinage à Jérusalem et la première
Pentecôte." *Revue d'Histoire et de Philosophie religieuses* 20 (1940): 120-41.

Chadwick, Owen.   *From Bossuet to Newman: The Idea of
Doctrinal Development.* Cambridge: At the University Press, 1957.

Chapman, D. J.   "St. Paul and the Revelation to St. Peter,
Matt. XVI, 17." *Revue Bénédictine* 29 (1912): 133-47.

Collingwood, R. G.   *The Idea of History.* Oxford: Oxford
University Press, 1946.

Conzelmann, Hans. *An Outline of the Theology of the New
Testament.* Translated by John Bowden. London:
SCM, 1969.

_____. "Literaturbericht zu den synoptischen
Evangelien." *Theologische Rundschau* 37 (1972):
220-72; 43 (1978): 3-51; 321-27.

_____. "Die Rechtfertigungslehre des Paulus: Theo-
logie oder Anthropologie?" In *Theologie als Schriftauslegung. Aufsätze zum Neuen Testament.* Beiträge
zur evangelischen Theologie 65. Munich: Kaiser,
1974. Pp. 191-206.

Coreth, Emerich.   *Grundfragen der Hermeneutik. Ein
philosophischer Beitrag.* Philosophie in Einzeldar-
stellungen 3. Freiburg-Basel-Wien: Herder, 1969.

Coulson, John. "Front-Line Theology — a Marginal Comment on Newman and Lonergan." In *Looking at Lonergan's Method.* Edited by Patrick Corcoran. Dublin: Talbot, 1975. Pp. 187-93.

Cullmann, Oscar. *The Christology of the New Testament.* Translated by S. C. Guthrie and C. A. M. Hall. Rev. ed. London: SCM; Philadelphia: Westminster, 1963.

Dahl, Nils Alstrup. "The Crucified Messiah." In *The Crucified Messiah and Other Essays.* Minneapolis: Augsburg, 1974. Pp. 10-36.

_____. "The Missionary Theology in the Epistle to the Romans." In *Studies in Paul. Theology for the Early Christian Mission.* Minneapolis: Augsburg, 1977. Pp. 70-94.

Davies, W. D. *The Gospel and the Land. Early Christianity and Jewish Territorial Doctrine.* Berkeley-Los Angeles-London: University of California Press, 1974.

Deichgräber, Reinhard. *Gotteshymnus und Christushymnus in der frühen Christenheit. Untersuchungen zu Form, Sprache und Stil der frühchristlichen Hymnen.* Studien zur Umwelt des Neuen Testaments 5. Gottingen: Vandenhoeck & Ruprecht, 1967.

Denis, A. -M. "La fonction apostolique et la liturgie nouvelle en esprit. Étude thématique des métaphores pauliniennes du culte nouveau." *Revue d'Histoire et de Philosophie religieuses* 42 (1958): 401-36; 616-56.

Dix, Dom Gregory. *Jew and Greek. A Study in the Primitive Church.* Westminster: Dacre Press, 1953.

Dülmen, Andrea van. *Die Theologie des Gesetzes bei Paulus.* Stuttgarter biblische Monographien 5. Stuttgart: Katholisches Bibelwerk, 1968.

Dunn, James D. G.   *Unity and Diversity in the New Testament. An Inquiry into the Character of Earliest Christianity.* Philadelphia: Westminster, 1977.

Dupont, Jacques.   "La conversion de Paul et son influence sur sa conception du salut par la foi." In *Foi et salut selon S. Paul (Epitre aux Romains 1, 16).* Analecta Biblica 42. Rome: Biblical Institute Press, 1970. Pp. 67-88. ET, "The Conversion of Paul and its Influence on his Understanding of Salvation by Faith." "In *Apostolic History and the Gospel.* [F. F. Bruce Festschrift.] Edited by W. W. Gasque and R. P. Martin. Grand Rapids: Eerdmans, 1970. Pp. 176-94.

Eichholz, Georg.   *Die Theologie des Paulus im Umriss.* 2nd rev. ed. Neukirchen-Vluyn: Neukirchener Verlag, 1977.

Ellis, E. E.   "The Circumcision Party and the Early Christian Mission." In *Prophecy and Hermeneutic in Early Christianity. New Testament Essays.* Tübingen: Mohr, 1978. Pp. 116-28.

Fitzmyer, Joseph A.   "The Letter to the Romans." In *The Jerome Biblical Commentary.* Edited by R. E. Brown, J. A. Fitzmyer, and R. E. Murphy. 2 vols. Englewood Cliffs: Prentiss-Hall, 1968. Vol. 2, pp. 291-331.

_____. "Reconciliation in Pauline Theology." In *To Advance the Gospel. New Testament Studies.* New York: Crossroad, 1981. Pp. 162-85.

——————. "Paul and the Law." In *To Advance the Gospel. Pp. 186-201.*

——————. See also under Reumann, John.

Friedrich, Gerhard. *Die Verkündigung des Todes Jesu im Neuen Testament.* Biblisch-Theologische Studien 6. Neukirchen-Vluyn: Neukirchener Verlag, 1982.

Goppelt, Leonhard. "Typos." In *Theological Dictionary of the New Testament.* Edited by Gerhard Kittel and Gerhard Friedrich, 9 vols. Translated by Geoffrey W. Bromiley. Grand Rapids: Eerdmans, 1964-74. Vol. 8, pp. 246-59.

——————. *Theologie des Neuen Testaments. 2. Vielfalt und Einheit des apostolischen Christuszeugnisses.* Edited by Jürgen Roloff, Göttingen: Vandenhoeck & Ruprecht, 1976.

Gray, John. *The Biblical Doctrine of the Reign of God.* Edinburgh: T. & T. Clark, 1979.

Gunkel, Hermann. *Zum religionsgeschichtlichen Verständnis des Neuen Testaments.* Göttingen: Vandenhoeck & Ruprecht, 1903.

Gunneweg, A.H.J. *Understanding the Old Testament.* Translated by John Bowden. Old Testament Library. Philadelphia: Westminster, 1978.

Güting, Eberhard. "Der geographische Horizont der sogenannten Völkerliste des Lukas (Acta 2.9-11)." *Zeitschrift für die neutestamentliche Wissenschaft* 66 (1975): 149-69.

Hahn, Ferdinand.   *Mission in the New Testament.* Studies in Biblical Theology 47. Translated by Frank Clarke. London: 1965.

_____. *The Titles of Jesus in Christology. Their History in Early Christianity.* Translated by Harold Knight and George Ogg. Cleveland: World, 1969.

_____. "Taufe und Rechtfertigung. Ein Beitrag zur paulinischen Theologie in ihrer Vor- und Nachgeschichte." In *Rechtfertigung.* [Ernst Käsemann Festschrift.] Edited by Johannes Friedrich, Wolfgang Pohlmann, and Peter Stuhlmacher. Tübingen: Mohr; Göttingen: Vandenhoeck & Ruprecht, 1976. Pp. 95-124.

Harnack, Adolf von. *Die Apostelgeschichte.* Leipzig: Hinrichs, 1908.

_____. *The Mission and Expansion of Christianity in the First Three Centuries.* Translated by James Moffatt. London: Williams and Norgate, 1908.

Harrington, Daniel J.   "The Reception of Walter Bauer's *Orthodoxy and Heresy in Earliest Christianity* During the Last Decade." *Harvard Theological Review* 73 (1980): 289-98.

Hawkin, David J.   "A Reflective Look at the Recent Debate on Orthodoxy and Heresy in Earliest Christianity." *Église et Théologie* 7 (1976): 367-78.

Hengel, Martin. "Die Ursprünge der christlichen Mission." *New Testament Studies* 18 (1971-72): 15-38.

_____. "Christologie und neutestamentliche Chronologie. Zu einer Aporie in der Geschichte des Urchristentums." In *Neues Testament und Geschichte* [Oscar

Cullmann Festschrift]. Zurich: Theologischer Verlag; Tübingen: Mohr, 1972. Pp. 43-67.

──────. "Zwischen Jesus und Paulus. Die 'Hellenisten,' die 'Sieben' und Stephanus (Apg 6, 1-15; 7,54-8,3)." *Zeitschrift für Theologie und Kirche* 72 (1975): 151-206.

──────. *Acts and the History of Earliest Christianity.* Translated by John Bowden. London: SCM, 1979.

Hickling, C. J. A. "Centre and Periphery in the Thought of Paul." In *Studia Biblica 1978: III. Papers on Paul and Other New Testament Authors.* Edited by E. A. Livingstone. Sheffield: JSOT Press, 1980. Pp. 199-214.

Hofius, Otfried. *Der Christushymnus Philipper 2, 6-11. Untersuchungen zu Gestalt und Aussage eines urchristlichen Psalms.* Wissenschaftliche Untersuchungen zum Neuen Testament 17. Tübingen: Mohr, 1976.

──────. "Erwägungen zur Gestalt und Herkunft des paulinischen Versöhnungsgedankens." *Zeitschrift für Theologie und Kirche* 77 (1980): 186-99.

──────. "'Gott hat unter uns aufgerichtet das Wort von der Versöhnung' (2 Kor 5:19)." *Zeitschrift für die neutestamentliche Wissenschaft* 71 (1980):3-20.

Holmberg, Bengt. *Paul and Power. The Structure of Authority in the Primitive Church as Reflected in the Pauline Epistles.* Coniectanea Biblica, New Testament Series, II. Lund: Gleerup, 1978.

Hooker, Morna D. "Interchange in Christ." *Journal of Theological Studies* 22 (1971): 349-61.

Jeremias, Joachim. *Jesus' Promise to the Nations.* Translated by S. H. Hooke. Studies in Biblical Theology 24. London: SCM, 1958.

_____. "Untersuchungen zum Quellenproblem der Apostelgeschichte." *Zeitschrift für die neutestamentliche Wissenschaft* 36 (1937): 205-21.

_____. *The Parables of Jesus.* Rev. ed. Translated by S. H. Hooke. London: SCM, 1963.

_____. "Die älteste Schicht der Menschensohnlogien in den Evangelien." *Zeitschrift für die neutestamentliche Wissenschaft* 58 (1967): 159-72.

_____. "The Key to Pauline Theology." *Expository Times* 76 (1964): 27-30.

_____. *New Testament Theology I. The Proclamation of Jesus.* Translated by John Bowden. London: SCM; New York: Scribners, 1971.

_____. *The Servant of God.* See entry under Zimmerli, Walther and Joachim Jeremias.

Jervell, Jacob. "Das gespaltene Israel und die Heidenvölker. Zur Motivierung der Heidenmission in der Apostelgeschichte." *Studia Theologica* 19 (1965): 68-96. ET: "The Divided People of God. The Restoration of Israel and Salvation for the Gentiles." In *Luke and the People of God. A New Look at Luke-Acts.* Minneapolis: Augsburg, 1972. Pp. 41-74.

_____. "The Mighty Minority." *Studia Theologica* 34 (1980): 13-38.

Jüngel, Eberhard. *Paulus und Jesus. Eine Untersuchung zur Präzisierung der Frage nach dem Ursprung der Christologie*. Hermeneutische Untersuchungen zur Theologie 2. 5th ed. Tübingen: Mohr, 1979.

Käsemann, Ernst. "The Problem of the Historical Jesus." In *Essays on New Testament Themes*. Translated by W. J. Montague. Studies in Biblical Theology 41. London: SCM, 1964. Pp. 15-47.

_____. "The Canon of the New Testament and the Unity of the Church." In *Essays on New Testament Themes*. Translated by W. J. Montague. Studies in Biblical Theology 41. London: SCM, 1964. Pp. 95-107.

_____. "A Primitive Christian Baptismal Liturgy." In *Essays on New Testament Themes*. Translated by W. J. Montague. Studies in Biblical Theology 41. London: SCM, 1964. Pp. 149-68.

_____. "Zum Verständnis von Römer 3, 24-26." In *Exegetische Versuche und Besinnungen*. 2 vols. Göttingen: Vandenhoeck & Ruprecht, 1960-65. Vol. 1, pp. 96-100.

_____. "'The Righteousness of God' in Paul." *In New Testament Questions of Today*. Translated by W. J. Montague. London: SCM, 1969. Pp. 168-82.

_____. "Justification and Salvation History in the Epistle to the Romans." In *Perspectives on Paul*. Translated by Margaret Kohl. London: SCM, 1971. Pp. 60-78.

_____. "On Paul's Anthropology." In *Perspectives on Paul.* Translated by Margaret Kohl. London: SCM, 1971. Pp. 1-31.

_____. *An die Römer*. Handbuch zum Neuen Testament 8a. Tubingen: Mohr, 1973.

_____. "Die Neue Jesus-frage." In *Jésus aux origines de la christologie*. Edited by Jacques Dupont. Gembloux: Duculot, 1975. Pp. 47-57.

Kasting, Heinrich. *Die Anfänge der urchristlichen Mission. Eine historische Untersuchung*. Munich: Kaiser, 1969.

Kertelge, Karl. "*Dikaioō*." In *Exegetisches Wörterbuch zum Neuen Testament*. Edited by Horst Balz and Gerhard Schneider. Vol. 1. Stuttgart: Kohlhammer, 1980. Col. 796-807.

_____. "*Dikaiosyne*." In *Exegetisches Wörterbuch zum Neuen Testament*. Edited by Horst Balz and Gerhard Schneider. Vol. 1. Stuttgart: Kohlhammer, 1980. Col. 784-96.

_____. "*Rechtfertigung" bei Paulus. Studien zur Struktur und zum Bedeutungsgehalt des paulinischen Rechtfertigungsbegriffs*. Neutestamentliche Abhandlungen (Neue Folge) 3. 2nd rev. ed. Münster: Aschendorff, 1967.

Klein, Günter. "Gottesgerechtigkeit als Thema der neuesten Paulus-Forschung." In *Rekonstruktion und Interpretation. Gesammelte Aufsätze zum Neuen Testament*. Munich: Kaiser, 1969. Pp. 225-36.

_____. "Der Synkretismus als theologisches Problem in der ältesten christlichen Apologetik." In *Rekonstruktion und Interpretation. Gesammelte Aufsätze zum Neuen Testament*. Munich: Kaiser, 1969. Pp. 262-301.

_____. "Sündenverständnis und theologia crucis bei Paulus." In *Theologia Crucis—Signum Crucis.* [Erich Dinkler Festschrift.] Edited by C. Andresen and G. Klein. Tübingen: Mohr, 1979. Pp. 249-82.

Kraabel, A. T. "The Disappearance of the 'God-Fearers.'" *Numen* 28 (1981):113-26.

Lash, Nicholas. *Change in Focus. A Study of Doctrinal Change and Continuity.* London: Sheed & Ward, 1973.

_____. *Newman on Development. The Search for an Explanation in History.* Shepherdstown, West Virginia: Patmos, 1975.

Lawrence, Frederick. "Method and Theology as Hermeneutical." In *Creativity and Method: Essays in Honor of Bernard Lonergan.* Edited by Matthew L. Lamb. Milwaukee: Marquette University Press, 1981. Pp. 79-104.

Leaney, A. R. C. *The Rule of Qumran and its Meaning. Introduction, Translation and Commentary.* Philadelphia: Westminster, 1966.

Léon-Dufour, Xavier. *Le partage du pain eucharistique selon le Nouveau Testament.* Parole de Dieu. Paris: Seuil, 1982.

Lohfink, Gerhard. "Christologie und Geschichtsbild in Apg 3, 19-21." *Biblische Zeitschrift* 13 (1969): 223-41.

Lohse, Eduard. *Märtyrer und Gottesknecht. Untersuchungen zur urchistlichen Verkündigung vom Sühntod Jesu Christi.* 2nd ed. Forschungen zur Religion und Literatur des Alten und Neuen Testaments 64. Göttingen: Vandenhoeck & Ruprecht, 1963.

_____. *Colossians and Philemon. A Commentary on the Epistles to the Colossians and to Philemon.* Translated by W. R. Poehlmann and Robert J. Karris. Philadelphia: Fortress, 1971.

Lonergan, Bernard J. F. *Insight. A Study of Human Understanding.* New York: Longmans, 1958.

_____. *Method in Theology.* New York: Herder and Herder, 1972.

_____. "The Ongoing Genesis of Methods." *Studies in Religion/Sciences Religieuses* 6 (1976-77): 341-55.

_____. "Philosophy and Theology." In *A Second Collection. Papers by Bernard J. F. Lonergan.* Edited by William F. J. Ryan and Bernard J. Tyrrell. New York: Herder and Herder, 1974. Pp. 193-208.

_____. "The Subject." In *A Second Collection. Papers by Bernard J. F. Lonergan.* Edited by William F. J. Ryan and Bernard J. Tyrrell. New York: Herder and Herder, 1974. Pp. 69-86.

_____. "Theology and Man's Future." In *A Second Collection. Papers by Bernard J. F. Lonergan.* Edited by William F. J. Ryan and Bernard J. Tyrrell. New York: Herder and Herder, 1974. Pp. 135-47.

_____. *The Way to Nicea. The Dialectical Development of Trinitarian Theology.* Translated by Conn O'Donovan. Philadelphia: Westminster, 1976.

Löser, Werner. "Dimensionen der Auslegung des Neuen Testaments. Zum Gespräch Heinrich Schliers mit Rudolf Bultmann." *Theologie und Philosophie* 57 (1982): 481-97.

Lubac, Henri de. "Le problème du développement du dogme." *Recherches de science religieuse* 35 (1948): 130-160.

Lutz, Hanns-Martin. *Yahwe, Jerusalem und die Völker. Zur Vorgeschichte von Sach 12, 1-8 und 14, 1-5.* Wissenschaftliche Monographien zur Alten und Neuen Testament 27. Neukirchen-Vluyn: Neukirchener Verlag, 1968.

Lyonnet, Stanislas. "Le sens de *eph' ho* en Rom 5, 12 et l'exégèse des pères grecs." *Biblica* 36 (1955): 436-56.

_____. "Conception paulinienne de la rédemption." *Lumiere et Vie* 36 (1958): 35-66.

_____. "Gratuité de la justification et gratuité du salut." In *Studiorum Paulinorum Congressus Internationalis Catholicus 1961.* Analecta Biblica 17-18. 2 vols. Rome: Biblical Institute Press, 1963. Vol. 1, pp. 95-110.

_____. "Pauline Soteriology." In *Introduction to the New Testament.* Edited by A. Robert and A. Feuillet. Translated by P. W. Skehan and others. New York-Rome-Paris-Tournai: Desclée, 1965. Pp. 820-65.

_____. "The Return of Christ to God according to St. Paul." In *Word and Mystery: Biblical Essays on the Person and Mission of Christ.* Edited by Leo J. O'Donovan. Baltimore: Newman, 1968. Pp. 201-30.

_____ and Léopold Sabourin. *Sin, Redemption, and Sacrifice. A Biblical and Patristic Study.* Analecta Biblica 48. Rome: Biblical Institute Press, 1970.

MacRae, George W. "Nag Hammadi and the New Testament." In *Gnosis.* [Hans Jonas Festschrift.] Edited by Barbara Aland. Göttingen: Vandenhoeck & Ruprecht, 1978. Pp. 144-57.

Maier, Johann. *Geschichte der jüdischen Religion.* Berlin-New York: De Gruyter, 1972.

Martin, Brice L. "Some Reflections on the Unity of the New Testament." *Studies in Religion/ Sciences Religieuses* 8 (1979): 143-52.

Meagher, John C. *The Way of the Word. The Beginning and the Establishing of Christian Understanding.* New York: Seabury, 1975.

Meeks, Wayne A. *The First Urban Christians. The Social World of the Apostle Paul.* New Haven and London: Yale University Press, 1983.

_____. "The Social Context of Pauline Theology." *Interpretation* 36 (1982): 266-77.

Meier, John P. See above, under Brown, Raymond E.

Meyer, Ben F. *The Aims of Jesus.* London: SCM, 1979.

_____. *The Church in Three Tenses.* Garden City: Doubleday, 1971.

_____. "The 'Inside' of the Jesus Event." In *Creativity and Method: Essays in Honor of Bernard Lonergan.*

Edited by Matthew L. Lamb. Milwaukee: Marquette University Press, 1981. Pp. 197-210.

Meyer, Rudolf. "Die Bedeutung des Pharisäismus für Geschichte und Theologie des Judentums." *Theologische Literaturzeitung* 77 (1952): 677-84.

_____. "*Peritemno.*" In *Theological Dictionary of the New Testament*. Edited by Gerhard Kittel and Gerhard Friedrich, 9 vols. Translated by Geoffrey W. Bromiley. Grand Rapids: Eerdmans, 1964-74. Vol. 6, pp. 72-84.

Moraldi, Luigi. *Espiazione sacrificale e riti espiatori nell' ambiente biblico e nell' Antico Testamento*. Analecta Biblica 5. Rome: Biblical Institute Press, 1956.

Moran, William L. "'A Kingdom of Priests.'" In *The Bible in Current Catholic Thought*. Gruenthaner Memorial Volume. Edited by J. L. McKenzie. New York: Herder and Herder, 1962. Pp. 7-20.

_____. "Deuteronomy." In *A New Catholic Commentary on Holy Scripture*. Edited by R. C. Fuller, Leonard Johnston, and Conleth Kearns. London: Nelson, 1969. Pp. 256-76.

Moule, C. F. D. *The Origin of Christology*. Cambridge: Cambridge University Press, 1977.

Müller, Christian. *Gottes Gerechtigkeit und Gottes Volk. Eine Untersuchung zu Röm 9-11*. Forschungen zur Religion und Literatur des Alten und Neuen Testaments 86. Göttingen: Vandenhoeck & Ruprecht, 1964.

Newman, John Henry. *An Essay on the Development of*

Christian Doctrine. 2nd rev. ed., 1878. Garden City: Doubleday, 1960.

Norris, F. W. "Ignatius, Polycarp, and I Clement: Walter Bauer Reconsidered." *Vigiliae Christianae* 30 (1976): 23-44.

Panikkar, Raimundo. "Some Notes on Syncretism and Eclecticism Related to the Growth of Human Consciousness." In *Religious Syncretism in Antiquity. Essays in Conversation with Geo Widengren.* Edited by Birger A. Pearson. Missoula: Scholars Press, 1975. Pp. 47-62.

Rad, Gerhard von. "The City on the Hill." In *The Problem of the Hexateuch and Other Essays.* Translated by E. W. Trueman Dicken. Edinburgh: Oliver and Boyd, 1966. Pp. 232-42.

Raeder, Maria. "Vikariatstaufe in I Cor 15:29?" *Zeitschrift für die neutestamentliche Wissenschaft* 46 (1955): 258-60.

Rahner, Karl. "The Development of Dogma." In *Theological Investigations. Vol. 1: God, Christ, Mary, and Grace.* Baltimore: Helicon, 1961. Pp. 39-77.

Räisänen, Heikki. "Legalism and Salvation by the Law. Paul's Portrayal of the Jewish Religion as a Historical and Theological Problem." In *Die Paulinische Literatur und Theologie. The Pauline Literature and Theology.* Edited by Sigfred Pedersen. Arhus: Aros; Göttingen: Vandenhoeck & Ruprecht, 1980. Pp. 63-83.

Reumann, John with Joseph A. Fitzmyer and Jerome D. Quinn. *"Righteousness" in the New Testament. "Justification" in the United States Lutheran-Roman*

Catholic Dialogue. Philadelphia: Fortress; New York: Paulist, 1982.

Robinson, James M. "The Pre-history of Demythologization. The Introduction to the Second Edition of Hans Jonas' *Augustin und das paulinische Freiheitsproblem.*" *Interpretation* 20 (1966): 65-77.

Roloff, Jürgen. *Die Apostelgeschichte.* Das Neue Testament Deutsch 5. Göttingen: Vandenhoeck & Ruprecht, 1981.

Ropes, J.H. "'Righteousness' and 'the Righteousness of God' in the Old Testament and in St. Paul." *Journal of Biblical Literature* 22 (1903): 221-7.

Sabourin, Leopold. "Christ Made 'Sin' (2 Cor 5:21); Sacrifice and Redemption in the History of a Formula." In *Sin, Redemption, and Sacrifice. A Biblical and Patristic Study.* Analecta Biblica 48. Rome: Biblical Institute Press, 1970. Pp. 187-296.

Sanders, E. P. *Paul, the Law, and the Jewish People.* Philadelphia: Fortress, 1983.

_____. *Paul and Palestinian Judaism. A Comparison of Patterns of Religion.* Philadelphia: Fortress, 1977.

Sanders, Jack T. *The New Testament Christological Hymns. Their Historical Religious Background.* Society for New Testament Studies Monograph Series 15. Cambridge: At the University Press, 1971.

Schlier, Heinrich. "Kerygma und Sophia. Zur Neutestamentlichen Grundlegung des Dogmas." In *Die Zeit der Kirche. Exegetische Aufsätze und Vorträge.* Freiburg: Herder, 1956. Pp. 206-32.

_____. *Der Brief an die Galater.* Meyers kritisch-exegetischer Kommentar uber das Neue Testament 7. 14th ed. Göttingen: Vandenhoeck & Ruprecht, 1971.

_____. "Die 'Liturgie' des apostolischen Evangeliums (Röm 15, 14-21)." In *Das Ende der Zeit. Exegetische Aufsätze und Vorträge III.* Freiburg-Basel-Wein: Herder, 1971. Pp. 169-83.

Schmid, Hans Heinrich. *Gerechtigkeit als Weltordnung.* Beiträge zur Historischen Theologie 40. Tübingen: Mohr, 1968.

Schmitt, Joseph. "L'Église de Jérusalem ou la 'Restauration' d'Israël d'après les cinq premiers chapitres des Actes." *Revue des sciences religieuses* 27 (1953): 209-18.

Schneider, Gerhard. "Die Idee der Neuschöpfung beim Apostel Paulus und ihr religionsgeschichtlicher Hintergrund." *Trierer theologische Zeitschrift* 68 (1959): 257-70.

Schutz, Alfred. *Collected Papers. II. Studies in Social Theory.* Phaenomenologica 15. Edited by Arvid Brodersen. The Hague: Nijhoff, 1964.

_____. *The Phenomenology of the Social World.* Translated by George Walsh and Frederick Lehnert. Edited by George Walsh. Evanston: Northwestern University Press, 1967.

Scroggs, Robin. "The Sociological Interpretation of the New Testament: The Present State of Research." *New Testament Studies* 26 (1980): 164-79.

Sjöberg, Erik. "Wiedergeburt und Neuschöpfung im palästinischen Judentum." *Studia Theologica* 4 (1950): 44-85.

_____. "Neuschopfung in den Toten-Meer-Rollen." *Studia Theologica* 9 (1955): 131-36.

Stauffer, Ethelbert. *Jesus and His Story*. Translated by D. M. Barton. London: SCM, 1960.

Stendhal, Krister. "Paul Among Jews and Gentiles." In *Paul Among Jews and Gentiles and other Essays.* Philadelphia: Fortress, 1976. Pp. 1-77.

Stuhlmacher, Peter. *Gerechtigkeit Gottes bei Paulus.* Forschungen zur Religion und Literatur des Alten und Neuen Testaments 87. Gottingen: Vandenhoeck & Ruprecht, 1965.

_____. "Erwägungen zum ontologischen Charakter der *kainē ktisis* bei Paulus." *Evangelische Theologie* 27 (1967): 1-35.

_____. *Das paulinische Evangelium I. Vorgeschichte.* Forschungen zur Religion und Literatur des Alten und Neuen Testaments 95. Göttingen: Vandenhoeck & Ruprecht, 1968.

_____. "The Gospel of Righteousness in Christ — Basic Features and Issues of a Biblical Theology of the New Testament." *Horizons in Biblical Theology* 1 (1979): 161-90.

_____. *Vom Verstehen des Neuen Testaments. Eine Hermeneutik.* Göttingen: Vandenhoeck & Ruprecht, 1979.

230   *Bibliography*

_____. "Achtzehn Thesen zur paulinischen Kreuzestheologie." In *Versöhnung, Gesetz und Gerechtigkeit. Aufsätze zur biblischen Theologie.* Göttingen: Vandenhoeck & Ruprecht, 1981. Pp. 192-208.

_____. "Schriftauslegung in der Confessio Augustana. Überlegungen zu einem erst noch zu führenden Gespräch." In *Versöhnung, Gesetz und Gerechtigkeit. Aufsätze zur biblischen Theologie.* Göttingen: Vandenhoeck & Ruprecht, 1981. Pp 246-70.

_____. *"Die Gerechtigkeitsanschauung des Apostels Paulus." In Versohnung, Gesetz und Gerechtigkeit. Aufsatze zur biblischen Theologie.* Göttingen: Vandenhoeck & Ruprecht, 1981. Pp. 87-116.

_____. "Jesu Auferweckung und die Gerechtigkeitsanschauung der vorpaulinischen Missionsgemeinden." In *Versöhnung, Gesetz und Gerechtigkeit. Aufsätze zur biblischen Theologie.* Göttingen: Vandenhoeck & Ruprecht, 1981. 66-86.

_____. "Zur neueren Exegese von Röm 3, 24-26." In *Versöhnung, Gesetz und Gerechtigkeit. Aufsätze zur biblischen Theologie.* Göttingen: Vandenhoeck & Ruprecht, 1981. Pp. 117-35.

_____. " 'Er ist unser Friede' (Eph 2, 14). Zur Exegese und Bedeutung von Eph 2, 14-18." In *Versöhnung, Gesetz und Gerechtigkeit. Aufsätze zur biblischen Theologie.* Göttingen: Vandenhoeck & Ruprecht, 1981. Pp. 224-45.

_____. "Zur paulinischen Christologie." In *Versöhnung, Gesetz und Gerechtigkeit. Aufsätze zur bibli-*

schen Theologie. Göttingen: Vandenhoeck & Ruprecht, 1981. Pp. 209-23.

—————. "'Das Ende des Gesetzes.' Über Ursprung und Ansatz der paulinischen Theologie." In *Versöhnung, Gesetz und Gerechtigkeit. Aufsätze zur biblischen Theologie.* Göttingen: Vandenhoeck & Ruprecht, 1981. Pp. 166-91.

Sundkler, Bengt. "Jesus et les païens." *Revue d'Histoire et de Philosophie religieuses* 16 (1936): 462-99.

Talmon, Shmarjahu. "Har, gibh'ah." In *Theological Dictionary of the Old Testament.* Edited by G. J. Botterweck and Helmer Ringgren. Translated by David E. Green. Grand Rapids: Eerdmans, 1974-. Vol. III, pp. 427-47.

Thüsing, Wilhelm. *Erhöhungsvorstellung und Parusieewartung in der ältesten nachösterlichen Christologie.* Stuttgart: Katholisches Bibelwerk, 1970.

Troeltsch, Ernst. *Writings on Theology and Religion.* Translated and edited by Robert Morgan and Michael Pye. London: Duckworth, 1977.

Vögtle, Anton. "Die ekklesiologische Auftragsworte des Auferstandenen." In *Das Evangelium und die Evangelien. Beiträge zur Evangelienforschung.* Düsseldorf: Patmos, 1971. Pp. 243-52.

Wagner, Günter. *Pauline Baptism and the Pagan Mysteries. The Problem of the Pauline Doctrine of Baptism in Romans VI. 1-11, in the Light of its Religio-Historical "Parallels."* Translated by J. P. Smith. Edinburgh-London: Oliver & Boyd, 1967.

Wanke, Gunther. *Die Zionstheologie der Korachiten in ihrem traditionsgeschichtlichen Zusammenhang.* Beihefte zur Zeitschrift für die alttestamentlichen Wissenschaft 97. Berlin: Töpelmann, 1966.

Wengst, Klaus. *Christologische Formeln und Lieder des Urchristentums.* 2nd ed. Studien zum Neuen Testament 7. Gütersloh: Mohn, 1973.

_____. "Der Apostel und die Tradition. Zur theologischen Bedeutung urchristlicher Formeln bei Paulus." *Zeitschrift für Theologie und Kirche* 69 (1972):145-62.

Wensinck, A. J. *The Ideas of the Western Semites Concerning the Navel of the Earth.* Amsterdam: Muller, 1917.

Wilckens, Ulrich. *Weisheit und Torheit. Eine exegetisch-religionsgeschichtliche Untersuchung zu 1. Kor. 1 und 2.* Beiträge zur historischen Theologie 26. Tübingen: Mohr, 1959.

_____. "Über Abfassungszweck und Aufbau des Römerbriefs." In *Rechtfertigung als Freiheit. Paulusstudien.* Neukirchen-Vluyn: Neukirchener Verlag, 1974. Pp. 110-70.

_____. "Die Bekehrung des Paulus als religionsgeschichtliches Problem." In *Rechtfertigung als Freiheit. Paulusstudien.* Neukirchen-Vluyn: Neukirchener Verlag, 1974. Pp. 11-32.

_____. "Lukas und Paulus unter dem Aspekt dialektisch-theologisch beeinflusster Exegese." In *Rechtfertigung als Freiheit. Paulusstudien.* Neukirchen-Vluyn: Neukirchener Verlag, 1974. Pp. 171-202.

_____. "Zu Römer 3, 21-4, 25. Antwort an G. Klein." In *Rechtfertigung als Freiheit. Paulusstudien.* Neukirchen-Vluyn: Neukirchener Verlag, 1974. Pp. 50-76.

_____. "Was heisst bei Paulus: 'Aus Werken des Gesetzes wird kein Mensch gerecht'?" In *Rechtfertigung als Freiheit. Paulusstudien.* Neukirchener Verlag, 1974. Pp. 77-109.

_____. *Der Brief an die Römer.* Evangelisch-Katholischer Kommentar zum Neuen Testament VI/1-3. Zurich-Einsiedeln-Cologne: Benziger; Neukirchen-Vluyn: Neukirchener Verlag, 1978-82.

Wildberger, Hans. "Die Völkerwallfahrt zum Zion. Jes. II 1-5." *Vetus Testamentum* 7 (1957): 62-81.

Wilken, Robert L. "The Christians as the Romans (and Greeks) Saw Them." In *Jewish and Christian Self-Definition. Vol I: The Shaping of Christianity in the Second and Third Centuries.* Edited by E. P. Sanders. Philadelphia: Fortress, 1980. Pp. 100-25.

Wilson, R. McL. "Nag Hammadi and the New Testament." *New Testament Studies* 28 (1982): 289-302.

Wilson, Stephen G. *The Gentiles and the Gentile Mission in Luke-Acts.* Society for New Testament Studies Monograph Series 23. Cambridge: Cambridge University Press, 1973.

Winter, Gibson. *Elements for a Social Ethic. The Role of Social Science in Public Policy.* New York: Macmillan, 1966.

Zimmerli, Walther and Joachim Jeremias. *The Servant of God.* Rev. ed. Studies in Biblical Theology 20. London: SCM, 1965.

Index Of Names

Althaus, Paul, 155.
Arens, Eduard, 63, 209.
Aus, Roger D., 113, 184, 209.
Bachmann, Michael, 197, 209.
Barrett, C.K., 55, 64, 108, 133, 195, 209.
Bauer, Walter, 14, 107, 108, 193, 194, 195, 210.
Bauer-Arndt-Gingrich, 123, 126.
Baur, Ferdinand Christian, 10, 14, 107, 108.
Beker, J. Christian 38, 160, 170, 210.
Betz, Otto, 152, 210.
Billerbeck, Paul — Front matter, 144.
Blank, Josef, 181, 210.
Blass-Debrunner-Funk — Front matter, 123.
Bornkamm, Günter, 152.
Botterweck, G.J., 8.
Brown, Raymond E., 105, 106, 210.
Brox, Norbert, 193, 210.
Bruce, F.F., 91, 211.
Bühner, Jan-Adolf, 63, 211.
Bultmann, Rudolf, 15, 40, 50, 84, 117, 134, 187, 188, 211.
Burkitt, F.C., 53, 54, 107, 211.
Butterworth, E.A.S., 60, 212.
Catchpole, David R., 172, 212.
Causse, Antonin, 55, 212.
Chadwick, Owen, 195, 212.
Chapman, D.J., 90, 212.
Collingwood, R.G., 16, 31, 32, 188, 212.
Conzelmann, Hans, 54, 73, 151, 212.
Coreth, Emerich, 157, 212.
Coulson, John, 190, 213.
Cullmann, Oscar, 49, 50, 213.
Dahl, Nils Alstrup, 49, 50, 109, 213.
Davies, W.D., 64, 213.
Deichgräber, Reinhard, 80, 213.
Denis, A.-M., 112, 213.

Dix, Gregory, 10, 15, 100, 191, 213.
Dülmen, Andrea van, 135, 214.
Dunn, James D.G., 185, 194, 196, 199, 214.
Dupont, Jacques, 162, 214.
Eichholz, Georg, 109, 114, 214.
Ellis, E.E., 68, 214.
Fitzmyer, Joseph A., 85, 124, 140, 152, 214.
Friedrich, Gerhard, 167, 215.
Gese, Hartmut, 154.
Goppelt, Leonhard, 42, 201, 215.
Grässer, Erich, 152.
Gray, John, 38, 62, 215.
Green, David E., 8.
Gunkel, Hermann, 186, 187, 215.
Gunneweg, A.H.J., 108, 215.
Güting, Eberhard, 55, 215.
Hahn, Ferdinand, 37, 102, 166, 216.
Harnack, Adolf von, 14, 69, 107, 108, 182, 216.
Harrington, Daniel J., 193, 216.
Hawkin, David J., 194, 216.
Hegel, G.W.F., 108, 146.
Hengel, Martin, 41, 54, 68, 69, 70, 77, 92, 97, 108, 111, 184, 216.
Hickling, C.J.A., 155, 217.
Hofius, Otfried, 80, 81, 82, 123, 124, 126, 134, 217.
Holl, Karl, 184.
Holmberg, Bengt, 100, 103, 169, 217.
Holtz, Traugott, 169.
Hooker, Morna D., 122, 125, 217.
Jeremias, Joachim, 42, 56, 59, 63, 69, 72, 75, 89, 126, 160, 161, 218.
Jervell, Jacob, 95, 96, 173, 218.
Jonas, Hans, 192.
Jüngel, Eberhard, 157, 219.
Käsemann, Ernst, 40, 84, 85, 150, 151,

Index of Scriptural Passages

OLD TESTAMENT

NON-CANONICAL JEWISH LITERATURE

NEW TESTAMENT

NON-CANONICAL CHRISTIAN LITERATURE